HOUSTON SYMPHONY
CELEBRATING A CENTURY

HOUSTON SYMPHONY
CELEBRATING A CENTURY

By Carl R. Cunningham

Terry Ann Brown and Ginny Garrett

Published by Herring Design
1216 Hawthorne Street
Houston, Texas 77006

Houston Symphony, Houston, Texas 77002
© 2013 by Houston Symphony Society
All rights reserved. Published 2013
Printed in the United States of America

Printed by R.R.Donnelly

Every effort has been made to trace the ownership of all copyrighted material included
in this volume. Any errors or omissions that may have occurred are inadvertent and
will be corrected in subsequent editions, provided notification is sent to the publisher.

ISBN 978-0-917001-277

Library of Congress Control Number: 2013946771

    Cunningham, Carl R.
    Houston Symphony: Celebrating a Century / Carl R. Cunningham,
    Terry Ann Brown and Ginny Garrett; with an introduction by Mark C. Hanson.
    Edited by Jennifer Mire.
    —1st ed.
    Includes index.

Unless otherwise indicated, all photographs are courtesy Houston Symphony Archives.

Jacket photo — Carl Cunningham, photo by Eric Arbiter. Terry Brown and Ginny
Garrett, photos by Gittings.

All other photo credits can be found on pages 191–192.

For more information on the history of
the Houston Symphony, visit
www.houstonsymphony.org

Previous spread: The 100th birthday concert of the Houston Symphony at Miller Outdoor Theatre, 2013.

The Houston Symphony gratefully acknowledges the generous financial support
of the following donors who made this book possible:

Ms. Charlotte A. Rothwell

Lilly and Thurmon Andress

Robin Angly and Miles Smith

Dr. Susan Gardner and Dr. Philip Scott

Christina and Mark Hanson

The Hood-Barrow Foundation

Mrs. Sybil F. Roos

Mr. and Mrs. Jesse B. Tutor

Mr. and Mrs. C. Clifford Wright

TABLE OF CONTENTS

APPENDIX

CREDITS AND INDEX

100 | 2013–14 CENTENNIAL SEASON CELEBRATION

F O R E W O R D

From a three-concert experiment in 1913 to a concert season that today consists of nearly 300 performances, the journey of the Houston Symphony now spans one hundred years. For an orchestra to attain such an age is something to celebrate indeed!

Within these pages, the growth of the Houston Symphony is shown through a recounting of the individual and collective efforts of music directors working in concert with hundreds of musicians, board members, administrators and volunteers. Our city can be proud of both the Houston Symphony and the people who have worked tirelessly to build it.

As we began an inclusive centennial planning process that drew on the ideas and work of 150 participants, a universal clamor to assemble this centennial book arose. Although begun barely a year before the print deadline, we hope it bears proper witness to our history. Some new research is revealed about our early history, and we have brought out long-forgotten tales of our early musicians. Chapters within chronicle the accomplishments and contributions of all constituency groups that make up the Houston Symphony organization. While it is impossible to capture every individual detail and individual contributor, a picture emerges that will hopefully inspire hundreds more over our second century to build upon the successes of the first.

On the occasion of the Houston Symphony's 50th anniversary, Miss Ima Hogg noted that "only great courage and dedication on the part of public-spirited citizens make it [a symphony orchestra] possible…" This centennial publication benefited immeasurably from the courage and dedication of three guiding forces: Carl Cunningham, Terry Brown and Ginny Garrett. To these three individuals, we say thank you and congratulations.

We hope you all enjoy this fascinating look back at the first one hundred years of the Houston Symphony and a season-long centennial celebration designed to honor our past and launch our exciting future.

Mark C. Hanson
Executive Director and Chief Executive Officer

Ima Hogg at Bayou Bend

Top, from left: Trombonist David Waters. Piles of tour luggage to be loaded. Dick Schaffer and trumpet. Center, from left: Desmond Hoebig and Hakeem Olajuwon. Ray Fliegel at his retirement party. Barbara and Byron Hester. Far left: Bassoonist and photographer Eric Arbiter. Left: Flutists Judy Dines and John Thorne, and oboist Anne Leek.

ACKNOWLEDGMENTS

It is no surprise that women are prominent in the long list of those to whom I am indebted for the completion of this long journey through the history of the Houston Symphony. Women have always been the bulwark of support for this orchestra and its peers throughout the United States.

My text is dedicated to Katherine Taylor Mize, who first proposed the idea of a new history to me at the Houston Symphony Society's fall board meeting in September 1985. She provided crucial advice and assistance during the early stages of the project.

I am indebted to the following for their early support of the extensive research needed for the book I intended to publish: The Cullen Foundation, the Cooper Industries Foundation, the Knox-Charitable Trust, the Rockwell Fund, the former Tenneco Inc., Browning-Ferris Industries, the late Mrs. Wesley West and the Brown Foundation. I am particularly indebted to the Houston Symphony Society for bringing this work to publication.

The process was beset by a series of personal crises: sudden unemployment with the demise of the *Houston Post*, a frightening health emergency, bereavement and finally Tropical Storm Allison, which destroyed the Houston Symphony Archives. But two brave women, Terry Brown and Virginia (Ginny) Garrett, accomplished a miracle in gathering and cataloging the materials for the new, much larger archive that made this book possible. Terry's painstaking work and Ginny's authorship of the chapters on the Houston Symphony League and on the orchestra's educational ventures were, again, crucial to the success of this project.

Historian Virginia Bernhard provided important counseling on Miss Ima Hogg's life during the early years of the orchestra. The staff of the Dolph Briscoe Center for American History at the University of Texas, Austin, provided a wealth of information from personal documents of the orchestra's first conductor, Julien Paul Blitz. The elegantly written 1972 history of the Houston Symphony by Hubert Roussel, my predecessor as music critic of the former *Houston Post*, illuminates the orchestra's earlier history in much greater detail than I could. Finally, countless Houston Symphony musicians, conductors, board presidents, orchestra managers and staff members provided valuable details about the life of this remarkable orchestra as it grew from infancy to the polished ensemble it is today.

Carl Cunningham

———————◆———————

This book would not have been possible without the generosity of many individuals and institutions. When Tropical Storm Allison caused a catastrophic flooding of the Houston Symphony offices a dozen years ago, nearly all photographs, programs, clippings and other historical materials were rendered unidentifiable or otherwise unusable. Since then, supporters and musicians of the Houston Symphony opened their hearts and collections and helped us build a new archive to document the century-long journey of the orchestra. The donors and archives volunteers are too numerous to list here, so we will content ourselves with those who actively assisted with materials and preparation for this publication.

Many thanks to Houston Symphony Librarian Tom Takaro and Assistant Librarian Mike McMurray for their assistance. Of invaluable help in providing photography for this book were: Eric Arbiter; Andrew Cordes of Gittings; Lorraine Stuart of the Museum of Fine Arts, Houston Archives; C. C. Conner from the Houston Ballet; Howard Decker and Joyce Lee of the *Houston Chronicle*; Brian Mitchell of the Houston Grand Opera; Joel Draut and Timothy Ronk at the Houston Metropolitan Research Center, Houston Public Library; Anne Peterson and Cindy Boeke of the DeGolyer Library at Southern Methodist University; and Aryn Glazier of the Dolph Briscoe Center for American History, University of Texas at Austin.

Many thanks are also due to the members of the Archives and Exhibits Centennial Committee, whose vision sparked the creation of this book.

Terry Brown and Ginny Garrett

CHAPTER

I

JULIEN PAUL BLITZ & PAUL BERGÉ

Today the Houston Symphony is an 87-member orchestra with a $30.4 million budget, annually performing nearly 300 concerts for audiences numbering some 300,000 at home and abroad. But it began in 1913 as a 36-member ensemble that grew out of a café orchestra, like those that entertained dinner patrons in turn-of-the-century Vienna. Its budget for the first season of three concerts was a mere $2,500.

In his book *The Houston Symphony Orchestra 1913–1971*, historian Hubert Roussel wrote that this café orchestra performed regularly at Sauter's Restaurant on the corner of Preston and Travis streets in Houston. Julien Paul Blitz, a cellist of Belgian ancestry, was the conductor, and his small ensemble typically entertained dinner patrons with waltzes of Strauss and Lehár, along with chamber music of the Viennese masters from Haydn to Brahms.

Go to the Symphony Concert!

YOU can do something "For the good of Houston" by attending the initial concert of the Houston Symphony Orchestra tomorrow afternoon.

Houston SHOULD have a permanent symphony orchestra! Houston CAN have such an organization. Whether she WILL or not, however, depends upon public appreciation.

The first concert tomorrow will be *your* first opportunity of expressing *your* wish for this new acquisition to Houston's greatness. Express yourself by your presence.

Let us all go to that concert and so pack the Majestic Theatre that there can be no doubt in the promoters' minds that Houston wants such an orchestra. Let us do that much for "musical Houston." Let us encourage the proposition all we can. The interest shown in this first concert will govern largely the activity of the organization's promoters in the future. Concert is at 5 p.m. Saturday afternoon. Tickets on sale at Doscher's Jewelry Store, Goggan's, Oliver's and Carter's Music Houses. Seats 25 cents to $1.00.

Blitz was born May 21, 1885, in Ghent.[1] His father, Edouard Emanuel Blitz, born in 1860, developed his talent as a violinist at the Royal Conservatory there, though he also studied dentistry and may have practiced professionally. The elder Blitz came to America in 1880, met an American pianist, Mattie Louise Miller, in Illinois and married her in 1884. The couple returned to Ghent where their only child, Julien Paul, was born a year later. The child traveled with his parents to the United States when he was two. According to some accounts, Edouard Blitz founded a predecessor of the Kansas City Symphony in 1887. That orchestra did not survive, but Mattie obtained a position as director of music at the small Cottey College in Nevada, Missouri, and both parents were listed as faculty members there from 1895 to 1904, when Mattie died unexpectedly.

In the meantime, young Julien Paul first studied violin and piano with his parents, but returned to Ghent where he enrolled in the Royal Conservatory in 1893 and learned the French solfège system of sight-singing.[2] A notation in his personal scrapbook indicates he returned to his parents in Nevada, Missouri, at some uncertain date and began cello studies "with great desire." Again, he went back to the Ghent conservatory in 1901, graduating with distinction four years later. He had completed an eight-year course in half that time and won first or second prizes in solo and chamber music competitions three times during his last two years.

After graduating in 1905, Julien Paul sailed from Antwerp to New York where his father maintained a teaching studio in Carnegie Hall and held classes at an extension service connected to the Institute for the Arts and Sciences at Columbia University.

But the younger Blitz developed a severe ear infection in the rigorous winter weather. Seeking a warmer winter climate, he obtained a teaching position at Mary Hardin-Baylor College (Baylor Female College) in Belton, Texas. By 1909 he was living in Houston, where he served as music director of the Treble Clef Club, the city's leading choral organization and a sponsor of touring musical artists. He organized and participated in numerous chamber music performances, winning great praise and respect for the quality of his playing. He also wrote reviews of visiting performers and other articles on music for the *Houston Chronicle*.

Blitz made one more trip to Ghent for post-graduate work in 1910–11. Back in Houston by September 1912, he had been hired by restaurateur G. F. Sauter and had authored a lengthy article on his hopes for establishing a symphony orchestra in Houston. During the months that followed, he made contact with Miss Ima Hogg, daughter of Texas Governor James Stephen Hogg. She is credited as the founder of the Houston Symphony, although she frequently minimized her role, insisting that the work of establishing and supporting the orchestra had been the labor of many volunteers. Miss Ima, as she was affectionately known in her home city, was a pianist who had studied music in New York and Germany during the early years of the 20th century, and her exposure to music and the arts in other American and European cities prompted her desire to establish an orchestra in Houston. After meeting with Blitz, she and other members of the Women's Choral Club and the Girls Musical Club gathered a group of 138 guarantors who responded to a growing desire among Houston's musicians for a symphony orchestra.

Previous spread: **Musicians of the orchestra presented a silver loving cup to Julien Paul Blitz when he departed the orchestra in 1916.** Above: **The newspaper advertisement for the first concert was written by Ima Hogg.** Right: **Julien Paul Blitz with music and cigar.**

Arrangements were made for a test concert to determine whether the people of Houston were ready to support a symphony. Tickets were issued to the public, and the New Majestic Theatre on Texas Avenue was filled to capacity on the hot historic late afternoon of June 21, 1913, when the Houston Symphony, with Blitz as its first conductor, made its debut. At age 28, he was the youngest of the conductors who have led the orchestra during the last century. The program began nobly with Mozart's Symphony No. 39, followed by an orchestral fantasy on Bizet's *Carmen*; an aria from Gluck's *Alceste*, sung by Houston soprano Blanche Foley; and the Waltz of the Flowers from Tchaikovsky's ballet *The Nutcracker*.

"At age 28, he was the youngest of the conductors who have led the orchestra during the last century."

The Majestic was the second of three Houston theaters bearing that name. Opened in 1910, before the days of air-conditioning, it boasted a modern rooftop exhaust fan designed to change 250,000 cubic feet of air every three minutes. A handwritten ledger of expenses personally maintained by Blitz indicates there were six rehearsals. Only 17 musicians showed up for the first rehearsal on June 8, but the number increased to 32 musicians by the final rehearsal on June 20, and 33 signed the ledger for the June 21 concert. Each musician was paid $2 per rehearsal and $5 for the concert. The total expense was $602.90, including $.40 for a telegram to Blitz, $2.00 for music copying services (provided by legendary Houston pianist Patricio Gutierrez)

and $1.50 for janitorial services. According to the ledger, Blitz was paid $25 for conducting the six rehearsals and the concert—and who can count all the other minutiae and personnel problems he encountered while setting a symphony orchestra in motion! For some reason, his name and payment are crossed off the ledger, so in the final analysis, he may not have received any remuneration for his efforts.

That fall, the orchestra inaugurated a season of three "twilight" concerts, also conducted by Blitz. He stayed on for the orchestra's first three seasons before resigning. A few days before the March 2, 1915, concert, Blitz' father died, following a tragic accident in which he unknowingly drank from a glass containing photographic developing chemicals instead of water.

The younger Blitz was deeply affected by the loss and rushed to New York, where he took over the teaching of his father's classes at Columbia University's extension program and played memorial concerts there and at his father's Carnegie Hall teaching studio.

His prolonged stay in New York prompted telegrams from Houston Symphony officials urging him to return. Though concertmaster Maurice Derdeyn substituted for him on the March concert, Blitz did return to conduct the final concert in May and stayed for a third season in 1915-16. In the March 1916 concert, Blitz himself was the soloist in the Saint-Saëns Cello Concerto No. 1—a valedictory piece he had played upon graduation from the Ghent conservatory 11 years earlier. He also had performed the concerto with the Chicago Symphony in May 1909, winning high praise from the Chicago newspapers for the quality of his playing.

"Blitz and the fledgling Houston Symphony won high marks from Leonard Liebling, editor-in-chief of the important, nationally distributed journal *The Musical Courier,* for that March 1916 concert."

Blitz and the fledgling Houston Symphony won high marks from Leonard Liebling, editor-in-chief of the important, nationally distributed journal *The Musical Courier*, for that March 1916 concert. Liebling was on a musical tour of the American South and West. He traveled from New York, stayed two nights at the Rice Hotel and expressed his reaction in a lengthy interview published in the *Houston Chronicle*. His observations are worth quoting extensively, for they bear directly upon the accomplishments and the challenges facing Houston's brand new orchestra:

"I was a bit disappointed at first when I saw the size of the orchestra," Liebling began, "but being a musician and a critic, I adjusted my mind to the conditions and based my estimates on quality rather than on quantity.

Left: **The New Majestic Theatre on Texas Avenue at Milam Street, 1913. Karl Hoblitzelle let the new orchestra have the space for free, as concerts were held between the afternoon and evening vaudeville shows.** Above: **The Houston Symphony Orchestra in the 1915–16 season at the New Majestic Theatre.**

"The first thing I look for in an orchestra is the evidence of rehearsal; it is the keynote of successful orchestral performance. An orchestra must be thoroughly acquainted with the matter it is handling before the manner can be perfected. In that respect, the Houston Symphony Orchestra gave me real pleasure in the Haydn score (the 'London' Symphony, No. 104). The 'attack,' as we musicians call it, was unanimous, the tone production was refined and well modulated, the dynamic signs were all carefully observed and executed, and the general effect was one of smoothness and ease. It is not necessary to have a very large orchestra for a reverent and correct reading of a Haydn symphony, for that composer wrote at a period when the modern-sized orchestra of our own day would have been considered a monstrosity."

Concerning Blitz, Liebling stated: "It was clear to me that he is a very capable and earnest musician who knows his score, exacts obedience in matters of rhythm, technic [sic] and phrasing, and does not cater in the slightest degree to sensationalism or other extraneous tricks that make for easy popularity. My respect for his musical ability was enhanced also by the fact that he was the soloist (as well as the conductor) of the concert. Not many conductors are able to do that. At present, we have only one other soloistic conductor in America, and that is Doctor (Ernst) Kunwald of the Cincinnati Orchestra… Mr. Blitz is unquestionably an accomplished virtuoso on the cello. His playing of the Saint-Saëns concerto was admirable in every way and I could not well imagine a more polished or authoritative performance. To tell you the truth, I was tremendously surprised, for I had been given no previous intimation that Mr. Blitz is such a master of his instrument. He would be given that title in any musical metropolis anywhere."

Liebling demurred when asked by the interviewer to compare the new Houston Symphony "to those of the larger Northern and Eastern cities." He replied: "Most of the large orchestras have from 65 to 100 men and therefore a comparison with the Houston body is neither fair nor of the least artistic value. But since you have brought up the subject," he continued, "I wish to say that I cannot understand why it is not possible for your city to have a bigger orchestra than it possesses at present. Houston does everything else in such a lavish and magnificent spirit that an orchestra representative of the wealth, culture and civic pride of this progressive community ought to number at least 60 men. There is no reason why Houston should not hear the latest and greatest musical masterpieces as well as all the standard classics, but as constituted at this time, your

Emil Lindenberg

Emil Lindenberg (1850–1919) was a prominent music educator who moved from Galveston to Houston after the 1900 hurricane. The German-born Lindenberg formed the early Houston Symphony Club (not affiliated with the later Houston Symphony Orchestra), which brought prominent solo artists from out of state to play with the group.

Lindenberg taught violin to the only two women to serve that first season in the Houston Symphony Orchestra's violin section, Marian Jenkins and Rosetta Hirsch. He also taught the young Josephine Boudreaux, who played in the orchestra in the mid-1910s and served as concertmaster from 1931 to 1937.

Lindenberg's daughter Grace Keller played viola in the Symphony's 1917–18 season and joined Josephine as a member of the Boudreaux String Quartet shortly before the orchestra's revival in 1931. Born in 1881, Grace had also been a 1908 charter member of the Thursday Morning Musical Club.

orchestra, through no fault of its own or of its leader, is unable to give you the whole of the symphonic repertory."

What was the measure of Houston's wealth in early 1916? With a population of nearly 102,000, according to the 1910 census, the city was unquestionably much smaller and newer than its Northeastern counterparts. But according to the Chamber of Commerce, Houston bank deposits stood at $370 per capita, compared with a national average of $194 per capita. Almost 1.3 million tons of freight—cotton, lumber, oil and rice, collectively valued at $37.5 million—passed over the city's wharves. In 1913, Houston had 347 factories producing goods valued at more than $50 million. By 1918, eight oil fields around Houston were producing 30 million barrels of oil a year. By 1920, Houston's population had grown to nearly 173,000, and the per capita bank deposits stood at $617, compared to a $392 national average. The problem did not seem to be a serious lack of money; rather, it was a lack of enough musicians to populate a full symphony orchestra and enough well-educated patrons to support such an ensemble.[3]

On June 9, 1916, the *Houston Press* carried an article detailing Blitz' strongly worded reasons for resigning his position: "I want to bring it (the Houston Symphony) nearer to the people," Blitz was quoted as saying. He wanted concerts at night instead of 5 p.m., so working men and their families, and businessmen could attend. He wanted regular weekly concerts instead of formal events every two to three months. And he wanted outside as well as local talent employed. In addition, he said the orchestra should be advertised in the local newspapers. "I want to see it made a popular institution of the city," he concluded.

Blitz' formal letter of resignation was posted on the bulletin board at the musicians' union and was forwarded to the *Houston Post*, which printed it in full on June 10. It read as follows:

To the Houston Symphony Orchestra Association, Houston, Texas.

Madam President—In view of the fact that the Houston Symphony Orchestra Association has not invested me with sufficient authority to alter such of their policies as are diametrically opposed to my conceptions of progressive orchestral management, I hereby tender my resignation to become effective immediately.

Owing to the pleasant features of our individual relations, both musical and social, it would be a source of great regret to me should the board of directors attribute any other motive to my resignation than a purely technical one.

I beg of you to accept the assurance of my most perfect consideration,

J. P. Blitz

Blitz' resignation followed an intense period when the matter of public funding came under discussion. On February 22, 1916, the *Houston Post* and *Houston Chronicle* both reported on a meeting Blitz convened at the Rice Hotel, asking that the mayor and city fathers reallocate $16,000 in annual public funding for band concerts and Sunday afternoon entertainment to include the Houston Symphony as part of that subsidy.

On March 19, 1916, the *Houston Press* reported on a financial report at the Symphony Association's March 13 business meeting, stating that the orchestra would come through its third season without having to draw upon the guarantors' fund.

Despite this balanced budget, the *Press* continued, "the orchestra must be enlarged to meet the demands of the progressive audience. They are asking for compositions which cannot be presented by our orchestra, with its present limited number of instruments, and until we can support the necessary musicians at home, we must send to other cities for them, involving considerable expense." The article ended by urging greater public support.

The program for Blitz' final concert on April 10, 1916, listed 46 members, so the orchestra had grown significantly from its initial size, and his published remarks failed to take a few practical matters into proper account. The reason the concerts were held at 5 p.m. had to do with the availability of musicians and a stage. The Majestic was a vaudeville theater, and the symphony concerts had to be scheduled between the end of the matinees and the beginning of the evening shows. The musicians who played in the Houston Symphony were largely the same musicians who played in the pit orchestra at the Majestic and other vaudeville theaters in Houston. Karl Hoblitzelle, the theater manager, made the stage available to the fledgling symphony orchestra free of charge.

Above: **Miss Ima Hogg in 1910, three years before the formation of the Houston Symphony.**
Top left: **Mrs. Edwin B. Parker was the first president of the Houston Symphony Orchestra Association. Photo circa 1932.**

The intensity of Blitz' feelings, expressed in that *Houston Press* article, other newspaper articles and his own personal writings, leave little doubt that the inaugural conductor of the Houston Symphony was a finely trained musician and a young man of strong artistic principles. In short, he wanted better things and a broader outreach for the Houston Symphony than the board was able to provide, and when that was not possible, he weighed the situation against his own talents and personal goals, and chose to serve the cause of music in Texas by other means in other places.

It was the first of many instances when the artistic element in the Houston Symphony came into conflict with its supporters, while a musically uneducated populace failed to understand or really care about the problems both parties were trying to solve for the betterment of all the people in the city. But frequently, the generosity and positive spirit emanating from both parties brought the Houston Symphony forward by leaps and bounds in its effort to meet the standards of its longer-established peers.

In the end, the *Houston Press* published an editorial, titled "Good Music for All," on June 15, 1916:

It is unfortunate for Houston's music lovers that Julien Paul Blitz and the directors of the symphony orchestra have come to the parting of the ways. Unfortunate, because Blitz, with his superior musical genius, gave the orchestra an appreciable distinction. Unfortunate, because the orchestra is deprived of the leadership and service of perhaps the most gifted musician in the city.

Blitz gave good reasons for desiring a change in policy for the orchestra, but the directors replied by declaring that they were going to do just the things he desired, so it appears there is not so great a difference of opinion between them, after all.

The directors say they have been working toward the establishment of an orchestra that will be for all the people of the community, not for the select few. They realize that to make it a success, it must be generally popular, and that the poor as well as the rich must be interested in it and enabled to enjoy its concerts. In view of this desire, they point out that popular prices have prevailed and that as many as possible of the concerts have been held on holidays, the opening concert each season being on Thanksgiving.

They state that the 5 o'clock hour was chosen because it was most convenient for the musicians.

So far, so good. The *Houston Press* congratulates the directors for their efforts and their aspirations in this direction. The problem is to make the orchestra MORE POPULAR THAN IT IS. This can be accomplished by a campaign of education in which the people of Houston are made fully acquainted with the ideals and aspirations of the orchestra and encouraged to patronize it.

Surely Houston has room and appreciation for a symphony orchestra of this sort.

> "He conducted the San Antonio Orchestra from 1917 to 1922, where he met and married pianist Flora Briggs in 1921."

> "Blitz was succeeded by Paul Bergé, a violinist who also had come from the ranks of café orchestra musicians in Houston."

When Blitz resigned, the orchestra members presented him with a silver loving cup, duly inscribed with his name and an expression of their thanks for his accomplishments. A month later, Blitz also resigned from the Treble Clef Club and left Houston for various activities throughout Texas and neighboring states. He conducted the San Antonio Orchestra from 1917 to 1922, where he met and married pianist Flora Briggs in 1921. He also served as director of San Antonio's Chaminade Choral Society, taught at music colleges or conservatories in San Antonio, Fort Worth and Sherman, and chaired the music department at Texas Technological College (later Texas Tech University) in Lubbock from 1934 to 1950, a year before his death. During that entire time, Blitz concertized throughout Texas, both with orchestras and in recitals with his wife. His only son, Edouard Marquis Blitz, became assistant principal cellist of the Dallas Symphony and, eventually, a cellist with the St. Paul Chamber Orchestra.

In a later summation of his career, Blitz counted his quiet, unheralded educational achievements—not the luster of the podium or solo performer's spotlight—as the most rewarding aspect of his long career in Texas. In a personal statement, he expressed special pride that the French system of solfège was taught at Baylor College in Belton as early as 1906, the year he arrived in Texas.

Blitz was succeeded by Paul Bergé, a violinist who also had come from the ranks of café orchestra musicians in Houston. Bergé, the son of a physician who maintained his practice in Louisiana, began pre-medical studies at Tulane University, combining them with violin playing. He was encouraged to pursue music rather than medicine. Following studies in Europe, he attempted to start a career as a touring violin soloist, but settled into orchestral playing. He became director of the café orchestra in the Italian Garden of New Orleans' St. Charles Hotel, but migrated to

Top right: **Jules and Theresa Hirsch, circa 1911.**
Bottom right: **Former conductor Paul Bergé at an October 21, 1968 concert with Mrs. Virginia McGregor.**

Houston in 1913, where he became director of the café orchestra at the old Brazos Hotel on Washington Avenue. Ima Hogg recruited Bergé to succeed Blitz, and in later years, he quoted her as saying: "Paul Blitz, our first conductor of the symphony here, has just left in a huff, which we're perfectly happy about, and I would love to talk to you about taking over."

Bergé conducted the orchestra through the spring of 1918, when it disbanded for 13 years. On April 6, 1917, the United States had entered World War I, and the orchestra's ranks were being depleted as Houston's young men went off to fight in European trenches.

Bergé continued to live in Houston, becoming music director at the newly enlarged Rice Hotel, where he had four café orchestras, according to a 1965 interview in the *Houston Chronicle*. After the orchestra was reorganized in 1931, its rosters never again listed him as a member of the Houston Symphony, but a seating plan in a 1943 program book shows his name at the back of the second violin section. Bergé taught violin until 1961, when an unsuccessful operation to remove cataracts from his eyes left him nearly blind. He lived out his last years in the obscurity of a healthcare retirement facility. On October 21, 1968—50 years after Bergé conducted his last Houston Symphony concert—a Jones Hall audience was startled to find the 86-year-old musician in its midst, acknowledging greetings from conductor André Previn who dedicated that evening's performance of Mozart's *Eine kleine Nachtmusik* to his early predecessor.

Though marches, dances, overtures, operatic arias and orchestral salon pieces filled out much of the repertoire during those first five seasons, there was almost always a full symphony on each program. Mostly they were early or late symphonies by Mozart or Haydn, especially during Blitz' three years. Bergé concluded the 1916–17 season with Mendelssohn's Overture to *A Midsummer Night's Dream*, Beethoven's First Symphony and Mozart's D minor Concerto featuring prominent Houston piano teacher Bessie Griffiths as soloist. She had been one of Ima Hogg's students. Violinist Rosetta Hirsch was another significant soloist, playing the Bruch G minor Concerto on March 2, 1915. She was the daughter of Mrs. Jules Hirsch, charter member and original board member of the Houston Symphony Orchestra Association. She was also the sister of Maurice Hirsch, a noted Houston attorney who was a dedicated supporter of the orchestra and became a very strongly committed president of the Houston Symphony Society from 1956 until 1970.

Paul Bergé

Houston suffragist, art collector and hotel owner Annette Finnegan was responsible for Paul Bergé's moving to Houston in 1913 from New Orleans as orchestra and general manager for the Brazos Court at the Brazos Hotel. Ima Hogg asked him to take over for Blitz in 1916.

Bergé recalled in 1965, "Sometimes we would give two rehearsals, which were just like concerts, at the old Central High School or perhaps San Jacinto High. Dress rehearsals they were—and very successful.

"The biggest problem was getting certain instruments such as the French horn, the oboe, the English horn, instruments in the oboe family. There was not much use for these in the small town that Houston was then."*

* Kay Pope, "Symphony's 2nd Conductor," *Houston Chronicle*, February 14, 1965.

WILLIAM REHER
Symphony Conductor

Director of the Reher String Quartet

Member of the
Cincinnati Symphony Orchestra
FRITZ REINER, Conductor

CHAPTER

II

DORMANCY AND REAWAKENING

When the fledgling Houston Symphony disbanded, with its musicians called away by World War I, the supporting Houston Symphony Association hung on, essentially as a social organization, sponsoring touring orchestras and other visiting artists who regularly circulated through the city's theaters. It has never been clearly understood why the Symphony Association abandoned its efforts on behalf of a resident orchestra just seven months before the armistice was declared, then left the musicians adrift for 13 long years.

External factors could have prevented the immediate resumption of symphonic activities. America entered the war on April 6, 1917, and troops were training for combat a month later. No one knew how long the war would last, and even though the armistice of November 11, 1918, brought an uneasy cessation of warfare, all of the troops did not return home until the middle of 1919. Also, the Spanish flu struck Houston in September 1918, and theaters could well have been closed during that time, as they were elsewhere in the nation.

> "On September 5, 1921, the *Galveston Daily News* reported that the Houston Symphony Association planned to offer monthly concerts beginning in October, employing Houston and Galveston musicians."

Another possible reason may have been a health crisis suffered by the organization's leading patron, Miss Ima Hogg. In 1917 she accepted the presidency of the Symphony Association for four years, but she was reported to have suffered from physical ailments and nervous disorders—including mental depression—for about four years, beginning in July 1918. According to historian Virginia Bernhard, she was under the steady care of a doctor in Philadelphia from May 1919 until April 1921. Without her energy, determination and constant presence in Houston, it is easy to understand how the Houston Symphony guarantors could have relaxed and faltered in their support.[1]

There were sporadic reports of musical activity in Houston on the part of a symphonic organization throughout the 1920s. On April 2–3, 1921, the *Galveston Daily News* reported that 2,500 school children attended a concert "given by the new Houston Symphony Orchestra at City Auditorium." The orchestra, which numbered some 50 Houston musicians, was "directed by William Reher, with B. J. Steinfeldt as concert manager." (Steinfeldt had served as the orchestra's first concertmaster in 1913.) Beethoven's First Symphony, Henry Hadley's suite *Ballet of the Flowers* and a couple of songs were on the program.

Reher was a violinist, conductor and educator who was born in Hamburg, Germany, and educated at the conservatory there. He studied with the noted Czech pedagogue Otakar Ševčík in Vienna, and became concertmaster of the Munich Philharmonic for four years, followed by a teaching position at the Hamburg Conservatory. He married Danish pianist Anna Callesen, and they concertized throughout Scandinavia, Germany and Italy before arriving in Los Angeles in 1914, where Reher became a member of the first violin section in the Los Angeles Symphony for four years. He also established the Reher String Quartet.

Reher's Houston concert was apparently another free test concert to see whether the Houston Symphony could be revived. The City of Houston's Recreation and Community Service Association sponsored the concert, meeting one of the demands Blitz had voiced before he resigned five years earlier: public tax funding for the Symphony. The orchestra was managed by Ernest Hail, a clarinetist with the original Houston Symphony. He was also president of Local No. 65 of the American Federation of Musicians and may have facilitated negotiations for sponsorship of the free concert.

On September 5, 1921, the *Galveston Daily News* reported that the Houston Symphony Association planned to offer monthly concerts beginning in October, employing Houston and Galveston musicians. In keeping with the Symphony Association's practice from 1913 to 1918, funding was to be guaranteed through private subscriptions. Based on that promise, the Rehers settled into a house on Drew Street in Houston. But by mid-October, Reher wrote privately in a letter that everything had fallen apart: the Symphony Association had raised no funds and was asking the musicians to play for "theater wages, $3.00 or $3.50 instead of $7.50. Of course, the union refused, now that means the end," he said. "Everything in vain, all my work." By December 11 the *Galveston Daily News* reported cancellation of the proposed concerts and the Rehers' return to Los Angeles. From 1925 to 1928, Reher occupied the third chair (presumably the first assistant concertmaster's position) with the Cincinnati Symphony. He also opened a school of orchestral playing for advanced student instrumentalists there, in conjunction with the Wurlitzer

Previous spread: **From an advertisement by Reher when he was later a member of the Cincinnati Symphony Orchestra.** Right: **The pit orchestra for the Majestic Theatre included many Houston Symphony musicians such as John Gottwald, J. G. Grace, William Ready, W. K. Russ, Lee Waters and Jake Wilkenfeld, circa 1928–29.**

Company. Eventually the Rehers settled permanently in Los Angeles, where their two sons became prominent members of the Los Angeles Philharmonic: Sven Reher as violist and Kurt Reher as principal cellist.[2]

William Reher was not the only conductor to seek a position with the dormant Houston Symphony. On April 15, 1921, shortly after Reher's free student concert, the *Galveston Daily News* reported that Josef Stransky, director of the New York Philharmonic, addressed a meeting of 30 Symphony Association guarantors (including Miss Hogg), offering to come to Houston during his vacation, rehearse the orchestra and give three concerts without remuneration.[3] Stransky had been the extraordinarily popular, energetic conductor of the New York orchestra since 1911, when he gained the position following the death of Gustav

Mahler. But a decade later, he apparently sensed the New York podium was getting a little unsteady under his feet because he was forced off in 1923 in favor of Wilhelm Mengelberg.[4]

The November 25, 1924, edition of the Waterloo, Iowa, *Evening Courier* carried a brief, mysterious notice that Houston radio station KPRC would broadcast a concert by the Houston Symphony as a special Thanksgiving evening attraction. There is no documentation that the dormant Houston Symphony assembled to play a concert that day, but the orchestra had traditionally begun its three-concert season on Thanksgiving evening. Interestingly, the New Majestic Theatre had been remodeled and reopened under a new name, the Palace Theatre, a year earlier with its seating capacity expanded to 1,500—and even a broadcast booth!

Records from this period are sketchy, but several items have been gleaned from newspapers of the time. On January 18, 1925, the *Galveston Daily News* reported that a massed band of Houston musicians, followed by the Houston Symphony, would entertain delegates to the national convention of the Associated Advertising Clubs of the World. Mrs. H. M. Garwood, Symphony Association president and guarantor, and Houston concert manager Edna W. Saunders were in charge of the event. And on May 7, 1927, the Houston Symphony "made a clean sweep of honors" in the orchestral division of Harris County's first band contest. The Rice Institute (now Rice University) band won first prize and then joined with a 300-member massed ensemble for the final concert, attended by 1,000 people.

By the end of the decade, competition from various quarters forced the Symphony Association to take action. Historian Hubert Roussel noted that by 1929, Houston's musicians had grown impatient to have an orchestra and formed the Houston Philharmonic, led by legendary Houston band director Victor Alessandro Sr., whose name is memorialized in Alessandro Hall at Houston's High School for the Performing and Visual Arts. Concert manager Saunders sponsored conductor Ellison Van Hoose and his Little Symphony in a series of concerts, and Mrs. John Wesley ("Ma") Graham, seeking to form an orchestra for her projected operatic production of Verdi's *Aida*, imported Italian operatic coach Uriel Nespoli as her conductor.[5]

Seeing rivals on the horizon, the Symphony Association finally began to take action. There was a flurry of telegrams between Miss Hogg and noted Italian composer, pianist and conductor Alfredo Casella early in June 1929, setting up a meeting in New York regarding "an opening for a conductor."[6] Casella was guest conducting the Boston Pops in a series of summer concerts at the time, and he had previously guest conducted the Boston Symphony. But as with Reher and Stransky, nothing came of the scheduled June 9 meeting prior to Miss Hogg's departure on a European trip.

Instead, the Symphony Association entered the orchestral fray in Houston, gaining the upper hand with the musicians and Nespoli, luring him away from Mrs. Graham in what finally became a successful effort to revive the Houston Symphony. Nespoli conducted two performances of another test concert on

Above: **The Boudreaux Quartet began its performances for the Houston Symphony Orchestra Association in 1929. Pictured in 1930 are: violinists Josephine Boudreaux and Octave Pimbert, cellist Athelstan Charlton and violist Grace Lindenberg Keller.** Right: **Drusilla Huffmaster in the early 1960s.**

Drusilla Huffmaster

Local pianist Drusilla Huffmaster (1917–2011) was the first soloist of the new 1931–32 season with Grieg's Piano Concerto in A minor, Opus 16. On that occasion, she had just turned 14 years old. Her father, Hu T. Huffmaster, was well known in Houston musical circles as the choirmaster and organist at St. Paul's Methodist Church.

Over the next 20 years, she had a successful international career and played five more programs with the Houston Symphony, performing with conductors Nespoli, St. Leger, Hoffmann and Kurtz. In 1957, she appeared with conductor Sir Malcolm Sargent, and in March 1963, with Sir John Barbirolli in the Music Hall. She joined Arthur Fiedler for the Houston Symphony's 1964 New Year's Eve concert, once again with the Grieg Piano Concerto.

Uriel Nespoli

Conductor Uriel Nespoli also supported himself by taking pupils, many of whom he presented in recital in Galveston in October 1932.

Among these were Houston Symphony violinist Soeurette Diehl, soprano Nancy Swinford and soprano Ina Gillespie Grotte, who was a Symphony Association board member and wrote a column for the *Houston Chronicle*. According to the *Galveston Daily News*, Nespoli was a friend of Puccini and was associated as a director with Mascagni.*

* "To Sing in Concert Here," *Galveston Daily News*, October 23, 1932, p. 9.

May 6 and 7, 1931, in the renovated, renamed and enlarged Palace Theatre. As many as ten members of the original 1913–14 orchestra returned to play in Nespoli's ensemble at some point during the 1931–32 season. Violinist Josephine Boudreaux, a resident of the Houston Heights, served as concertmaster. She had been a little girl in the second violin section from 1916 to 1918 under Bergé. In 1921, Boudreaux won a scholarship to study at the American Conservatory in Fontainebleau, France, returning in 1929 to found her own string quartet and perform as soloist with the theater orchestra in the small Isis vaudeville theater on Prairie Avenue. (Remnants of the theater still existed in 2012 in its newest reincarnation as a small brewery.) She remained in that prime orchestral position for six seasons—a noteworthy achievement for a woman in the 1930s. Other returning orchestra members from the 1910s included Ben Grossman and Jesus Gutierrez, horn player Patricio Gutierrez, flutist Arthur Hussman, trombonist Ernest Kuhnel, violinist William R. Patrick, clarinetist Franz Roman, Galveston violinist Conway Shaw, violist Grace Keller, timpanist Herman Weiss, trombonist John C. Willrich, violinists Iva Carpenter and Henry G. Thayer and cellist Athelstan R. Charlton.[7] Violinist Soeurette Diehl was the daughter of original orchestra violinist Anton Diehl, founder of the Houston Conservatory. Principal cellist Michael De Rudder also had a son playing in the orchestra, Louis DeRudder, who remained a member for nearly 50 years until the end of Lawrence Foster's tenure as music director in 1978.

Since Nespoli had a background in opera, the repertoire for the test performances leaned heavily on overtures and orchestral excerpts from operas: The Prelude and Love-Death from Wagner's *Tristan und Isolde*; Beethoven's Fifth Symphony (apparently its Houston Symphony premiere); the Good Friday Music from Wagner's *Parsifal*; Saint-Saëns' The Swan; Schumann's Reverie; and the "Hymn to the Sun" from Mascagni's rarely heard opera *Iris*. Somewhere between 65 and 80 choristers for the Mascagni piece were borrowed from church choirs and/or "Ma" Graham's fledgling opera company (newspaper accounts vary). This may have been the very first choral/orchestral work played by the Houston Symphony.

Admission to the test concert was by free tickets—except for the box seats—and both performances were apparently well attended. The two performances cost the Symphony Association $2,000. Based on this, the Association firmly announced that tickets for the six programs that followed during the 1931–32 season would be distributed by paid admission only. "Success or failure of the Houston Symphony Orchestra will be up to the public," the newspapers reported. "The concerts will not be underwritten, but will be given by means of subscription only."

Subscriptions were sold as follows: $10 for 12 tickets (two for each performance); $25 for 36 tickets (six per performance); $100 for 25 tickets for each performance (or for a box with six seats for each performance). They were marketed to the public in Houston, Galveston, Beaumont and Port Arthur. Large corporations bought blocks of tickets to distribute to their employees. By the end of August, the Symphony Association had taken in $7,000 in subscriptions. They estimated the season would cost $16,000, meaning that pledges amounting to $9,000 would have to be collected from the guarantors.

A key factor in the reorganization was a contract with the musicians' union enabling the Symphony Association to hire union, non-union and amateur musicians "all chosen on the basis of talent." This new clause allowed the Association to import qualified musicians from other cities, in an effort to build up the orchestra to symphonic strength. That clause met another of Blitz' demands when he resigned 15 years earlier.

During the 1931–32 season, Nespoli led a 75-member orchestra in six programs at the 3,500-seat City Auditorium (site of the present Jones Hall). The repertoire remained much the same as in the two test concert performances: an overture and a symphony or concerto almost always began each program, followed by operatic excerpts and/or shorter orchestral pieces at the end. Soloists were drawn from resident Houston talent—pianists Drusilla Huffmaster and Rhodes Dunlap, violinist Josephine Boudreaux and singers Card Elliott, Daisy Elgin, Nancy Yeager Swinford and

> "Initially, the orchestra rehearsed on a platform in the warehouse of the cavernous Merchants and Manufacturers Building (now part of the University of Houston Downtown campus)."

Walter Jenkins. Initially, the orchestra rehearsed on a platform in the warehouse of the cavernous Merchants and Manufacturers Building (now part of the University of Houston Downtown campus). The M&M Building, built in 1928 on the banks of Buffalo Bayou, was filled with acoustically deadening cotton bales. It had been patterned after the Chicago Merchandise Mart, using water, rail and road to transport goods to market. But its opening coincided with the Great Depression, and the building remained largely vacant, falling into bankruptcy in 1934.

Musically solid, but apparently excitable and animated in his motions, Nespoli lasted only one season. He spoke little if any English, and his limited ability to communicate apparently caused misunderstandings both in business matters and doubtless in rehearsals with the orchestra. His rotund stature, physical gestures and squeaky shoes brought unfortunate ridicule from the press and public.

Nespoli was followed by the handsome, sociable (but apparently uninspiring) conductor Frank St. Leger for the next three seasons. Born in India of Scotch-Irish parents, St. Leger studied in London and Paris, toured extensively with Australian soprano Nellie Melba and joined the Australian army in 1915. He conducted operatic and symphonic performances in Chicago, London and Australia before and during his three years with the Houston Symphony.

For his opening concert, St. Leger invited former conductor Blitz to make a return appearance as cello soloist in French-Alsatian composer Léon Boellman's Symphonic Variations for Cello and Orchestra. Blitz was pleased and honored with the invitation, calling the Houston Symphony "the best orchestra I ever performed with." But in his personal papers, he privately grieved that so many of the musicians had lost their theater jobs in the Great Depression. The Symphony Association, also aware of their unemployed state, noted that by reviving the Houston Symphony, it was able to distribute some $15,000 to $20,000 among the musicians in salary payments.

Above: Inscribed "To the Houston Symphony Orchestra with my best wishes for a glorious future! Alfred Hertz, San Francisco, Sept. 1936." Right: Houston Symphony Orchestra in the early 1930s with Frank St. Leger.

An historic note: 14-year-old Raphael Fliegel, who was to become a 59-year orchestra member and concertmaster for 25 years, made his Houston Symphony debut as soloist in the Mendelssohn Violin Concerto under St. Leger in January 1933.

The 1935–36 season brought three guest conductors: Vittorio Verse, former San Francisco Symphony conductor Alfred Hertz and Dr. Modeste Alloo. Each of them conducted two programs. Verse, who had been recruited to replace Nespoli as conductor of "Ma" Graham's Texas Grand Opera production of *Aida*, was also the featured soloist in Mozart's D major Piano Concerto, K.537, at the December 9 concert. Alloo was of Belgian ancestry and had been a trombonist with the Boston and Cincinnati orchestras. He also conducted the Cincinnati Conservatory Orchestra. He later became a band director at the University of California, Berkeley, and the University of Miami, Florida.[8] According to the *New York Times*, Alloo was a member of the conducting staff of the Federal Music Project at one point in his career. He conducted the season's final two concerts.

Hertz was far better known. Born in 1872 in Frankfurt, he held several positions in Germany before taking over the German-language repertoire at the Metropolitan Opera where he conducted for 13 years. He conducted the San Francisco Symphony for 15 seasons, and he inaugurated the famed Hollywood Bowl concerts in Los Angeles during the summer of 1922. According to historian Roussel, Hertz was appalled at the sound of the orchestra when he arrived, insisting that additional instrumentalists be imported, and insisting on several extra rehearsals to bring the playing up to some decent standard. But his two concerts made the musicians, audiences and the Symphony Association realize what could be accomplished—and what needed to be done to achieve a creditable symphonic sound.

If it seems senseless that all this floundering occurred in the southern United States' second largest city (Atlanta was the largest) when prosperity abounded during the Roaring Twenties, one should remember that it was a tale told earlier by young orchestras in several regional cities across America. The venerable Cincinnati Symphony went through several starts and stops between 1857 and 1909, when Leopold Stokowski ascended the podium. The Kansas City Philharmonic went through a few demises and reincarnations in the late 19th century—and again in the 1980s. The histories of several more orchestras—each with its own tale of interruptions, renaming, mergers, etc.—characterize the establishment of orchestral music from San Francisco to New York. Though Houston was chartered as a city as far back as 1836, the labor pains, growing pains and childhood tantrums associated with the birth and establishment of the Houston Symphony were entirely confined to the 20th century. The city was exactly 100 years old before its young orchestra got its feet on the ground and started catching up with its peers in the rest of the nation.

CHAPTER
III

ERNST HOFFMANN

The 23-year-old Symphony Association renamed itself the Houston Symphony Society when Ernst Hoffmann became conductor in 1936, but the orchestra had performed under the organization's auspices only ten seasons. So, Hoffmann can be credited as the orchestra's first great builder, who nurtured its growth and survival, paving the way to its present status.[1]

Ernst Heinrich Hoffmann was born June 18, 1899, in Boston. His father was a Boston Symphony violinist who had immigrated to the United States from Czechoslovakia in 1890. His paternal grandfather had been born in Hungary. Though his mother, Paula Schwitzer (Hoffmann), was born in Poland, both of her parents also came from Hungary.[2]

Hoffmann became an accomplished pianist during his youth and graduated cum laude from Harvard University with a major in anthropology. He furthered his musical studies at Berlin's Hochschule für Musik, where he met and married Annemarie Clara Hoffman in 1922 (her maiden name was the same as his but spelled differently), and he played in theater orchestras there. In 1924, he became conductor of the opera and orchestra in Breslau, where Christoph Eschenbach was born 16 years later.

He retained his position for ten years until Hitler came to power; then he was banned because of his American citizenship and his opposition to the Nazi movement. He returned to Boston where he founded the Commonwealth Symphony, a Depression-era orchestra funded by the Works Progress Administration. That was where Walter Walne, president of the Houston Symphony Society, located him, based on a recommendation by Boston Symphony conductor Serge Koussevitzky.

The prospective new conductor was brought to Houston for an interview by the board, but according to Roussel, he alighted from the train and accepted the board's invitation before the Symphony Society had a chance to decide whether it wanted him. Arthur Judson, Hoffmann's New York manager, cited his ability "to sense the future in almost virgin territory."[3]

The six-concert format remained in place for the 1936–37 season, and dramatic music (selections from opera, ballet and theater) were strongly represented on all six programs. But Hoffmann deployed the music skillfully. The third program was a concert performance of Puccini's *Madama Butterfly*, employing resident singers and the combined choirs of Christ Church Episcopal Cathedral and St. Paul's Methodist Church. In a politically astute gesture, Hoffmann awarded the role of the Consul to Christ Church's choirmaster, George W. Barnes, while Mrs. Huffmaster (wife of St. Paul's choirmaster) sang the role of Suzuki. The fourth program contained music based on Shakespearean plays, including such rarities as American composer John Knowles Paine's orchestral work *The Tempest*. There were no concertos and only three symphonies all season long: Schubert's Ninth, Tchaikovsky's Fourth and Brahms' Second.

From the *Galveston Daily News*, January 11, 1940:

"Mr. Hoffmann's father was Jacques Hoffmann… who owned two famed Guarnerius violins which are now the property of the younger Hoffmann and are used in the orchestra. The Houston Symphony also boasts two violins made by Guadanini, famous Italian violin-maker of bygone years. …It is the only orchestra in the U.S. which has a rotary valve trumpet. Hoffmann… plays every instrument in the orchestra, he admits the harp and the French horn give him trouble."

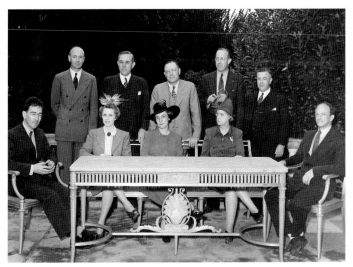

Hoffmann rounded out his cycle of Puccini favorites with a fully staged production of *Tosca* in April 1944 and *La Bohème* in 1945. Both featured Houston soprano Elva Kalb Dumas in the respective title roles, tenor Myron Taylor as Cavaradossi and Rodolfo, and baritone Edward Bing as Scarpia and Marcello. (A decade later, Bing was to become a charter member of the Houston Grand Opera board.) The trio also sang the third act of Verdi's *Aida* on the closing concert of the 1941–42 season.

For two seasons, 1939–40 and 1940–41, the number of subscription programs increased from six to ten, and then settled into nine programs for five of Hoffmann's remaining six seasons with the orchestra. But the orchestra's exposure to the citizenry grew in other ways. As early as 1937, his second season in Houston, there were four student concerts and five pops concerts. These were confined almost entirely to light classics, but Hoffmann also reached out to younger audiences with a "college night" in the pops series, inviting the Rice University Band and Glee Club, and the University of Houston Singers to perform. Brass and drum sections of the Rice Band returned in 1942 to play a prelude and fugue on "Dixie." The Singing Cadets from Aggieland (Texas A&M University) sang a group of male choruses on an operatic program in 1942, and Wilfred Bain's North Texas State Choir sang Rachmaninoff's choral/orchestral work *The Bells* on an all-Rachmaninoff program in 1944.

The standard orchestral repertoire also began to be regularly surveyed, although at least half of each program was still peppered with short overtures, marches, dances, arias and orchestral excerpts from operas, and other salon pieces. A program limited to an overture, a big piano concerto and a major symphony was pretty hard to come by.

But there were significant items here and there. Hoffmann opened the December 6, 1937, program with Mendelssohn's huge, rarely performed symphony/cantata *The Hymn of Praise*, featuring a choral group called the Houston Symphony Society Chorus. That was 12 years before the Houston Chorale became the orchestra's regularly constituted chorus. On March 23, 1942, Hoffmann conducted what was apparently the first Houston Symphony performance of Beethoven's Ninth Symphony, with vocal soloists Frances Lockhart, Helen Havens, Fred Kendall and Hugh Martin, and choirs from the city of Denton and its North Texas State Teachers College prepared by its famed choral conductor and dean, Wilfred C. Bain.

Previous spread: **New conductor Ernst Hoffmann on September 24, 1936.** Top: **City Auditorium was built in 1910 and served as the Symphony's home from 1932–38 and from 1939–53.** Bottom: **An early 1940s Symphony business meeting on the veranda of the Cullen house. Seated, left to right: Ernst Hoffmann, Hazel Ledbetter, Fredrica Dudley, Lillie Cullen and Isaac Arnold, Sr. Standing, left to right: Ted Swigart, Hugh Roy Cullen, Leopold Meyer, Harry Bourne and Joe Henkel.** Left: **Concertmaster Joseph Gallo in 1940.**

For the first time, a list of distinguished guest soloists began to appear with the orchestra: pianists Robert Casadesus, Harold Bauer (Hoffmann's former teacher), Artur Schnabel, Claudio Arrau and William Kapell; violinists Albert Spalding and Zino Francescatti; violist William Primrose; sopranos Helen Jepson, Bidú Sayão, Rose Bampton, Grace Moore and Helen Traubel; mezzo soprano Gladys Swarthout; baritone Mack Harrell; and bass Ezio Pinza. Resident Houston and Texas musicians continued to figure prominently as soloists: pianists Drusilla Huffmaster, Monte Hill Davis and Jacques Abram (a former student of Miss Hogg), and violinist Fredell Lack, playing the Bruch G minor Concerto in the first of numerous Houston Symphony engagements over the next several decades.

Weekly radio broadcasts, sponsored by the Texas Gulf Sulphur Company (now Dow Chemical), began in February 1945. They continued—with some possible interruptions—during the orchestra's winter series through the end of the 1950–51 season. Thirty-minute broadcasts were carried by Houston radio station KPRC and were broadcast to Amarillo, Dallas, Fort Worth, San Antonio, Weslaco and the Rio Grande Valley by the Texas Quality Network. Hoffmann designed the repertoire to include lighter fare, along with individual movements from standard symphonic works, so the half-hour broadcasts would appeal to a broad swath of musical tastes. Thus, the radio series did not broadcast the orchestra's subscription programs. They were separate and emanated from the 250-seat performance hall at the Carter Music Company, Houston's Steinway piano dealership. At age 12, pianist Van Cliburn was featured on the April 12, 1947, broadcast, playing the first movement of the Tchaikovsky Piano Concerto in B-flat minor after winning a student competition sponsored by the Houston Symphony.

National exposure on the airwaves came on February 22, 1947, when Hoffmann and the Houston Symphony were featured on NBC's weekly broadcast series *Orchestras of the Nation*. Hoffmann began the hour-long program with Don Gillis' Overture to an Unwritten Opera, following it with the Rondo movement from Mozart's *Haffner* Serenade, featuring violinist Raphael Fliegel as soloist. Brahms' Fourth Symphony was the major work on the program, performed in honor of the 50th anniversary of the composer's death.

The orchestra participated in two other national broadcasts during Hoffmann's tenure. At the behest and under the sponsorship of Symphony patron Hugh Roy Cullen, soprano Lucille Manners and the entire production staff of NBC's *Cities Service* program were brought to Houston to broadcast a pops concert from the Houston Music Hall, which was then followed by a special concert for military servicemen stationed at Houston's Ellington Field, on January 15, 1943. The live broadcast was transmitted by NBC affiliate KPRC from City Auditorium, and orchestra manager Francis Deering struggled with the problem of having only 4,000 seats available for a crowd of 10,000 Houstonians who wanted to attend. On January 25, 1944, the orchestra was featured on the *Voice of Firestone* program, with tenor Richard Crooks and violist William Primrose as soloists.

During the height of World War II, between 1942 and 1945, 15 to 19 Houston Symphony members were called into military service. But Hoffmann did not let the orchestra die, as had been the case during the first World War. Replacements were found and the orchestra made many patriotic gestures to the American cause.

Cullen personally sponsored extended tours by the Houston Symphony to military bases coordinated by the United Service Organization over three seasons (1942–45). Hoffmann and the orchestra performed a total of 55 concerts in Texas and Louisiana on these tours. Mostly, they were performed in short groups of three to four concerts, scheduled after one of the orchestra's regular monthly programs in City Auditorium. But some of those tours took the orchestra hundreds of miles away—as far as San Angelo, Waco, Abilene, Wichita Falls, Corpus Christi, Laredo and Harlingen. Other patriotic orchestral activities included a notorious wrestling match accompanied by groaning sound effects from the Symphony during a highly successful $7 million war bond drive in 1944. In addition to its commitment to military audiences, the orchestra made three civilian tours to 15 cities in Texas, Louisiana and Mississippi in the 1941–42 season; to 24 cities in Texas and Louisiana in the 1942–43 season; and another Texas/ Louisiana tour that ventured into Mexico for its first international exposure during the 1943–44 season.

Hoffmann's most enduring legacy was the establishment of the free summer concert series at Miller Outdoor Theatre in

Hermann Park. More than anything, this gesture fulfilled the wish of his early predecessor, Julien Paul Blitz, to "bring it (the orchestra) closer to the people." The original Grecian-style Miller Memorial Theatre was designed by architect William Ward Watkin and built in 1923, thanks to a $50,000 bequest to the City of Houston from mining engineer Jesse Wright Miller.

In the summer of 1940, music critic Hubert Roussel quoted a letter to the *Houston Post* from an unnamed greengrocer, wondering why there were no free summer concerts. Thanks to a flood of incoming letters, underwriting from cotton and real estate broker N. D. Naman and Hoffmann's enthusiasm for the project, test concerts were held soliciting audience contributions and the series began. After a few years, it was jointly sponsored by the City of Houston and the Symphony Society. With additional funding from numerous corporations and foundations, it has now survived for more than 70 years.

The stage of the original theater could accommodate only 45 musicians, so nearly half the orchestra was laid off during the summer months. The Houston Symphony's participation reached a height of 18 concerts in the late 1960s when a new steel batwing structure replaced the original theater, accommodating the entire orchestra. But then the number of concerts was gradually reduced to five, to make way for a broad range of free summer events in Houston's burgeoning performing arts community. As an extension of the Miller Theatre series, Houston Symphony musicians performed at neighborhood parks throughout the city for several decades during the middle of the century.

In February 1942, the orchestra's seventh subscription program at City Auditorium began as usual at 8:15 p.m. President Roosevelt's speech was broadcast from the stage at 9 p.m. This was his Fireside Chat number 20 on the progress of the war.

Two very special events were scheduled early in March 1947, as Hoffmann's tenure came down to its last two months. As part of the first annual Texas Creative Arts Festival, conceived by Ima Hogg and held in conjunction with the Houston convention of the Texas Federation of Music Clubs, the Houston Symphony gave its first performance of Bach's B minor Mass, featuring national soloists and Wilfred Bain's North Texas State choirs on March 7 in City Auditorium.

Late the next afternoon, the orchestra staged an outdoor performance of Gluck's *Orpheus and Eurydice* on the terraced lawn of Bayou Bend, Miss Hogg's estate. The project suggests that Hoffmann may have been reminded of the outdoor theaters in European cities, where manicured lawns, shrubbery, hedges and sloping hillsides were shaped and trimmed to provide stage, backdrop and seating areas for performances alfresco. Alas, a sudden March windstorm swept through Miss Hogg's famed azalea garden, blowing costumes, scenic properties and sheet music to the four corners of her River Oaks neighborhood, while chilled singers, dancers and musicians sought shelter wherever they could.

Throughout their 11 years in Houston, the Hoffmanns accepted humble tasks at a time when volunteerism meant survival. He arrived an hour before rehearsals to set up chairs, music stands and orchestra parts. He bought musical instruments to help certain musicians improve their performance. He and his wife, Annamarie, housed, clothed, fed and found jobs for refugee musicians fleeing Nazi horrors.

Alas, when the war ended, Houston had grown tired of Hoffmann's many years of hard, monumental work, which he accomplished on a mere $10,000 salary. Historian Roussel tells us he was dismissed amid a bitter schism on the Symphony board. Hugh Roy Cullen opposed the change and threatened to withdraw all his support of the Symphony. His fury forced incoming president Joseph S. Smith to resign after only a week in office. Cullen sent Hoffmann an extra $10,000 to tide him over.

Thanks to his old friend Wilfred Bain, Hoffmann found a worthy conducting position at Indiana University, establishing an historic annual Eastertide performance of Wagner's *Parsifal* and helping to build the university's school of music into the powerful institution it is today. Life ended tragically for the Hoffmanns, who were killed in an automobile accident early in 1956, after visiting their son in Houston during the Christmas holidays.

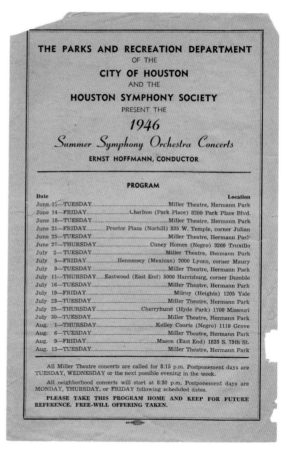

Top: **The Symphony helped to sell war bonds in 1944 in the world's first wrestling match and symphony concert. Wrestler Ellis Bashara was a bit upset at the orchestra's playing of Chopin's *Funeral March* and took the slender conductor Ernst Hoffmann in a headlock.** Bottom: **The City of Houston Parks and Recreation Department sponsored outdoor concerts of the Symphony at Miller Memorial Theatre.** Right: **The Houston Symphony (Summer Symphony) at Miller Memorial Theatre, August 17, 1946.**

Symphony

OFFICIAL PUBLICATION
HOUSTON SYMPHONY SOCIETY

EFREM KURTZ, *Guest Conductor*

MARCH 8, 1948

CHAPTER
IV

EFREM KURTZ

The uproar within the Houston Symphony board of directors caused by the dismissal of Ernst Hoffmann caused a season's delay in naming his successor. Efrem Kurtz had been a guest conductor during Hoffmann's final season and was the intended heir to the podium, but Hugh Roy Cullen's furious opposition and threat to withdraw all support of the orchestra resulted in a series of guest conductors for 1947–48, letting tempers cool down for a season.[1]

The list of candidates included some impressive names: Charles Munch, the young Leonard Bernstein and Maurice Abravanel. There were two composer/conductors: Carlos Chávez and George Enescu. Kurtz was on the list, conducting Mahler's First Symphony—the initial performance of any Mahler symphony by the orchestra. Others included Hans Schwieger, Dr. Frieder Weissman, Walter Hendl, Tauno Hannikainen, Igor Buketoff and the young Massimo Freccia, who was then music director of the New Orleans Philharmonic. Eventually, Kurtz was named music director and conductor for the 1948–49 season.

Russian-born Kurtz was no stranger to Houston audiences, for he had conducted yuletide engagements by the touring Ballet Russe de Monte Carlo during an eight-year term (1933–41) as the troupe's music director. He was also no stranger to orchestral music, having been conductor of the Stuttgart Philharmonic from 1924 to 1933, and music director of the Kansas City Philharmonic from 1943 to 1947.[2]

Roussel indicated that Kurtz' accomplishments had more to do with refurbishing the orchestra than making inherently great music. The 1948–49 budget grew to $311,000, $111,000 over Ernst Hoffmann's final year. There was also a large turnover in the orchestra's roster: two-thirds of its players were new members.[3] Kurtz did not wait for applicants to come knocking on his door. He held auditions at leading music festivals on the East and West Coasts, bringing in several new musicians from elsewhere in the nation.

The number of women in the Houston Symphony became a matter of interest during Kurtz' tenure. The 1947–48 season of guest conductors preceding his appointment saw the number of women rise to 21—over a quarter of the 79-member roster. During his first season, it fell to 19, then fluctuated between 14 and 21 women musicians for the remainder of his term. During his first season, he had special attire designed for the women, with white vests, black jackets and floor-length skirts, so that they closely matched the men's formal attire.

Olin Downes, music critic of the *New York Times*, discussed the matter of women in symphony orchestras at considerable length in the May 15, 1949 edition. He cited George Szell, music director of the Cleveland Orchestra, who deplored the dearth of qualified orchestral string players coming out of American music schools at the time. Male string players left conservatories and quickly sought work as soloists, knowing only a few flashy concertos, whereas women stayed longer and were more thoroughly trained in the refinements of string playing.

Kurtz was also interviewed for the article and he proposed two solutions to the problem: increase the pay of orchestral string players so that it equals the pay of wind players, and admit more women to the ranks of symphony orchestras. At the time, Downes noted that the New York Philharmonic and the Boston Symphony had no women players and the NBC Symphony had only one. As a point of comparison, violinists Rosetta Hirsch and Marian Jenkins were charter members of the Houston Symphony in 1913. There were four women by the 1917–18 season, when the original orchestra disbanded, and there were 17 women among the 72 orchestra musicians, with Josephine Boudreaux as concertmaster, for the February 18, 1932, concert during Uriel Nespoli's tenure.

Orchestral rosters during Kurtz' term indicate the number of musicians grew suddenly from 79 members during the 1947–48

Previous spread: **Efrem Kurtz program cover, 1948.**
Above: Oboist **Laila Storch was one of the 1948 recruits of Efrem Kurtz. She is wearing the new women's costume created by Paris designer Gisèle de Biezville.** Right:
Efrem Kurtz, left, discusses the score of *The Red Pony* suite with composer Aaron Copland, October 31, 1948.

"There had regularly been nine to ten programs throughout Hoffmann's tenure. During the 1947–48 season of guest conductors, the number of programs grew to 12."

season (the season of guest conductors) to 90 musicians during his first season. Thereafter, the numbers declined steadily, reaching a low of 78 during his final season. However, the number of subscription programs doubled. There had regularly been nine to ten programs throughout Hoffmann's tenure. During the 1947–48 season of guest conductors, the number of programs grew to 12. There were only 11 during Kurtz' first season (1948–49), but the number jumped to 19 programs in 1949–50 and 20 programs throughout his remaining four years with the orchestra.

The list of soloists had already represented a broad sampling of international concert artists during Hoffmann's

tenure and that level was maintained—and possibly raised—during Kurtz' tenure. But regular guest conductors were new to the scene and there was an astute group of names on the list: Sir Thomas Beecham, Leopold Stokowski, André Kostelanetz, Milton Katims—all of whom developed future commitments to the orchestra—plus Dmitri Mitropoulos, Bruno Walter, Eugene Ormandy, Vladimir Golschmann, Maurice Abravanel and Ferenc Fricsay. In comparison to Hoffmann who had conducted virtually all the subscription programs during his tenure, Kurtz' policy of featuring several guest conductors brought new faces and different interpretive styles to the orchestra and audiences.

There was also a decent taste of 20th-century music. Roy Harris' *Elegy and Paean* was a solo vehicle for violist William Primrose in December 1948, followed by Harold Shapero's overture *The Travelers*, in February 1949. New works by Houston and other Texas composers Thomas Beversdorf, David Guion, John Rice and Merrills Lewis also made their way onto Symphony programs. With his broader international background, Kurtz also brought Houston Symphony musicians and audiences their first performances of Albert Roussel's Third Symphony, Shostakovich's Ninth Symphony, Prokofiev's Sixth Symphony and the acclaimed Short Symphony by African-American composer Howard Swanson.

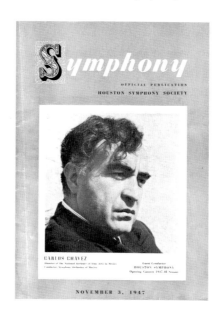

Kurtz led the orchestra on its first national tour in 1949–50, playing in 20 cities including Chicago. He lived for another 41 years after his tenure ended in 1954. He shared the music directorship of the Liverpool Philharmonic Orchestra with John Pritchard for two seasons, then limited his conducting activities to guest engagements on a worldwide basis. He returned as a guest conductor in 1971, again for a single appearance during the 1978–79 season and twice in the 1979–80 season, when the orchestra was between music directors.

In 1948, Tom M. Johnson began a 25-year career as manager of the Houston Symphony. And at the end of the 1948–49 season, the Houston Chorale (predecessor of the Houston Symphony Chorus) was officially affiliated with the Houston Symphony. (It had been organized by Symphony cellist/personnel manager Alfred Urbach in 1946.) The Chorale made its debut singing the finale of Beethoven's Ninth Symphony on April 11, 1949. External glamour was added that season by the commissioning and premiere of Aaron Copland's Children's Suite from *The Red Pony*, extracted from his film score, and the guest engagement of Igor Stravinsky to conduct his own music.

Top: **The Houston Symphony with Efrem Kurtz in 1952–53.** Bottom: **Carlos Chávez made his first Houston Symphony appearance in 1947.** Right: **Ray Fliegel, left, making music with Jack Benny at KTRH Radio.**

CHAPTER

V

FERENC FRICSAY & LEOPOLD STOKOWSKI

Following Kurtz' departure in 1954, the Houston Symphony Society began to look for conductors with a higher international profile. First came Hungarian-born Ferenc Fricsay, 39-year-old founding conductor of the orchestra in what was then West Berlin's RIAS (Radio Station in the American Sector).

Fricsay had previously been a guest conductor at the November 23, 1953, concert, during Kurtz' final season.[1] His conducting brought unprecedented rounds of enthusiastic applause from the audience, followed by letters and telephone calls to the Symphony offices urging his permanent appointment. He was signed to a contract as "principal conductor" for the 1954–55 season, conducting 16 of the 20 subscription programs, some pops concerts and regional concerts. His salary was reportedly set to exceed the $30,000 paid annually to Kurtz.[2]

He arrived at the moment a renovation had been completed on Houston's Music Hall, a Depression-era theater that had been physically attached to the Houston Coliseum. Alas, a common wall separating the rear of the Music Hall stage and the arena in the adjoining Coliseum transmitted the sounds of sporting events into the midst of musical and theatrical performances. While the renovation achieved some improvements, the acoustical deficiencies and limited stage space were not eliminated, and Fricsay's blunt requests for a new set of costly remedies—including a new hall, expansion of the orchestra, lengthening of the season, tours and facilities for recording—quickly alienated board members.[3] These sudden new financial demands brought about a rupture before the 1954–55 season was half finished. When Fricsay and his wife returned to Europe for a contractually scheduled vacation over the Christmas holiday, the Houston Symphony Society sent letters offering to release him from his obligation to return. After a brief retort, Fricsay pleaded illness and remained in Europe, gaining major positions with the Munich Opera and his former orchestra in Berlin. He died in 1963 at age 49.

Nevertheless, Fricsay's conducting left an indelible impression on at least one Houston Symphony musician. Concertmaster Raphael Fliegel carried a violin part with the conductor's markings for bowings and phrasing in his violin case for the rest of his career, employing them as an example for his colleagues and students. He cherished his brief opportunity to perform under Fricsay, holding him in the highest esteem.[4] Throughout his

career, the conductor was noted for his extremely clean, precise performances, achieved without the use of a baton. He guided his orchestral musicians using only his two expressive hands. (Stokowski was also noted for this practice.)

Sir Thomas Beecham presided over most of the remaining concerts in the 1954–55 season, while the Houston Symphony Society scored a behind-the-scenes coup in engaging Leopold Stokowski. Miss Hogg, founding board member and president of the organization at the time, was credited with bringing both conductors to Houston.[5]

At age 73, Stokowski had enjoyed major careers with the Cincinnati Symphony and Philadelphia Orchestra, and his white-maned profile was known worldwide, thanks to his involvement in conducting the film score of Walt Disney's *Fantasia*. Substituting cajolery for Fricsay's bluntness, he persuaded Symphony benefactors to make acoustical adjustments to the recently remodeled Music Hall. He was credited with polishing the orchestra's sound more than any of his predecessors. He was an advocate of free bowing among string players, allowing them to individually choose when to change the movement of the bow (up or down) within a given musical phrase. He also instituted a regular series of recordings, including Carl Orff's *Carmina Burana*, Reinhold Glière's Third Symphony, the first commercial recording of Shostakovich's 11th Symphony and excerpts from Wagner's *Die Walküre*. These and other Stokowski Houston Symphony recordings are still commercially available at this writing.

> "Concertmaster Raphael Fliegel carried a violin part with the conductor's markings for bowings and phrasing in his violin case for the rest of his career, employing them as an example for his colleagues and students."

Previous spread: **Leopold Stokowski in the late 1940s. He was first a guest conductor of the Houston Symphony in 1950.** Above: **Ferenc and Silvia Fricsay at the Houston airport, 1954.** Right: **Ferenc Fricsay and Tom Johnson with a sold-out concert sign at City Auditorium, 1954.**

But Stokowski's reputation for providing his audiences too steady a diet of new and unfamiliar music was soon made manifest in Houston, and empty seats quickly proliferated. While some of his repertoire was most worthwhile, some of it was music from the fringes of the standard repertoire. Numerous Stokowski transcriptions also kept popping up on programs—not only of works by Bach, but also Handel and Chopin. Periodically, allegations also circulated about his insulting, threatening behavior toward orchestra musicians,[6] and the inscrutable Stokowski grew increasingly alienated, sometimes condescending in his attitude. He terminated his association with the orchestra in the middle of the 1960–61 season, citing his desire to be closer to his two sons in New York, following a protracted and bitter divorce proceeding from his fifth wife, Gloria Vanderbilt.

Stokowski's frustrated effort to mount a production of Schoenberg's *Gurrelieder*, featuring mezzo-soprano Shirley Verrett with the Texas Southern University Chorus, exacerbated his alienation at the very end of his Houston career and became a matter of national embarrassment for the Houston Symphony during the last years of racial segregation. After initially declining, the Symphony Society granted his request during a guest engagement to perform the work during the 1961–62 season. But two additional white choruses that were needed to perform the work declined to participate and the Symphony Society had to withdraw the invitation—apparently without fully explaining the matter to Stokowski, who publicized it widely.[7]

The orchestra numbered 89 members when Stokowski began his conductorship in 1955, but it quickly grew to between 91 and 93 members through most of his tenure. Interestingly, specific musicians were named on the roster when additional wind, brass and percussion instruments were needed for large works requiring more than the normal complement. Stokowski's orchestral roster also called for 12 violas and 12 cellos, enriching the middle and lower tonal resources of the orchestra's string section. Stokowski also placed all the cellos in a line across the back of the stage, with the double basses on risers behind them.

During Stokowski's tenure, the orchestra's schedule began a crucial period of consolidation. Previously, the Houston Symphony had played single performances of 20 different subscription programs under Kurtz in the larger 3,500-seat City Auditorium.[8] That number was reduced to 18 single programs during

Sir Thomas Beecham

Although conductor Sir Thomas Beecham was only here briefly, he made quite an impression on the Houston Symphony board and audience. He was the darling of English society and came from a wealthy family who made its fortune from Beecham's Little Liver Pills.

The Symphony's late concertmaster Ray Fliegel related this story:
The orchestra was playing a pops concert, so they were not in black tie, but were wearing suits. Beecham strolled onstage to applause, stood at the podium, and leaned over to Ray, saying in a semi-soft voice, "I like your suit." Ray thanked him and fought not to laugh, and they were off on the first movement. When the movement ended, Beecham leaned over once more and in a normal-volume voice said, "Where'd you get the suit?" So Ray told him where, and they went on with the concert, with the whole section struggling to keep straight faces. At the next rehearsal, Beecham came in wearing the same suit.*

"When Beecham was conducting the Houston Symphony at Texas A&M, the cadets applauded every time there was a pause. Finally, Beecham turned around and told them: 'No matter how hard you try, we're going to play to the end.'"†

* Interview with Ray Fliegel, December 9, 2002, Houston Symphony Archives.
† Interview with Ray Fliegel, *Upbeat*, newsletter of the Orchestra Committee of the Houston Symphony, vol. 1, no. 1 (May 1989).

Alan Hovhaness

Alan Hovhaness' compositions were championed by conductor Leopold Stokowski, who led the world premiere of Symphony No. 2, Opus 132, *Mysterious Mountain* in 1955 on a nationwide broadcast on NBC radio. The next year, Stokowski programmed *As on the Night* and in 1957 gave another world premiere performance with *Ad Lyram*, commissioned by the Houston Symphony. Yet another Hovhaness piece, *Meditation on Orpheus*, was performed in the 1958–59 season. When the time came to choose a composer to commemorate the opening of Jones Hall in 1966, Hovhaness returned with *Ode to the Temple of Sound*.

Stokowski's second season (1956–57) in the smaller 3,000-seat Music Hall. This evolved largely to 15 pairs of subscription concerts from his third season onward. Also in contrast, Kurtz had conducted most of the standard 20 subscription programs throughout his tenure, but Stokowski's schedule called for a gradually diminishing presence on the podium: 10 of the 20 single subscription concerts during his initial 1955–56 season, 12 of the 18 single concerts in 1956–57, eight of the 12 subscription pairs in 1957–58, and eight of the 15 subscription pairs that became standard over the 1958–59 and 1959–60 seasons. He only conducted four of the 16 subscription pairs in the 1960–61 season before resigning in December 1960. André Kostelanetz and Sir Malcolm Sargent substituted for six of the remaining concerts, aided by single engagements from Laszlo Somogyi, Vladimir Golschmann, Georges Sebastian and Erich Leinsdorf.

Top, clockwise from left: **Gerald Fippinger and horn section during the recording of _Carmina Burana_ in City Auditorium. Leopold Stokowski, circa 1957. Marquee of the Music Hall in February 1960, when the orchestra played for the Houston Foundation for Ballet in ballet director Tatiana Semenova's _Enigma_. Leopold Stokowski at the sound boards during the recording of _Carmina Burana_, 1958. United Press named it the finest classical recording of 1959.** Bottom: **Winifred Hirsch with Esme Gunn and Leopold Stokowski.** Next spread: **The Houston Symphony plays for Houston Grand Opera's production of _Salome_, 1955.**

CHAPTER
VI

SIR JOHN BARBIROLLI

Sir John Barbirolli first raised his baton over the Houston Symphony as a guest conductor in February 1960 and began his tenure as conductor-in-chief in the fall of 1961. The eight and one-half years he spent with the orchestra can be considered its happiest time until the arrival of Christoph Eschenbach in the late 1980s.

Barbirolli was a world-renowned conductor who had followed Arturo Toscanini on the New York Philharmonic podium in 1937, then returned to his native England in 1943—the middle of World War II—to resuscitate Manchester's venerable but ailing Hallé Orchestra. He shared the two podiums during his entire tenure in Houston and also guest conducted the world's leading orchestras, becoming especially beloved by the musicians of the Berlin Philharmonic.

Under Barbirolli, the Houston Symphony's roster grew to 90 members, and the subscription concerts held steady at 16 pairs, 12 of which were conducted by him. He held the title of conductor-in-chief of both the Hallé Orchestra and the Houston Symphony, starting the Hallé's season in September and then coming to Houston to begin the season here in October. He would fly back to Manchester for midwinter concerts, returning to Houston in late January or February.[1]

Essentially a traditionalist in his choice of works, Barbirolli professed a special love for the music of Mahler and Elgar. His Houston performances included six of the nine Mahler symphonies (Nos. 1–5 and 9), and all but Mahler's First Symphony were new to the Houston Symphony's repertoire. He was also famed for his interpretations of Debussy, Ravel and Sibelius. Works of other English composers, particularly Vaughan Williams and Delius, were prominently featured among 33 compositions by 13 British composers he conducted in Houston.

He conducted 23 works by 19 American composers on his Houston programs. These included pieces by Houston composers Elmer Schoettle and Merrills Lewis and a handsome string symphony by Ukrainian-born Fort Worth composer Serge Saxe. Overall, Barbirolli conducted music by some 90 different composers during his Houston years,[2] and he was thoroughly comfortable with the entire standard orchestral literature. His finest asset was his ability to let the music speak naturally, as though the composer were on the podium leading the orchestra without interference from a conductor.

Barbirolli almost never interrupted a musical performance to address the audience, but there was a memorable exception at the Houston Symphony premiere of Sir Edward Elgar's Second Symphony on February 13–14, 1967. He prefaced the performance with a few words, revealing how important the Elgar symphony had been to his own career as a struggling 27-year-old conductor four decades earlier. He told of receiving a sudden call to replace ailing Sir Thomas Beecham and learning the score to the Elgar symphony on 48 hours' notice. With a touch of Barbirollian humor peeking out of the story, he recalled the London Symphony management saying, "Let's give young Johnny a try."

Barbirolli turned serious as he defined the work's message and relevance to his own life. "It is a masterpiece of the first order and the last of the symphonies in the formal manner," he said. He set the 1911 symphony and his own adolescent years against the dark, looming clouds of World War I. Recalling Sir Edward Gray's much quoted statement, "The lights have gone out all over Europe, never to be lit again," Barbirolli said, "I am… I was… an Edwardian boy. I was even a Victorian boy. It is an epilogue that brings tears to my eyes. It symbolizes a certain world that unfortunately exists no more."[3] Then, turning to the orchestra, he conducted a heartfelt interpretation of the Elgar symphony, expressing the nobility and magnificence of the music along with its

> "Essentially a traditionalist in his choice of works, Barbirolli professed a special love for the music of Mahler and Elgar."

sense of impending tragedy in one of his most long-remembered performances with the Houston Symphony.

In the spring of 1967, Barbirolli also settled an agonizing financial dispute, winning a $78,855 settlement from the estate of the conductor's former personal business manager, Kenneth Crickmore.[4] In October 1965, Barbirolli had filed a $100,000 claim against Crickmore's estate in San Diego Superior Court[5], charging Crickmore with having converted that amount of money, which he handled for the conductor, to his own use.[6] Lady Barbirolli said the diversion of funds had been going on for several years, unknown to them. In a 1965 letter, Barbirolli indicated that "at [age] 66, I have practically to begin again."[7] Lady Barbirolli credited Houston Symphony Society president Maurice Hirsch with helping the Barbirollis find legal counsel in the United States to pursue their suit against Crickmore's estate.[8]

Previous spread: **Sir John Barbirolli and concertmaster Raphael Fliegel, 1960s.** Top: **Houston Symphony in the Music Hall with Sir John Barbirolli, 1961–62.** Bottom: **Musician Hugh Gibson's invitation for a White House tour.** Left: **Sir John Barbirolli at the Mahler Symphony No. 2 rehearsal, March 1962.**

Settlement of the suit roughly coincided with the announcement that Barbirolli would relinquish his position as conductor-in-chief to André Previn at the end of the 1966–67 season, becoming conductor emeritus and returning for fewer concerts each fall and spring.

Barbirolli's greatest glories came during the Houston Symphony's 50th anniversary celebration in 1963–64, and again during the orchestra's inaugural season in Jesse H. Jones Hall for the Performing Arts, 1966–67. The 50th anniversary season embraced the orchestra's most tragic and triumphant observances. President John F. Kennedy visited Houston on the eve of his assassination in Dallas. Three days later, Barbirolli prefaced the November 25–26, 1963, subscription program with a performance of the "Nimrod" movement from Elgar's *Enigma Variations*, connecting it by way of a muted drumroll to a solemn account of "The Star-Spangled Banner."

Though the orchestra's Golden Anniversary tour had been booked long before the orchestra set out in February 1964, Lyndon Johnson had succeeded Kennedy as president in November, months before Barbirolli and the orchestra arrived for their Washington, D.C., concert in Constitution Hall. Letters had flown back and forth between Houston and Washington, making detailed arrangements and issuing invitations for numerous social engagements including a private White House tour and reception for the orchestra and a luncheon honoring Miss Hogg, who joined the presidential entourage in its Constitution Hall box for the concert itself. Indeed, the Houston Symphony's delegation of touring supporters was the toast of several gala events hosted by fellow Texans living in Washington. Much the same reception greeted the Houston Symphony and its supporters on their arrival in New York. The press lavished high praise upon the orchestra, greatly boosting its status as one of the nation's leading symphonic ensembles. And *Time* magazine dubbed Miss Hogg "Empress of the Symphony," headlining a feature article on the orchestra's first tour to Washington and New York.

The Golden Anniversary tour was the first of four annual tours the orchestra took under Barbirolli's leadership and the first the orchestra had undertaken under its chief conductor since the one led by Kurtz in 1949–50. Stokowski had relegated touring

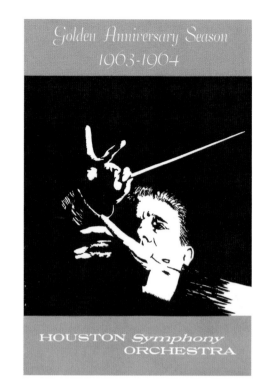

activities to guest conductors Walter Susskind, Milton Katims and his associate conductor Maurice Bonney. That practice left the Houston Symphony at a disadvantage in competition with other touring orchestras for the best locations and tour dates. But under Barbirolli, the Houston Symphony toured major cities from Miami all the way up the East Coast to Boston and Montreal, Canada. On its first tour through Western states in 1967, there were major engagements in Missoula, Montana, San Francisco, Los Angeles, Phoenix and Albuquerque. The orchestra played 78 concerts at 75 venues in 29 states during Barbirolli's four tours.

The Houston Symphony's inaugural concert in Jones Hall on October 2, 1966, was another highlight of Barbirolli's Houston career. He opened the new hall with a magical performance of Ravel's second *Daphnis et Chloé* suite and ended that season with a celestial Houston premiere of Mahler's Third Symphony. He was named conductor emeritus in 1967 and conductor laureate of the Hallé Orchestra the following year.

Sir John was beloved by his musicians for encouraging and helping them play better, as opposed to replacing those of lesser talent. While that made for a happy, secure orchestra, it also resulted in occasional problems of intonation, less-than-crisp ensemble playing and jarring moments of skewed notes, particularly in the horn and trombone sections. These problems were to persist for several seasons beyond his tenure.

As Barbirolli's health declined during his emeritus years, his Houston visits diminished in number, and there was a division of loyalty to a seasoned outgoing conductor who had headed four major orchestras, versus the appeal of André Previn, a young conductor who was taking over the helm of his first major orchestra—all complicated by the challenge of dealing with the non-profit world of the performing arts.

Age, failing health, the rigors of transatlantic travel in the middle of winter and the extended Houston Symphony tours gradually took their toll on Sir John's energy, but there was rarely an evening that he did not produce a glowing performance of at least one work. He collapsed on the Houston podium during a morning rehearsal in February 1968, and he was hospitalized overnight when he suffered a severe bronchial condition between two performances of Mahler's *Resurrection* Symphony a year later.

Barbirolli returned for a pair of November–December programs in the fall of 1969, in time to celebrate his 70th birthday on the podium with the Houston Symphony on December 2. But as Lady Barbirolli later recounted, there had been additional cardiopulmonary crises in Mexico City, Munich and other places around the world during the last years and months of Barbirolli's life. He was again hospitalized following a collapse on the podium during a New Philharmonia Orchestra rehearsal for a tour to Japan. His death in London on July 29, 1970, at age 70, was deeply mourned by musicians and audiences on both sides of the Atlantic Ocean.

Top: **Sir John Barbirolli takes a break from a Saturday morning rehearsal to watch a rodeo parade in 1964.** Bottom: **Ticket stub to a 1963 performance at the Music Hall.** Top left: **Sir John Barbirolli presided over the Houston Symphony's 50th anniversary season.** Center left: **Composer Alan Hovhaness and Ima Hogg at the opening of Jones Hall.** Bottom left: **Jones Hall opening night crowd, October 3, 1966.**

ANDRÉ PREVIN

Although André Previn's career with the Houston Symphony lasted barely two seasons (1967–69), he had appeared as guest pianist playing the Gershwin Concerto for a 1956 pops concert, as conductor for a *Houston Chronicle* Dollar Concert in January 1964 and as guest conductor for annual subscription concerts for three seasons beginning in the fall of 1964. The announcement of his appointment as conductor-in-chief was hailed as a bold move to place a young musician on the podium following the example of Leonard Bernstein at the New York Philharmonic.

The result was inconclusive. Though Previn was greatly admired by orchestra members for his keen ear, his clean baton technique, his generally fine musicianship and his impressive ability to absorb music quickly, he was nevertheless relatively new to the symphonic experience. Houston Symphony audiences were familiar with him from his previous guest appearances, which had been well attended, but they did not seem inspired by his interpretations.

Season subscriptions fell off severely in each of his two seasons, though single ticket sales experienced a turnaround during Previn's second season. In the face of rising costs that accompanied the move to Jones Hall and a difficult contract negotiation with the musicians that coincided with Previn's appointment, it was probably a miscalculation on the part of management to increase the number of subscription programs from 16 to 18 for the 1967–68 season. The orchestra numbered 91 musicians during Previn's short tenure.

Other events began to cause problems. In October 1967, the Houston Symphony Society declined a self-financed invitation to send the orchestra to Lincoln Center for three concerts during an annual festival of American and European orchestras in June–July 1968. The Houston Symphony's annual maintenance fund was $78,000 short of completion, and the Symphony Society was in the midst of matching a five-year, $2 million Ford Foundation grant. Even with the best box-office income, such a limited tour would have added $32,000 to the deficit in the orchestra's budget. Furthermore, the orchestra had already been scheduled to appear in Lincoln Center under Previn's baton during its Eastern tour, less than two months before the festival. So, Previn accepted a guest engagement conducting the Pittsburgh Symphony at the Lincoln Center Festival.

Within seven months of beginning his Houston engagement as conductor-in-chief—the same title Barbirolli had held—Previn's international career took a major leap forward when he was named principal conductor of the London Symphony Orchestra. Its extensive recording schedule was tailor-made for his efficient conducting skills, which had been honed during his 20-year career in the Hollywood film-music industry. At the time of his London appointment, Previn said it would not conflict with his position in Houston and that he was not leaving the Houston Symphony.[1]

Meanwhile, relations deteriorated between Previn and the Houston Symphony management and board as he voiced concerns about touring conditions, the lack of recording opportunities and his desire to be named music director. Despite attempts to include the Houston Symphony in Previn's RCA recording contract, officials from RCA had come to Houston, heard the orchestra in a live concert at Jones Hall and concluded they were not yet ready to record the orchestra. And Previn's attempt to upgrade the quality of playing by replacing certain musicians had mixed results, since the orchestra's players' committee vetoed his effort in at least one instance. Though the breakup of Previn's second marriage and his budding relationship with actress Mia Farrow drew a lot of colorful commentary in the press and gossip among the public, they were not central to his severance in May 1969.

The central issue involved his failure to sign a renewal and favorable upgrading of his contract, offered four months earlier. The Symphony Society announced on January 9, 1969, that Previn had agreed to a two-year renewal of his contract, upgrading his title to music director, a title that granted him more authority over the orchestra's artistic affairs. While there was apparently verbal agreement among Previn, his New York manager, Ronald Wilford, and the Houston Symphony Society, the press announcement noted that the new contract was not yet signed.

Then, Previn cited a conflict of dates between London Symphony concerts he had been awarded and several pre-season

Previous spread: **André and Dory Previn, left, with Maurice and Winifred Hirsch at the Petroleum Club on opening night, October 8, 1967.** Above: **André Previn and the four winners of a Pennzoil-sponsored competition: Joseph Gatwood, Jonathan Purvin, Ralph Kirshbaum and Joyce Arce, May 1969.** Right: **The Houston Symphony with André Previn, 1967–68 season.**

"Previn had asked for the extra regional pre-season concerts for the same reason Broadway plays were historically tried out in Hartford and Boston: he wanted to polish up the opening program out of town before bringing it to Jones Hall."

regional concerts with the Houston Symphony, which he had previously requested and which were booked, listing him as conductor of the orchestra. During his first season, Previn had asked for the extra regional pre-season concerts for the same reason Broadway plays were historically tried out in Hartford and Boston: he wanted to polish up the opening program out of town before bringing it to Jones Hall. He had already conducted a pre-season set of concerts in September 1968 and they had accomplished the result he wanted. So, the new contract sat unsigned for four months, while Wilford and Houston Symphony manager Tom Johnson negotiated fruitlessly to resolve the issue.

With the issue of Previn's contract renewal still unresolved at the end of the Houston Symphony's second tour under Previn in April 1969, there were only about four months remaining before the orchestra was to begin its 1969–70 season. The Symphony Society had to have one or more conductors on the podium for the bulk of the season. Repertoire had to be approved and subscription tickets had to be sold. Symphony manager Tom Johnson met the orchestra for its final tour concert in New York. Then, he delivered a letter from Symphony Society president Maurice Hirsch to Wilford the next morning and withdrew the unsigned contract.

The schedule conflict over the pre-season regional concerts for the 1969–70 Houston Symphony season was cited in Hirsch's letter. Hirsch also cited several instances when the Houston Symphony either could not get bookings for Previn and the orchestra in major U.S. cities, or drew poor attendance because Previn had recent or upcoming engagements with the London Symphony or some other orchestra in those same cities. In short, the Houston Symphony, which had given Previn his first chance for a symphonic career, was quickly being placed at a disadvantage as far as the ticket-buying public was concerned. Despite Previn's earlier statements that his London Symphony appointment would never conflict with his earlier commitment to Houston, that was precisely the problem.[2]

Unhappily, the rupture occurred at the very moment Previn's performances were beginning to show expressive merit. He brought some welcome new repertoire to Houston Symphony audiences, including works of several major American composers: the Sixth Symphony of Walter Piston, the Third Symphony and the Symphony for Strings of William Schuman, several works by Aaron Copland and a Concertino for Orchestra by his former teacher, Nikolai Lopatnikoff.

There were also several symphonic works by composers who gained their principal living in the film industry. These included Previn's own Cello Concerto, which he composed for Houston Symphony principal cellist Shirley Trepel, and Miklós Rózsa's Piano Concerto. Previn also gave the world premiere of the First Symphony by composer-conductor John Williams and symphonies by two prominent British composers, Richard Rodney Bennett and Oliver Knussen, both of whom had extensive credits in the world of film music.

While the concert works of the film composers did not excite more than polite interest, Previn and the orchestra did give the Houston Symphony premieres of two major 20th-century compositions: Stravinsky's *Symphony of Psalms* and Krzysztof Penderecki's *Threnody to the Victims of Hiroshima*. He introduced the Penderecki with a particularly telling remark, reminding the audience that symphony orchestras are often likened to museums with their nearly constant programming of traditional 19th-century works: "Tonight, we're going to hang a new painting," he said.

———————◆———————

The controversy that exploded on news of Previn's departure was followed by a second explosion when it was suddenly announced that Antonio de Almeida had been named principal guest conductor for the next two seasons and would conduct six of its 18 programs beginning in September 1969. Almeida's name was totally unfamiliar in Houston. It turned out, Symphony Society president Maurice Hirsch had made his acquaintance during one of Hirsch's globe-trotting vacations, and that was the source of his sudden appointment.[3] The orchestra musicians were furious at having an unknown, untried conductor suddenly thrust upon them without any consultation from management, and Almeida was unwittingly brought into a hostile working environment. Many years later, he said that if he had known the circumstances surrounding his appointment, he never would have signed a contract accepting it.[4]

Almeida was a highly intelligent, very cordial man who brought some sophisticated repertoire to the orchestra and its audiences. However, those assets did not translate into memorable performances, and his two seasons on the podium—six concerts in 1969–70, four in 1970–71—were essentially a period of marking time for the Houston Symphony. During the 1970–71 season, four prospective replacements for Previn were invited to conduct one to three concerts apiece: Belgian conductor André Vandernoot, American conductor Lawrence Foster, Polish conductor Georg Semkow and British conductor Maurice Handford, Barbirolli's former assistant at the Hallé Orchestra.

By coincidence, Foster was principal guest conductor of Britain's Royal Philharmonic Orchestra at the time and had conducted that orchestra in Jones Hall the preceding October on its independently scheduled tour sponsored by another Houston concert agency. He became the clear favorite and was appointed in December 1970 as conductor-in-chief for the 1971–72 season.

Above: **Carlos Chávez, composer and conductor, and Beatrice Schroeder Rose, principal harpist, discuss his works at rehearsal in February 1969.** Bottom right: **Hirsch reception for the Almeidas and Barbirollis on November 23, 1969. From left to right: pianist Lili Kraus, Maurice Hirsch, Cecilia and Antonio de Almeida, Lady Evelyn and Sir John Barbirolli, and Winifred Hirsch.**

NASA and the Houston Symphony

New guest conductor Antonio de Almeida and his family, center, visited NASA with NASA Public Affairs Officer Ben James, on the right. Miss Ima Hogg's opening night guests on September 22, 1969, were astronauts and space team members. From that evening's program: "The Opening Concerts are a salute from the Houston Symphony Society to the dedicated men and women who made possible the recent landing on the Moon."

In February 1971, he conducted a pair of weekend concerts, including a special Barbirolli memorial program, featuring the orchestra in Barbirolli's arrangement of Elizabethan music, Vaughan Williams' Eighth Symphony and Verdi's *Stabat Mater* and *Te Deum*. He returned in April for two additional programs.

During the 1970–71 season, the orchestra added two more subscription programs, bringing the total from 18 to 20. In addition, nine Sunday afternoon concerts were added to the traditional Monday–Tuesday evening concerts. The orchestra also achieved a full 52-week employment contract in 1971, marking an important milestone in its history.

If the years without a permanent conductor were a period of marking time artistically, they were also a period when old ways gave way to newer thinking throughout the entire organization. The death of Sir John Barbirolli in July 1970 signaled a change to a younger generation of conductors in the future. In May of that year, General Hirsch ended his 14-year term as Symphony Society president, becoming president emeritus. His parents had been original guarantors of the Houston Symphony, his mother had served on the original board of directors, and his sister had been a charter member of the violin section. After guiding Lawrence Foster through his first year as conductor-in-chief, Tom Johnson retired from his 25 years as manager in 1973. Clyde Roller concluded his eight-year career as associate conductor, then resident conductor, during the same year.

And for health reasons, Raphael Fliegel concluded his 26-year career as concertmaster, ceding his position to young Denver Symphony concertmaster Ronald Patterson in the fall of 1972. As noted earlier, Fliegel had debuted with the orchestra as soloist in the Mendelssohn Concerto under St. Leger in 1933. He joined the orchestra in 1936, served in the military in 1942 and returned to become concertmaster in 1946. When Patterson succeeded him, he continued playing in the position of principal second violinist, celebrating his 50th anniversary with the orchestra in 1986 and his 75th birthday in 1993, just prior to the orchestra's 80th anniversary season. He finally retired in 1995, at the end of a 59-year career with the Houston Symphony.

Fliegel treasured his many years playing under a vast number of the world's most famous conductors—both music directors and guest conductors. He shared what he learned with generations of colleagues in the violin section, and finally with numerous students at the University of Houston, Houston Baptist University and Rice University's Shepherd School of Music during the last two decades of his life.

CHAPTER
VIII

LAWRENCE FOSTER

Lawrence Thomas Foster was born October 23, 1941, in Los Angeles, the only surviving child of Romanian parents whose ancestry has been a source of great pride throughout his life. His musical studies in piano, conducting, music theory and counterpoint were taken privately with prominent Los Angeles-area musicians.

Before he was 20, Foster's conducting career started to rise up through conductorships with orchestras of the Los Angeles Young Musicians Foundation and San Francisco Ballet, master classes under Karl Böhm at the Bayreuth Festival and the Koussevitzky Memorial Conducting Prize at the Tanglewood Festival.

After three years as assistant conductor of the Los Angeles Philharmonic, his big break came in April 1967 with an unscheduled Albert Hall debut, replacing Hungarian conductor Christoph von Dohnányi in a concert with the London Philharmonic Orchestra. Engagements with major British orchestras led to his appointment as the youngest chief guest conductor of the Royal Philharmonic Orchestra in 1969. That fall, he shared conducting duties with RPO

music director Rudolf Kempe, conducting the orchestra on the Houston engagement during its American tour that resulted in his appointment to the Houston Symphony.

Given the two years under Almeida with a series of guest conductors and potential candidates, there seemed to be an interminable hiatus before Foster finally claimed the podium in the fall of 1971 ready to build the orchestra's artistic future. That delay was extended by three extra weeks, because the 1971–72 season began under the baton of still another guest conductor. This time it was Erich Leinsdorf, who had been engaged by Symphony manager Tom Johnson long before Foster's appointment, in order to ensure that the season would open with a big-name artist. To bolster the opening weeks with added name recognition, Van Cliburn was engaged to play the Rachmaninoff Second Piano Concerto on Leinsdorf's third and final program.

At last, Foster arrived on October 14, little more than a week before his 30th birthday. Beethoven's music was prominently featured on his first two concerts, but rather than the standard Beethoven one might expect, Foster cannily used this inaugural occasion to expose his listeners to valuable but rarely heard Beethoven works: the C major Mass; his Incidental Music to Goethe's drama *Egmont*; and a scintillating performance of

Beethoven's Second Piano Concerto featuring Malcolm Frager on the second program. The performance of the C major Mass nearly coincided with the 25th anniversary of the founding of the Symphony's official chorus, the Houston Chorale, which had held its first rehearsal on October 29, 1946.

After a year as conductor-in-chief, Foster assumed the full title of music director at the beginning of the 1972–73 season. His seven-year tenure was to become a period of great change throughout the Houston Symphony organization. The retirement of Maurice Hirsch and election of Charles Jones as president indicated a firmer corporate attitude on the board; the retirement of Clyde Roller brought a succession of younger associate conductors to the podium; the change of the orchestra's concertmaster from Ray Fliegel to Ronald Patterson signaled significant changes to come among orchestra personnel. The impending retirement of Tom Johnson after 25 years as general manager inaugurated a long period of transition and instability in the management of the orchestra. And the growth of the Houston Symphony's three sister organizations—Houston Ballet, Houston Grand Opera and Society for the Performing Arts—put intense pressures on the Houston Symphony for time and space in Jones Hall, as well as audience growth and financial support.

Correcting fuzzy orchestral ensemble playing was one of many giant tasks Foster faced in shoring up the orchestra's weaknesses, while building bridges between its past glories and present needs. He repeatedly said throughout his Houston career, "My goal has been to maintain the warm Barbirolli sound of the orchestra, but to clean it up." As one sign of his respect for Barbirolli, Foster was the only conductor to scrupulously maintain bow markings Barbirolli established for works he had conducted

"As one sign of his respect for Barbirolli, Foster was the only conductor to scrupulously maintain bow markings Barbirolli established for works he had conducted in Houston."

in Houston. It is doubtful that any conductor could maintain the sound of one of his predecessors, particularly after the hiatus of two intervening conductors and the long string of podium guests the Houston Symphony experienced in those years. In Foster's case, however, one could say that the robust, forthright character of the orchestra's sound under his direction was indeed closer to the warm, full sound of Barbirolli's era than the slender but generally clear tone heard during Previn's years.

As for cleaning up the sound, Foster prescribed heavy doses of classical and neo-classical music. He began with a four-year cycle of Haydn's *London* symphonies, supplemented by the *Sinfonia concertante* and *The Creation*; a brace of Mozart works; Stravinsky's Violin Concerto and Symphony in Three Movements; and touches of early Schubert, Kurt Weill, Jean Françaix, Hindemith and neo-classical Ravel works. Much of this was repertoire that appealed to Foster's musical tastes and drew from his strength in solid control of complex rhythms. The Stravinsky works were also welcome additions to the Houston Symphony's repertoire. Although the composer had visited the orchestra twice,

Previous spread: **Lawrence Foster in the conductor's dressing room at Jones Hall.** Above: **Lawrence Foster and the Houston Symphony, 1970–71 season.** Left: **Ima Hogg and Lawrence Foster at a 1975 Annual Fund meeting.**

in 1949 and in 1957, his lesser known neo-classical works were not extensively performed in Houston until Foster's arrival.

In addition to a steady infusion of Stravinsky's works, Foster periodically programmed works by the Second Viennese School of composers, regular servings of Prokofiev and Shostakovich, all the Bartók concertos, compositions by Barber, Copland, Roberto Gerhard, Ginastera, Lutosławski, George Rochberg, Wallingford Riegger, Honegger, Ligeti and Nielsen, and such craggy works as Ives' Fourth Symphony, Harrison Birtwistle's *The Triumph of Time* and Charles Koechlin's *Les Bandar-log*.

The standard Mozart-to-Mahler repertoire was also well represented, including two complete cycles of Beethoven piano concertos, one featuring Radu Lupu at the end of the 1972–73 season and a second featuring Alfred Brendel at the end of the 1975–76 season.

Foster displayed his interest in dramatic music with concert performances of Wagner's *Flying Dutchman*, Acts One and Three of *Die Walküre* and a complete performance of Berlioz' *The Damnation of Faust*. Guest conductor Robert Shaw brought Houston Symphony audiences their first performance of Britten's *War Requiem* in 1975, and Foster conducted the orchestra's first performance of Bach's *St. Matthew Passion* at the end of the 1975–76 season. His 1972 performance of Prokofiev's *Alexander Nevsky*, employing clips from the Eisenstein film and featuring Houston mezzo-soprano Earline Ballard with combined choruses from the Houston Symphony, Rice University and Houston Baptist College, drew a near-sellout crowd.

Foster also looked to resident talent within the orchestra and the Houston-area musical community. Numerous principal players were featured as soloists, especially during his first few years. He scheduled two works by Houston-area composers for performances with the orchestra. Music for Orchestra by Ned Battista, the Symphony's second trumpeter and a native Houstonian, was performed on March 13–14 during Foster's first season. A Trumpet Concerto by Fisher Tull, composer and music department chairman at Sam Houston State University, was scheduled on the 1972–73 season. The works were chosen from 17 scores submitted by 15 composers. Battista's work had been composed two years earlier at the request of André Previn, whose intention to perform it was forestalled by his sudden departure from the orchestra.

After auditioning 16 applicants, the Symphony announced on January 23, 1972, that 27-year-old Denver Symphony concertmaster Ronald Patterson would succeed Fliegel in the fall. Patterson, a former student of Eudice Shapiro and Jascha Heifetz, had been a colleague of Foster's as concertmaster of the Young Musicians Foundation Debut Orchestra in the 1960s.

Above: **Van Cliburn and Ima Hogg, September 1971, when Eric Leinsdorf conducted Cliburn in the Rachmaninoff Piano Concerto No. 2, Opus 18.**

A significant strengthening of the trombone section was heralded with the simultaneous announcement that 25-year-old John McCroskey would become principal trombonist in the fall of 1972. McCroskey, second trombonist of the Dallas Symphony, was chosen from 80 applicants, including 40 who auditioned for the position. They included trombonists from the orchestras in Pittsburgh, Cleveland, New York and Philadelphia, as well as two who flew across the Atlantic from Hanover, Germany, and The Hague in the Netherlands, to audition.

McCroskey succeeded Albert Lube, who had joined the orchestra under Hoffmann in 1940. Lube became second trombonist, replacing Ralph Liese, who stopped performing to devote full time to his other position as personnel manager of the orchestra. David Waters, who had joined the orchestra as bass trombonist in 1966, remained as a valuable anchor to the section for 41 years, until his retirement in 2007, three years before his untimely death. The horn section remained stable for about half of Foster's seven-year term, then its membership began to fluctuate as 19-year principal James Tankersley was briefly replaced by Robin Graham, who was succeeded by Thomas Bacon during Foster's final season.

The assets and inadequacies of Foster's still-developing talent and the liabilities of an unevenly secure orchestral ensemble were periodically on display throughout his early years. Strong, secure performances of 20th-century piano concertos by Ginastera and Bartók were offset by less convincing interpretations of standard repertoire by Haydn, Brahms, Dvořák and Debussy. Intonation and clean ensemble could still suddenly go awry, especially in the string and brass sections, indicating an unrelenting need for the strong orchestral discipline Foster had prescribed with his emphasis upon classically oriented repertoire.

But there were also glorious moments for the orchestra. Legendary conductor Paul Kletzki provided the first of them on November 13–14, 1972, with a breathtaking interpretation of Mahler's *Song of the Earth*, featuring mezzo-soprano Anna Reynolds and tenor Kenneth Riegel. And in a special December 16 concert, pianist Arthur Rubinstein joined the Houston Symphony in richly rewarding performances of the Chopin F minor and Brahms D minor Concertos, celebrating the 90th birthday year of Miss Ima Hogg. Rubinstein was one of many leading soloists who were delighted to perform and make recordings with Foster during those years. Visiting soloists and Houston Symphony orchestra members repeatedly praised him as a superb orchestral accompanist, a conductor who was able to anticipate and accommodate their slightest interpretive nuances, making for seamless performances of concertos, song cycles and operatic performances. One of the finest examples of this expert collaboration occurred in April 1978, when 49-year-old Marilyn Horne, in the prime of her performing years, joined baritone John Shirley-Quirk, Foster and the orchestra in a most memorable performance of Mahler's song cycle *Des Knaben Wunderhorn*.

Earlier, Foster had offered the position of associate conductor to his former Los Angeles colleague, violinist/conductor Akira Endo, who declined in favor of remaining in his current position as conductor of American Ballet Theatre. Foster eventually chose Mario Benzecry, who was briefly succeeded by Endo in 1975.[1]

When the 1972–73 season was completed, the first three weeks of June 1973 became a period of contractual strife between orchestra musicians and the Houston Symphony Society. Perennial issues of salary, vacation and retirement benefits erupted as the deadline for contract renewal came and went. But the most serious issue involved the question of whether the music director or a players' committee set up by the orchestra had the final authority to fire or demote musicians whose abilities did not meet satisfactory artistic and technical standards.

Rumblings of discontent over the treatment of musicians extended back to the tenure of Leopold Stokowski, and the players' committee had been established in the 1971 contract, negotiated during the interim between Previn and Foster. The musicians finally won that self-governing right when the contract was ratified on June 19. But several other issues, including health insurance and

"In a special December 16 concert, pianist Arthur Rubinstein joined the Houston Symphony in richly rewarding performances of the Chopin F minor and Brahms D minor Concertos, celebrating the 90th birthday year of Miss Ima Hogg."

"Visiting soloists and Houston Symphony orchestra members repeatedly praised him as a superb orchestral accompanist, a conductor who was able to anticipate and accommodate their slightest interpretive nuances" work-related rules, were left unresolved for further consideration during the third year of the new contract.

The three-year period between 1973 and 1976 was peaceful and productive, but then the impasse that occurred when the contract expired very nearly destroyed the orchestra.

The deficit kept mounting while Foster's popularity began to wane. James Wright, the manager who had been hired to replace Tom Johnson, resigned in May 1976, just as negotiations were beginning in earnest, leaving his assistant, Carlos Wilson, to function in his place. Tensions rapidly escalated, and by the middle of June, the Symphony Society issued a two-day deadline for the musicians to vote on a one-year extension of the existing contract, with a $20-per-week increase in salaries.

A violent rainstorm flooded much of Houston the evening of June 16, preventing orchestra members from assembling to vote on the proposed contract extension, so the Symphony Society ordered a cessation of all rehearsals and performances. Orchestra members called it a lockout; the Symphony Society maintained it was a strike. The stalemate lasted nearly five full months, while the two sides hired lawyers, and then had to educate them about the special working conditions involved in a symphony orchestra contract.[2]

For their part, suddenly unemployed musicians scrambled to find work wherever they could. Two string players quickly left the orchestra and found positions with the San Francisco Opera and the Minnesota Orchestra. Four others also found positions with other orchestras. Nearly a third of the orchestra members relied on teaching and free-lance work at weddings, dance jobs and pops concerts. Others found odd jobs, working in a glass-cutting plant, at a moving company, and as a legal secretary, an airport security guard, a messenger, a house painter, a shoe salesman and a paint salesman.

In an effort to raise money and preserve their sense of a musical ensemble, the musicians periodically gathered and performed four Houston Symphony Musicians Benefit concerts.

The Symphony Society maintained hospitalization benefits for the musicians, as well as paying them five weeks of vacation pay they had accrued. And it gradually canceled the orchestra's entire series of free summer outdoor concerts and the first five fall subscription programs in Jones Hall. The musicians soon found themselves struggling to meet expenses and feed their families, while the Symphony Society saw its ticket income and fundraising efforts dry up.

Foster returned to Houston in early September to address the situation with the Symphony board's 13-member executive committee, and then had to wait two weeks until enough committee members could assemble to constitute a quorum for the meeting to take place. Setting aside the disputed contract issues and the $1.4 million accumulated debt, he concentrated upon the larger issue of "how to maintain and nurture a first-class organization. Taking sides is of no interest or concern to me," he said. "Defining conditions for excellence is."

He called for "a clear and unequivocal commitment to maintain the present quality and numerical strength of the orchestra over the next three years"[3] and "the willing and cooperative improvement of pensions, hospitalization and, particularly, disability insurance" for orchestra members.[4] He asked the Symphony Society to facilitate credit for the musicians to purchase high-quality musical instruments and guarantee insurance costs for them. (This request echoed one Ferenc Fricsay had made 22 years earlier.) He asked the board to be more active in securing the use of Jones Hall for the Symphony, especially making the stage available for all rehearsals as well as performances.[5] Finally, he asked the board to stop subsidizing

Above: **Houston Ballet principals Anthony Sellers and Judith Aaen, with Laura, Nathanne, Joyce and Jim Tankersley, December 1971. The Houston Symphony had provided the orchestra for ballet performances from the Houston Ballet's inception.** Right: **Foster conducted a special concert featuring cellist Gregor Piatigorsky, who played Dvořák's Concerto in B minor, Opus 104, in September 1972. Piatigorsky had not appeared with the orchestra since 1955 with Sir Thomas Beecham on the podium.**

Houston Grand Opera by nearly $100,000 and make HGO pay the full cost of subcontracting Houston Symphony musicians for its six annual productions.

After four months had passed, the Symphony Society hired Michael Woolcock, a young British record producer with Decca/London Records, to succeed Wright as executive director of the orchestra. Though Woolcock had engineered recordings for several major international orchestras, he had never managed one. He succeeded in getting the two sides to start negotiating meaningfully and a new contract was settled on November 3. It granted the musicians carefully scaled minimum weekly salary increases over the three-year life of the agreement, plus increased insurance and pension benefits. For its part, the Symphony Society gained flexibility in scheduling the orchestra, including a vast increase in the number of days it could tour the orchestra. A special clause allowed it to subdivide the orchestra into as many as three smaller ensembles in order to enhance earnings when the full orchestra was not being used for any given concert.

But the work stoppage took its toll on the embittered orchestra. When performances resumed, some 12 to 15 orchestra members had either left permanently or announced plans to retire, take leaves of absence or take positions elsewhere. Several had been members for 20 to 30 years. Some of the titled or longtime players who left included associate concertmaster Albert Muenzer, principal trumpeter James Austin, principal tubist William Rose, trombonist Albert Lube, and violinists Marcella Boffa and Dorothe Robinson.

Foster had been granted permission to seek conducting engagements elsewhere during the work stoppage. As a result, he was unable to conduct the delayed November 8 season-opening concert because he had been asked to replace André Previn for a revival and recording of Sir William Walton's opera *Troilus and Cressida* at London's Royal Opera House in Covent Garden.[6] Michael Palmer, associate conductor of the Atlanta Symphony, served capably as guest conductor for that concert and for the 1977 free outdoor Miller Theatre series.

GREGOR PIATIGORSKY

with

THE HOUSTON SYMPHONY ORCHESTRA

LAWRENCE FOSTER Conducting

September 15, 1972

Several other conductors—David Zinman, Stanislaw Skrowaczewski, Carmen Dragon, Samuel Jones and Alexander Gibson—fulfilled their previously scheduled mid-winter engagements until Foster made his scheduled return, conducting an impressive performance of Stravinsky's opera-oratorio *Oedipus Rex*, featuring mezzo-soprano Joy Davidson and tenor George Shirley on February 6–8. That was followed by a brilliantly played Houston Symphony debut from cellist Mstislav Rostropovich on February 13 and an immensely expressive performance of Brahms' Fourth Symphony on the orchestra's regular subscription concert on February 14–15.

The deeply felt, tragic-heroic feelings Foster coaxed from the orchestra in that Brahms performance left one wondering what had aroused such powerful emotion from his exacting baton. The answer was not long in coming. Five days later, Foster and his wife joined Symphony board chairman Charles Jones and Woolcock in the Symphony offices. With a very heavy heart, he announced that he would no longer be conductor of the Houston Symphony when his contract expired at the end of the following season, 1977–78.[7]

He felt honored, he said, to have followed Kurtz, Fricsay, Stokowski, Barbirolli and Previn on the podium, and was proud to have brought such world-famed soloists and conductors as Rubinstein, Kletzki, Menuhin, Piatigorsky and Rostropovich to appear with the orchestra. After six seasons "of hard work," he felt the orchestra was well on the way to realizing many of his artistic ambitions, but he listed seven disappointments and "difficulties beyond my control": no regular recording sessions, no international tour, "a national tour of substance has not been possible," not enough onstage rehearsal time, constant interruptions to the Symphony season because of opera and ballet productions in Jones Hall, the Symphony Society's financial problems and, "for whatever reasons," poor attendance at concerts.

Lawrence and Angela Foster both expressed sadness at the death of Houston Symphony founder Ima Hogg, whose heart had failed several days after surgery for a fractured hip she suffered in a fall on August 14, 1975, while traveling in London.[8] Individually, the conductor cited her constant support of his efforts to establish modern works in the Houston Symphony repertoire, while Angela cited her personal friendship and outreach to a young person from a foreign country who had few close friends in Houston. The Fosters were the first podium family to actually buy a house in Houston, with a yard and trees, since Ernst and Annamarie Hoffmann in the 1930s.

He also expressed appreciation for the opportunity to "grow in the job," building the orchestra and providing it a comprehensive repertoire without interference. He promised to give the orchestra and audience "the best of what is within me" during his final 1977–78 season. During that season, Foster provided his listeners the debuts of conductors Michael Tilson Thomas, James Conlon, British conductor Sir Charles Groves conducting Tippett's oratorio *A Child of Our Time*, Spanish conductor Antoni Ros-Marbà and Romanian conductor Erich Bergel; the return of composer-conductor Aaron Copland; the debuts of pianists Murray Perahia, Rafael Orozco and Rudolf Buchbinder; and singer Marilyn Horne in the aforementioned Mahler *Wunderhorn* songs, all capped with glorious performances of Bruckner's *Te Deum* and Beethoven's Ninth Symphony as a finale to his tenure here.

When Foster set down his baton after that Beethoven Ninth Symphony, the Houston Symphony was a mature, confident orchestra, reliably able to produce a clean, hearty tone and to slice its way through major 20th-century scores with a sense of authority. Though his reputation suffered because of the steady diet of modern works, he largely ended the Houston Symphony audience's aversion to that segment of the orchestral literature.

The program book for that final concert printed three separate tributes from the leadership of the board, the orchestra and the management, saluting Foster's accomplishments and wishing him well in his future career. The orchestra's tribute was the most circumscribed, proudly reminding him that "we were an orchestra with a high performance standard from many years past when you arrived. It took some time for you to learn our strengths and weaknesses, as it did for us to learn yours. But it can be said that you maintained that standard in demanding our best and in knowing how to elicit just that with your rehearsal time. And you were always as quick with praise as with criticism."

He was commended for his support of modern music and for featuring orchestra members as soloists. "Certainly, your gift for sensitively articulated orchestra accompaniments for (visiting) soloists will not be matched easily by any other conductor, nor will the clarity of your beat—a real treasure.

"These seven years of change and crisis in this orchestra have not been the easiest in terms of musical growth or stability for any of us. We had our differences: personal and musical sparks occasionally flew, but your wit and humour always helped."

Recognizing that "we face a new transition period, as you do," the orchestra wished Larry and Angela Foster happiness. "May we all do as well in terms of musical excellence in our future encounters."[9]

Foster had stood alone, speaking with one clear voice amid confusion and shifting sands all around him. Fortunately, the musical maturity he had attained in Houston was properly acknowledged by the regular invitations he accepted, returning as guest conductor to bring the Houston Symphony many fine performances over the next four decades.

Above: **Lawrence Foster at the Jones Hall entrance, late 1970s.** Right: **Tom Johnson, right, escorted Miss Ima Hogg and her entourage at her 90th birthday concert featuring pianist Arthur Rubinstein, December 15, 1972.**

CHAPTER

IX

SERGIU COMISSIONA

There was an air of confidence in the playing of the Houston Symphony as it entered the search for a new music director during the last half of 1978. Lawrence Foster had cleaned up the orchestral sound and technique, and although several prominent players had left after the work stoppage, some fine new players gradually replaced them.

They included two new principal players: trumpeter Charles Geyer who came from the Chicago Symphony to succeed James Austin, and horn player Thomas Bacon who had been sought for years by Foster and was finally available during Foster's final season. Concertmaster Ronald Patterson took a leave of absence in 1979 and was replaced by British violinist Alan Traverse as acting concertmaster that season, then co-concertmaster in 1980 when Patterson resigned.[1] Argentinian violinist Ruben Gonzalez became guest concertmaster in 1980, then assumed the post permanently for six more seasons.

Numerous staff members joined the musicians and subscribers in leaving the orchestra during the lockout, and it took the better part of two seasons to replenish their ranks. Much credit was owed to Dolores Johnson, who had come from the Minnesota Orchestra management team to assume the post of concerts manager in January 1977. Essentially, she worked with executive director Woolcock, directing the operations of the orchestra. Her efficiency, thoughtfulness and foresight quietly solved many problems behind the scenes over a crucial 3½-year time period.[2]

But the search for a new conductor was a protracted affair. Though a promising list of guest conductors paraded across the podium during the 1978–79 season, attention gradually focused upon two Romanian-born conductors, Erich Bergel and Sergiu Comissiona, Viennese conductor-violinist Walter Weller and British conductor Sir Alexander Gibson. Weller, who was principal conductor of the Royal Liverpool Orchestra, was appointed to the Royal Philharmonic Orchestra in 1980, eliminating his candidacy for Houston.

So, Bergel was appointed principal guest conductor for two seasons, 1979–80 and 1980–81, while the Houston Symphony began negotiating with Comissiona, who had been music director of the Baltimore Symphony since 1969 and had greatly built up its status. On June 23, 1979, the Symphony Society announced that Comissiona would become "artistic advisor" to the Houston Symphony under a three-year contract beginning in September 1980. He would conduct the two opening weeks of the 1979–80 season, at least six of the 20 subscription programs in 1980–81, at least eight programs in 1981–82 and at least ten programs in 1982–83.

The delay involved Comissiona's heavy obligation to the Baltimore Symphony and its mentor, Joseph Meyerhoff, who had been the principal donor for a new concert hall that was about to be constructed for that orchestra. Meyerhoff strongly objected to Comissiona's leaving Baltimore, especially before its new hall was completed. So, the day before Comissiona signed his three-year Houston Symphony contract, he renewed his Baltimore Symphony contract for another three years. It contained a clause preventing him from using the words "conductor," "musical" or "director" with any other orchestra; hence, the strange title in Comissiona's Houston Symphony contract. His Baltimore contract also called for him to conduct 16 subscription programs with the Baltimore Symphony during each of those three seasons.[3]

Comissiona was born in Bucharest June 16, 1928, and he and his future wife, Robinne, spent their teenage years enduring World War II under a fascist, Nazi-affiliated government, and then the Communist regime. His aspiration to conduct bore fruit when he replaced an ailing conductor at a Romanian State Ensemble production of Gounod's *Faust* in 1946. His mother was singing the leading role of Marguerite. Robinne was a dancer with the ballet company attached to the Romanian ensemble.

In 1958, Sergiu and Robinne Comissiona were both fired from their positions when he applied for an exit visa to immigrate to Israel. After nine months of being denied work, they had to sell most of their belongings and pay heavy taxes before being sent out of Romania on a midnight train.[4] He began again with the Haifa Symphony in 1959, commuting to Jerusalem to build up Israel's Ramat Gan Chamber Orchestra the following year. That orchestra's

1963 U.S. debut tour, along with London engagements, led to his musical directorship of the Göteborg Symphony (1966) before he was appointed to the Baltimore Symphony in 1969.

Comissiona's long tenure in Baltimore was probably the most secure period of his career, and he was torn between remaining there and moving on. With the prospect of a limited presence in Houston during his early seasons with the orchestra, a plan was devised that limited principal guest conductor appointments to two seasons. Thus, Gibson succeeded Bergel as principal guest conductor during the 1981–82 and 1982–83 seasons until Comissiona was completely free of his Baltimore Symphony obligations. After that, the concept of "principal guest conductor" vanished from the Houston Symphony's lineup of podium occupants.

Nevertheless, there were other conductorial aspirants on the Houston Symphony scene during those years. Michael Palmer, who had filled in for Lawrence Foster at the first concert after the 1976 work stoppage, had continued on, making himself available for occasional subscription programs, student programs, special concerts and the entire summer series of free Miller Outdoor Theatre concerts for the 1977, 1978 and 1979 seasons. He elevated those programs to a serious, respectable level, so that audiences for those free outdoor concerts were offered a genuine symphonic experience. He left a favorable public impression while helping the Houston Symphony Society rebuild its audiences as he gradually built his own professional career conducting orchestras in Wichita, Kansas, and Denver, Colorado.

Previous spread: **Sergiu Comissiona, Music Director.**
Above: **Comissiona, seated center, in a 1982 recording session. Assistant conductor Toshiyuki Shimada is on the right. Among those standing in the rear are executive director Gideon Toeplitz, concertmaster Ruben Gonzalez and trombonist Allen Barnhill.**
Left: **Composer Sir Michael Tippett celebrated his 80th birthday with the Houston Symphony in January 1985. He conducted an all-Tippett program on two evenings, was feted at luncheon and evening events, and also gave a talk at Rice University.**

In the fall of 1977, Palmer was joined by C. William Harwood, who gained a dual position as assistant conductor of the Houston Symphony and music director of Houston Grand Opera's touring satellite company, Texas Opera Theater, under sponsorship of Exxon Corporation and the National Endowment for the Arts. Harwood became an extremely active conductor for both organizations, gradually taking over Palmer's duties with the Houston Symphony while touring with Texas Opera Theater throughout the state and beyond. He even took Houston Grand Opera's acclaimed revival of Gershwin's *Porgy and Bess* to Broadway.

Harwood was promoted to the position of associate conductor in the fall of 1980, and his most distinctive work with

"Throughout Comissiona's tenure, there was a steady effort to shift audiences away from an historic Monday-Tuesday schedule toward weekend nights."

the Houston Symphony included an annual series of four new chamber orchestra concerts, titled the Stokowski Legacy Series, at St. Luke's United Methodist Church. These concerts blended newly commissioned works by American composers with standard chamber-orchestra repertoire extending back to the Baroque era. Harwood continued Palmer's policy of building the quality of symphonic repertoire at Miller Theatre, while increasing the popularity of the free summer concerts.[5]

When Harwood's term as associate conductor ended in the fall of 1983, he became music director of the Arkansas Philharmonic. During the early years of the 1980s, he also gained significant conducting opportunities with the Opera Theater of St. Louis and Santa Fe Opera. But his blossoming career was cut short by an early death at age 36 from viral pneumonia in the spring of 1984. He was warmly remembered by Houston Symphony musicians, staff and audiences as a talented, outgoing, energetic young conductor who provided five years of continuity on the podium in the midst of a seemingly endless parade of podium occupants with titles other than music director.

By the 1981–82 season, the orchestral roster listed four names: Sergiu Comissiona, artistic advisor; Sir Alexander Gibson, principal guest conductor; C. William Harwood, associate conductor; and Toshiyuki Shimada, assistant conductor. Shimada remained with the orchestra, first as assistant conductor, then as conducting associate until the end of the 1986–87 season. He became the very popular conductor of the Portland Symphony (Maine) for two decades (1986–2006) and conductor of the Yale University Symphony and other orchestras in Connecticut and Western New York State after that time.

Though Comissiona was absent from the Houston Symphony podium for at least half of his first three winter seasons, he directed the orchestra's artistic policies from a distance and was available for major summer activities. In 1981, he instituted a series of summer festivals that brought regular symphonic activity to Jones Hall in July. He began with a complete survey of Tchaikovsky's symphonies, concertos, numerous shorter orchestral works and some choral music. Much of the music was strongly performed and it drew several large audiences.[6] It was followed annually by summer festivals saluting major anniversaries for Haydn, Stravinsky and Ravel in 1982, Beethoven, Brahms and Tchaikovsky in 1983, Rachmaninoff, Tchaikovsky and Gershwin in 1984, a panorama of classical and pops favorites in 1985 and 1986, and finally Mozart,

featuring conductor and pianist Christoph Eschenbach as the headliner in the summer of 1987.[7] While it became an increasing challenge to attract an audience indoors for paid-admission summer concerts in Jones Hall throughout the mid-1980s, the festivals were a valued component of the Houston Symphony's growth during that decade.

Comissiona continued the Stokowski Legacy Series until Harwood left the orchestra, while also instituting a Contemporary Trends series, which did not survive beyond its inaugural 1982–83 season. A different satellite series, called The Performer Conducts, was begun in the 1981–82 season. It featured prominent soloists who also had conducting skills, performing chamber orchestra repertoire at suburban houses of worship or education: Memorial Drive Presbyterian Church, Temple Beth Israel and Klein Forest High School. Pianist Philippe Entremont, flutist James Galway, violist-conductor Milton Katims, pianist Anton Kuerti, oboist Heinz Holliger, violinists Alexander Schneider and Joseph Silverstein (a former Houston Symphony member who became concertmaster and associate conductor of the Boston Symphony), and numerous other soloist/conductors were featured with a chamber orchestra of Houston Symphony musicians. This briefly evolved into a baroque music series led by concertmaster Ruben Gonzalez during the 1983–84 season.

Throughout Comissiona's tenure, there was a steady effort to shift audiences away from an historic Monday-Tuesday schedule toward weekend nights. Monday nights had been the preferred concert night for the Houston Symphony dating back to the time of the orchestra's reorganization under Uriel Nespoli in 1931.[8] Ernst Hoffmann tried to inaugurate a second performance on Tuesday nights during the 1938–39 season, but a paltry subscription rate forced its abandonment the following season. During the 1951–52 season, Efrem Kurtz alternated concert nights between Mondays and Tuesdays each week, trying to encourage Tuesday night attendance. But it was not until the 1957–58 season, when the orchestra had moved from the larger City Auditorium to the smaller Music Hall, that Leopold Stokowski was able to attract enough subscribers to Tuesday nights, making a Monday-Tuesday pair viable.

Fast-forward to the 1970s in Jones Hall, when the Houston Symphony, Houston Grand Opera, Houston Ballet, Society for the Performing Arts and others were all competing for rehearsal and performance time and space on the Jones Hall stage.[9] This

Above: **Tchaikovsky Festival logo for the Symphony's first summer festival in Jones Hall, July 1981.** Left: **Mayor Kathy Whitmire presents a proclamation to Executive Director Gideon Toeplitz, Sergiu Comissiona and Houston Symphony Society president Ellen Kelley.**

congestion worsened over a 21-year period until Houston Grand Opera and Houston Ballet moved into the newly completed Wortham Theater Center in the fall of 1987.

Former symphony manager Tom Johnson had inaugurated the move toward weekend concerts by adding ten Sunday matinees to the schedule in the 1969–70 season. By the mid-1970s, the weekend schedule had become so crowded that James Wright, Johnson's successor, had to leap four seasons ahead on the City of Houston's schedule for Jones Hall to reserve 20 Saturday evenings and Sunday afternoons for the Houston Symphony during the 1978–79 season. Monday evening concerts were reduced to ten that season and the Tuesday concerts, which had never gained popularity, were eliminated.

By the middle of the 1986–87 season, Comissiona and executive director Gideon Toeplitz, who had replaced Woolcock, had worked out a complicated season schedule called The Classical Spectrum, allowing subscribers to choose five-, ten-, 15- or 20-concert subscriptions on Fridays, Saturdays, Sundays or Mondays, ranging from the season's full symphonic repertoire all the way down to popular orchestral pieces. Sometimes the orchestra had to rehearse and substitute alternate works on a single weekend, depending upon different labels given to programs on adjacent nights. The Classical Spectrum persisted during Comissiona's final season, 1987–88, although the number of subscription programs was reduced from 20 to 18.[10]

Toeplitz replaced Michael Woolcock as executive director in the fall of 1981, and he became a major stabilizing force throughout the last six years of Comissiona's Houston career. He had been operations manager of the Boston Symphony and held a management position with the Rochester Philharmonic prior to that. His father had been principal flutist with the Israel Philharmonic, and Toeplitz also had a musical background before immigrating to the United States for arts management training with the Los Angeles Philharmonic and UCLA.

Toeplitz drew heavily upon contacts made during his eight years with the Boston Symphony and can be credited with coaxing several major guest conductors and soloists to the Houston Symphony stage: Gerd Albrecht, Leonard Bernstein, Dennis Russell Davies, Charles Dutoit, Christoph Eschenbach, Günther Herbig, Neeme Järvi, Raymond Leppard, prizewinning composer-conductor Witold Lutosławski, Sir Neville Marriner and the debut of soprano Jessye Norman. He also encouraged Israel Philharmonic concertmaster Uri Pianka to apply for the position vacated by Gonzalez, resulting in Pianka's 18-year appointment that stretched from Comissiona's final season through Eschenbach's entire tenure until his retirement at the end of Hans Graf's fourth season. Pianka set a standard of strong orchestral leadership throughout his Houston career.[11]

On the financial side, Toeplitz claimed credit for nearly doubling, and sometimes tripling, the orchestra's annual earned income, achievements in fundraising and in the number of donors, increasing the endowment, reducing the orchestra's long-term debt and finally eliminating its annual deficit. This temporary balanced budget was accomplished during the board presidency of John Platt, an unyielding fiscal hawk. But the relentless drive for budgetary thrift was accompanied by considerable turnover among staff members, and it left orchestra musicians disheartened at freezes and reductions in wages that resulted from contract negotiations in the middle of the 1980s. These events coincided with a serious recession in Houston's economy.

Toeplitz's most enduring achievement was his quick work in securing Eschenbach as a replacement for the orchestra's Carnegie Hall concert during the 1985 tour, after Comissiona collapsed in his hotel room following an earlier concert in Wisconsin. The success of that Carnegie Hall concert set the stage for Eschenbach's 11-year music directorship that began three years later.

Periodically, Comissiona expressed concern that Houston audiences were not responding to concert occasions that would have drawn sold-out houses in Baltimore. In the spring of 1985, he made a special effort to establish his identity in a more public way. He appeared as guest conductor for Houston Grand Opera's March production of Tchaikovsky's *Eugene Onegin*.[12] He appeared as guest conductor with the Texas Chamber Orchestra and its conductor/violinist, Sergiu Luca, in a 300th-anniversary concert of J. S. Bach's birth. He conducted a magnificent semi-staged performance of Béla Bartók's opera *Bluebeard's Castle*, featuring Norwegian soloists Edith Thallaug and Aage Haugland. He conducted a special pops concert featuring Romanian pan flutist Catalin Tircolea.[13] He also conducted two performances

Above: **Sergiu Comissiona.** Right: **String principals during the early 1980s: seated, Raphael Fliegel, second violin, and Shirley Trepel, cello; standing, Ruben Gonzalez, concertmaster, and Wayne Crouse, viola.**

of Beethoven's Ninth Symphony at Miller Outdoor Theatre on July 3 and 5, as well as the traditional July 4 patriotic concert and fireworks display there.[14]

Comissiona led the orchestra in all the standard Mozart-to-Mahler orchestral repertoire, but he also freshened it with less frequently heard works, especially from French and Eastern European composers. Berlioz was the most prominent among them. Comissiona included his Requiem, *The Damnation of Faust*, *Romeo and Juliet*, his song cycle *Les nuits d'été* (sung by Frederica von Stade) and, above all, a combined performance of the *Symphonie fantastique* and its companion piece, the melodrama *Lélio*.

He invited Polish composer-conductors Krzysztof Penderecki and Witold Lutosławski to conduct complete programs of their own music and British composer Sir Michael Tippett for an 80th birthday program of his works. Russian conductor Maxim Shostakovich conducted a program of his father's music, including a performance of Dmitri Shostakovich's Concerto for Piano and Trumpet played by the composer's grandson, Dmitri Shostakovich II.

Comissiona conducted the first Houston performances of Schoenberg's *Gurrelieder* and his Violin Concerto, as well as a symphony by the little-known Swedish composer Allan Pettersson. He commissioned several large works: the Second Concerto for Orchestra by Bulgarian-American composer Henri Lazarof, an attractive Violin Concerto by Marc Neikrug, Houston composer Paul Cooper's Symphony in Two Movements, the Sixth Symphony of Ezra Laderman and a contrabassoon concerto by Donald Erb.

At his best, Comissiona's conducting style emphasized lyricism (hence his predilection for the music of Berlioz) rather than the precision found in the conducting of Foster and Eschenbach, who, respectively, preceded and followed him. He also had a rather soft voice, a significant foreign accent and a habit of speaking quite rapidly. Problems of verbal communication resulted from these mannerisms, and as the years went on, they increasingly caused feelings of frustration among orchestra members, who struggled to understand his verbal instructions during rehearsals.

Personally, Comissiona shared that sense of frustration, though he always maintained an optimistic attitude in public. On June 20, 1986, it was announced that he would begin a new appointment as music director of the New York City Opera in July 1986, and that he had extended his Houston Symphony contract and would conclude his tenure at the end of the 1987–88 season. After three seasons in New York, he became music director of the Vancouver Symphony for nine years, and held conducting appointments with the Radio Television Orchestra of Madrid and the University of Southern California School of Music. He died at age 76 of an apparent heart attack the night of March 5, 2005, in an Oklahoma City hotel room, following the dress rehearsal for a concert with the Oklahoma City Philharmonic.

Tobias Picker was appointed composer-in-residence in 1985 and he worked meaningfully to bolster the orchestra's contemporary music image. For the 1986 sesquicentennial celebration of the founding of the State of Texas, he engaged 21 mostly American composers to write short fanfares that Comissiona premiered throughout the last half of the 1985–86 and 1986–87 seasons.[15] He also instituted a lively chamber music series devoted to 20th-century music. It was called the Tower Series when it met at the refurbished Tower film theater and later on the unfinished top floor of a skyscraper, the Transco Tower.[16]

Periodically, several of Picker's compositions were featured on Houston Symphony programs, notably his quiet, reflective fanfare *Old and Lost Rivers*, named after the confluence of two small streams east of Houston, his Second Symphony *Aussöhnung*, his orchestral work *The Encantadas* and his piano concerto *Keys to the City*, celebrating the centennial of the Brooklyn Bridge.[17]

Comissiona recorded Picker's Second Symphony on the Nonesuch label and made several other recordings with the Houston Symphony: Franck's D minor Symphony, an album of Debussy's *Nocturnes* and his symphonic sketches *La Mer* on the Vanguard label; two CDs containing the four Schumann symphonies; and four other CDs of short orchestral works, all on the Pro Arte label.

The roster of musicians was still being rebuilt after the work stoppage, and it fluctuated between 89 and 91 musicians during Comissiona's first season in 1979–80. After that, it ranged between 94 and 97 musicians for his remaining eight seasons.

CELEBRATING A CENTURY

1912

Rice Institute opens

First concert by Houston Symphony – Julien Paul Blitz conducting

1914

Archduke assassinated – World War I begins

1913

Houston Symphony reorganizes and plays a six-concert season with Uriel Nespoli

Uriel Nespoli

Frank St. Leger becomes conductor of Houston Symphony

1931

1933

Houston Symphony Society Women's Committee is formed with Ima Hogg as chairman

1939

Germany invades Poland – World War II begins

1937

Houston Symphony
suspends concerts
during WWI

William Reher conducts
one concert by the
newly reorganized
Houston Symphony

1918

1921

1935

First class graduates from
the University of Houston

Ernst Hoffmann begins
11-year tenure as Houston
Symphony conductor

1936

First Houston Symphony
performance in Miller
Outdoor Theatre

Efrem Kurtz named
music director and
conductor of
Houston Symphony

1940

1948

Houston Symphony makes first national tour. The Houston Symphony Endowment is created.

Houston Symphony moves from City Auditorium to Music Hall. First television broadcast of a concert on KTRK Channel 13

1950

1954

Stokowski begins recordings with Houston Symphony

1957

Houston International Airport (now Hobby) opens ten miles south of city

1956

Barbirolli leads Houston Symphony on a three-week tour celebrating the Golden Anniversary

1965

Astrodome, "Eighth Wonder of the World," opens in Houston

1964

Houston Symphony makes first West Coast tour / André Previn named Conductor-in-Chief of Houston Symphony

1969

Apollo 11 lands men on the moon

1967

Ferenc Fricsay and
Sir Thomas Beecham
serve as Houston
Symphony conductors

Leopold Stokowski named
music director/Houston
Symphony's first national
television broadcast

1955

Sir John Barbirolli named
Houston Symphony
Music Director

1963

President John F. Kennedy
assassinated in Dallas

1961

Jesse H. Jones Hall for the
Performing Arts opens

1966

Houston Symphony signs
first 52-week contract with
musicians / Lawrence Foster
named music director

Houston Symphony
League begins
Ima Hogg National
Young Artist Competition

1971

1976

Sergiu Comissiona
named music director
of Houston Symphony

Houston Symphony
begins open rehearsals
and summer festivals

1980   **1981**

1987

George R. Brown Convention Center,
Wortham Theater Center and
Menil Collection open in Houston

Christoph Eschenbach
named music director

1988

Second successful
European tour

Hans Graf named music
director / Symphony
offices flooded in
Tropical Storm Allison

1997   **2001**

Houston Symphony performs
in Moscow at the Festival of
the World's Symphony
Orchestras

Houston Symphony names
Andrés Orozco-Estrada
music director designate

2012   **2013**

1981

U.S. launches first space
shuttle, Columbia

Houston Symphony creates
Fanfare Project – a series of
commissions to celebrate
Texas Sesquicentennial

1986

Houston Symphony
tours to Japan

Houston Symphony
makes first European
tour

1991

1992

2001

9/11 Terrorists attack
the U.S.

2008

Hurricane Ike strikes
Texas Gulf Coast

Houston Symphony performs
world premiere of film
commission *The Planets–
An HD Odyssey*

2010

From a three-concert experiment in 1913 to a concert season that today consists of nearly
300 performances, the journey of the Houston Symphony now spans one hundred years. For
an orchestra to attain such an age is something to celebrate. While it is impossible to capture
every individual detail and individual contributor, a picture emerges that will hopefully inspire
hundreds more over our second century to build upon the successes of the first.

CHAPTER

X

CHRISTOPH ESCHENBACH

Christoph Eschenbach may have been the first Houston Symphony conductor to be greeted with a standing ovation just for walking onstage at a press conference. Such was the jubilation the morning of March 3, 1988, when he was announced as the orchestra's next music director, effective September 1 of that year. He responded with a short speech containing the kernel of his philosophy and his goal for the orchestra on the cusp of its 75th anniversary.

He referred to the musicians seated behind him on the Jones Hall stage as "an assembly of artists, which an orchestra on this level is always for me. I think we should all collaborate. We should be one family and create a very strong island of value with music in this very difficult time," he said. "Our goal will be reached through quality, *only* through quality. I will put all my capabilities to that work."[1]

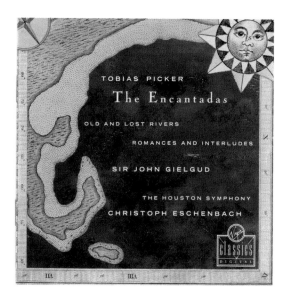

Eschenbach's appointment was hardly a surprise, because rumors had circulated since the preceding summer that he would be chosen to succeed Sergiu Comissiona. In July 1987, he had headlined the opening weekend of the Houston Symphony's Mostly Mozart Festival with a musical triathlon, joining the orchestra's principal players in performances of two Mozart chamber music works on a Thursday night, conducting an orchestral program Friday night and serving as soloist and conductor in three Mozart piano concertos on Saturday night.

He returned in November of that season to conduct a magical performance of Mahler's First Symphony, in what became the opening installment of a complete multi-year cycle of Mahler's nine symphonies.[2] Judie Janowski, his personal manager at Columbia Artists, soon followed, and by early December, he was among a small number of candidates discussing with the conductor search committee what each of them would expect from the Symphony Society.

Eschenbach had greatly advanced his credentials for the position as early as 1985, when he stepped in on short notice to rescue the Houston Symphony's final tour concert in Carnegie Hall after music director Sergiu Comissiona had suddenly collapsed with a heart problem three nights earlier. The concert cemented a relationship between Eschenbach and the orchestra that extended into a musical "love affair" throughout his 11-year tenure as music director.

Those 11 years became a period of sustained triumph for conductor and orchestra, and seemingly the apex of a life that had begun quite bleakly for Eschenbach. He was born February 20, 1940, in Breslau, Germany (now Wroclaw, Poland). He never knew his real mother, who died in childbirth. His father was Heribert Ringmann, the noted musicologist who had published a modern edition of the *Glogauer Liederbuch*, a celebrated Renaissance manuscript of 15th-century sacred music and secular songs. Because Ringmann opposed the Nazis, he was recruited into the German army and sent to the Eastern Front, where, as Eschenbach said, "it was certain he would be killed."

The child was raised by his grandmother throughout World War II, and when it was ending, they fled westward to escape advancing Soviet armies. The grandmother died in a refugee camp near Mecklenburg, but Christoph—gravely ill and unable to speak at all—was found by his dead mother's cousin. She was a singer and piano teacher named Wallydore Eschenbach, who took him to her home near Hamburg. "There," he said, "after these very, very dark years at the end of the war, I had the opportunity to live a very beautiful, quiet, sheltered childhood—*with* music, which I wholly, unconsciously longed for. From my bed, I could hear her giving lessons and playing, and this fascinated me. The moment I could talk again, I asked to study and I had my first three years of lessons with her."

At age eight, Eschenbach began three years of piano study with Eliza Hansen. Later he studied with the noted Swiss pianist Edwin Fischer. At 11, he heard the touring Berlin Philharmonic Orchestra conducted by Wilhelm Furtwängler. The experience left a deep imprint on his mind. "Consciously or unconsciously at

"In the 1960s, he won piano competitions in Munich and Lucerne, and began the exhausting life of a touring pianist while studying conducting."

this age, I already decided I wanted to be a conductor," he said. I wanted to be in front of an orchestra and I wanted to get that kind of sound."[3]

In the 1960s, he won piano competitions in Munich and Lucerne, and began the exhausting life of a touring pianist while studying conducting, first with noted German pedagogue Wilhelm Brückner-Rüggeberg, later with George Szell and Herbert von Karajan. He made his conducting debut in 1973 and directed the Rheinland-Pfalz State Philharmonic from 1979–81, then conducted the Tonhalle Orchestra in Zurich from 1981–85.[4]

Because of a prior commitment to tour with the Australian Youth Symphony, Eschenbach could not conduct the Houston Symphony's second Mostly Mozart Festival in July 1988, which was parceled out to guest performers. The 1988–89 subscription series had also been announced a month before his appointment and had been planned months earlier by Comissiona and Toeplitz as a season of guest conductors and a 75th anniversary revival of works commissioned by the Houston Symphony in past seasons. Those previously commissioned works and several of the guest

conductors were tabled by Toeplitz's successor, David Wax, in an effort to provide more podium dates for Eschenbach and a greater focus on standard repertoire during his opening season.

So, Eschenbach's first season was something of a hodge-podge, assembled by many hands. But some of Toeplitz's long-planned efforts remained: an 80th birthday celebration for composer Elliott Carter on November 26–28, conducted by Michael Gielen and featuring pianist Ursula Oppens in Carter's Piano Concerto. The program included his fanfare *A Celebration of some 100 x 150 Notes*, commissioned by the Houston Symphony two seasons earlier. Famed Russian conductor Gennady Rozhdestvensky and his wife, pianist Viktoria Postnikova, made their Houston Symphony debuts in a Tchaikovsky program. Morton Gould conducted a novel program featuring his Symphony of Spirituals and tap dancer Fred Strickler in Gould's Tap Dance Concerto. Walter Weller conducted the world premiere of composer-in-residence Tobias Picker's Third Symphony, a work for string orchestra, and the first Houston Symphony performances of Prokofiev's rarely heard Seventh Symphony. And because Eschenbach had his own future plans to conduct Beethoven's Ninth Symphony, Lawrence Foster had to substitute the composer's *Missa Solemnis* for his season-ending engagement on April 8–10, 1989.[5]

The 1989–90 season could be considered the first one that bore something of Eschenbach's personal stamp. He preceded his performance of the Beethoven Ninth Symphony with the string-orchestra version of Beethoven's *Great Fugue*. He cited that work and the string-orchestra Adagietto from Mahler's Fifth Symphony as important technical exercises for the orchestra's string section.[6] Eschenbach broke the normal sequence of his Mahler cycle, skipping from the First and Second Symphonies to the Fifth Symphony in his opening concert of the 1989–90 season. There was a rather hard-edged patina to the orchestral tone in the work, a quality that carried over into the normally velvety Adagietto. A week later, the Beethoven *Great Fugue* was played at a relatively reasonable pace. Although Eschenbach had improved orchestral discipline during his first season, the results suggested the strings needed further refinement on one hand, greater virtuosity on the other, to meet the standard Eschenbach sought. He also spoke of a need for more players, reminding the board of the strain on musicians who were constantly playing "at the limit of their reserves."

There were 94 members on the orchestral roster throughout Eschenbach's first season in 1988–89, including 15 first violins and 14–15 second violins. The full roster went below that number only once during the next decade, in the fall of 1996, and for the most part, it stayed at or above 95 musicians, reaching an all-time high of 99 musicians at the end of the 1995–96 season. But that momentary decline in 1996 was a signal of much worse things to come, because the funds that had been heroically raised to support Eschenbach's ambitions were being seriously depleted, and the roster suddenly fell to 91 musicians in the spring of 1998 and remained there for two years. It returned to the original 94 musicians only at the very end of his "conductor emeritus" season in the spring of 2000.[7]

Among the 94 players Eschenbach inherited from Comissiona, 24 musicians—essentially one-quarter of the orchestra—had been contracted members of the Houston Symphony at least since 1966, Sir John Barbirolli's final year as conductor-in-chief. Ten of those musicians had joined the orchestra under Stokowski: violinists Doris Derden, Elena Diaz and Vera Jelagin Harrin; violists Kyla Bynum,[8] Hugh Gibson and Violeta Moncada; cellist Marian Wilson; bass player William Black; oboist Barbara Hester; and principal clarinetist Richard Pickar. Three of them, violinist Dorothe Robinson, violist William Welch and principal flutist Byron Hester, had joined under Kurtz. Principal second violinist (and former concertmaster) Raphael Fliegel's 59-year Houston Symphony career had begun under Hoffmann in 1936.

But by the time Eschenbach left, performance traditions learned from playing under some famous past conductors had thinned out considerably. Only four members of Barbirolli's final orchestra—violists Thomas Molloy and Joy Plesner, double bassist Robert Pastorek and bass trombonist David Waters—remained to continue on with Hans Graf, the music director who carried the orchestra on to the 21st century and the brink of its centennial season.

Eschenbach was a commanding presence on the podium, standing as erect as a Marine, issuing decisive gestures to the musicians and bowing almost unsmilingly to the audience. He was trained, of course, by two of the most commanding "dictators of the baton" in orchestral history: Herbert von Karajan and George Szell. As a special trick to demonstrate his utter control over the orchestra, he would conduct the Scherzo and Trio of Tchaikovsky's Fourth Symphony with arms held rigidly against

his body, using only his eyes and eyebrows to signal cues and expressive indications.[9]

His interpretations were unvaryingly dramatic, mirroring in sound his stance on the podium. He strove for—and often achieved—a clean sound throughout the orchestra. He also challenged the players—particularly the strings—to achieve a new, higher level of technical excellence and virtuosity. This resulted in some of the fastest final movements of Mozart and Haydn symphonies on record, often taken at speeds the musicians could barely maintain. It was comparable to a runner winning a marathon, gasping for breath.

Above all, Eschenbach reveled in the sound of the brass. In the climaxes of big 19th-century symphonies, he could demand—and get—a bigger… and bigger… and still bigger sound from the brass in each succeeding phrase, oftentimes to the detriment of the strings, the basic orchestral foundation, which became drowned out in all that brass tone. This was definitely in contrast to Foster, who claimed he was unpopular with the trumpets because he was always shushing them.[10] And Barbirolli would tell the brass, "You must be quiet, so we strings over here can be heard."[11]

Although Hoffmann and Erich Bergel took the Houston Symphony briefly to Mexico, it was Eschenbach who led the Houston Symphony on major international tours: first, a brief tour to Singapore in 1990, then a two-week tour to Japan in 1991, where Eschenbach was co-director (with Michael Tilson Thomas) of the Pacific Rim Music Festival on the island of Hokkaido. Single concerts in Tokyo and Osaka followed their weeklong stay in Sapporo. A major 3 ½-week tour of Germany, Switzerland and Austria followed in the fall of 1992. Seven cities in Japan were visited in 1995. Two additional European tours followed in 1997 and 2000, at the very end of Eschenbach's tenure. These were interspersed with four national tours—mainly to major cities along the Eastern seaboard, with occasional forays as far west as Chicago and Lexington, Kentucky.

In the summer of 1993, the Houston Symphony Chamber Players were founded, in response to an invitation for Houston Symphony principal musicians and Eschenbach to perform a special private chamber concert during the orchestra's 1992 European tour. They were formally organized to perform and give

> "Eschenbach was a commanding presence on the podium, standing as erect as a Marine, issuing decisive gestures to the musicians and bowing almost unsmilingly to the audience."

> "Although Hoffmann and Erich Bergel took the Houston Symphony briefly to Mexico, it was Eschenbach who led the Houston Symphony on major international tours."

workshops for three weeks at Japan's Pacific Rim Music Festival in July and August 1993. Eschenbach believed this was an excellent way to improve ensemble playing among the orchestra's principals and throughout the orchestra itself. In essence, the Chamber Players were successors to the earlier Houston Symphony Chamber Players that former concertmaster Ronald Patterson had briefly organized during the spring of 1975. Eschenbach joined the 15 principals and also took them to perform at Chicago's Ravinia Festival in 1997, where he had become the festival's music director in 1994, and to the Schleswig-Holstein Music Festival in Germany, where he also served as co-artistic director during those years. They made four tours to Japan and maintained a regular Houston series in Rice University's Stude Hall.

Orchestral programs ranged broadly over the entire standard repertoire throughout Eschenbach's tenure. Because of the annual summer Mozart festivals during his early years in Houston, there was considerable emphasis upon the works of Mozart, Haydn, Beethoven and Schubert. Christopher Rouse was featured among living American composers with performances of his first two symphonies, his Flute Concerto, his tone poems *Jagannath* and *Phaethon* and his chamber music work *Compline*. The very moment Eschenbach's conductorship was announced, March 6, 1988, he led off that weekend's program with a stunningly brilliant performance of Bernd Alois Zimmermann's short tone poem *Photoptosis*, and later glimpses of his keen insight into the modern German repertoire came with the world premieres of Aribert Reimann's Nine Pieces for Orchestra and Hans Werner Henze's Eighth Symphony, which had been dedicated to Eschenbach.

Above all, Eschenbach's performances of the nine complete Mahler symphonies and the Adagio from the Tenth Symphony were treasured experiences for Houston Symphony audiences.[12] Once he had completed the cycle, he began a second one.

A summation of Eschenbach's Houston Symphony career would conclude that he brought the orchestra to its highest level of technical excellence. Leading musicians who came as soloists and guest conductors raved about the quality of the Houston Symphony. While he lavished care and prominence upon the orchestra's principal players, he enjoyed a corps of associate principals of unparalleled high caliber, so that he felt free to take the principals on Chamber Players tours without sacrificing the quality of the orchestra left behind. Unfortunately, the associates were never given a competitive opportunity to show off their own talents as solo and chamber players.

Eschenbach's keenly analytical mind brought new insights into the standard repertoire. Inner voices in a familiar work could be highlighted against the main melody, so that new meaning was imparted to any given composition. While his penchant for long pauses at phrase endings, extreme loud and soft volume levels and elastic tempos enhanced his interpretations of some works—notably those of Mahler—at other times they stretched musical works out of their appropriate shape. His deeply philosophical interpretations of Bruckner's larger symphonies could become ponderous. Eschenbach's record on Bruckner performances ran a fairly close second to his annual Mahler performances. During his 11 seasons as music director (1988–99) and the two subsequent seasons as conductor laureate, Eschenbach conducted nine performances of six different Bruckner symphonies, including an alternate version of the popular Fourth Symphony.

In the end, Eschenbach proved to be a very costly conductor for the Houston Symphony Society.[13] Even before he was named music director, the Wortham Foundation issued a $6 million challenge grant to erase the orchestra's deficit and build the endowment to $30 million. While the subsequent $41 million capital campaign succeeded, costs began to mount in the 1990s, and the musicians' contract renewal of 1993–94 was a time of considerable tension. A second capital campaign had to be abandoned in the mid-1990s, and contract negotiations came to the brink of a strike in 1997, with no settlement for more than a year.

In the midst of these difficulties, at the opening of Chicago's 1997 Ravinia Festival, which Eschenbach had directed since 1994, he was quoted as telling *Chicago Magazine*'s Ted Shen: "To be number one, like Berlin, Vienna, or Chicago, (an orchestra) needs financial involvement. But not always the rich people give their money. And we'd have to tour and record. If the folks in Houston don't want this, I'm ready to leave."[14] Around Thanksgiving time 1997, he wrote a gracious letter directly to the musicians, stating that he would end his tenure as music director at the conclusion of the 1998–99 season.

Eschenbach made the Houston Symphony internationally famous through his near-constant tours with the orchestra to Europe and Japan. But the Houston Symphony and the supporting Houston Symphony Society made him equally famous as a conductor. Both parties were searching for a new partner in the mid-1980s and they discovered each other almost by accident. It was a great symphonic romance, but like all things in life, it couldn't last forever.

> "Eschenbach made the Houston Symphony internationally famous through his near-constant tours with the orchestra to Europe and Japan."

Right: **Christoph Eschenbach**

XI

HANS GRAF

The new millennium was hardly 18 months old when the fateful warning that France's King Louis XV issued, "Après moi, le déluge," seemed to echo down the centuries and land directly upon the Houston Symphony, Jones Hall, the city of Houston and the nation.

During the night of June 8–9, 2001, Tropical Storm Allison completed its five-day rampage in Southeast Texas, dumping some 40 inches of rain all over the city. A concrete wall in the underground parking garage leading to Jones Hall gave way during the storm, allowing the adjoining Buffalo Bayou to flood the entire garage, a system of underground tunnels leading throughout downtown Houston, and the underground office and rehearsal spaces for the Symphony, two other major performing arts organizations and the civic center.

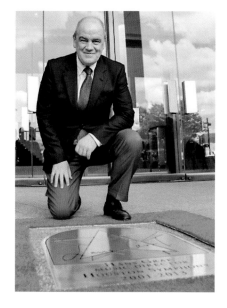

Most of the orchestra's library of music was flooded, including cherished string parts whose bowings had been personally marked by Sir John Barbirolli. Orchestra librarian Tom Takaro was the hero who overcame that calamity. He quickly turned his own home into a temporary library, borrowing materials from other orchestras across the nation to meet the orchestra's immediate needs. Two concert grand Steinway pianos, two double basses and other instruments were destroyed, along with the Symphony's entire computer and communications system, and the extensive photo archives and other materials.[1] Fortunately, the stage, ground level auditorium and lobby areas were spared.

As a side effect of the devastating September 11 al-Qaeda attack upon New York's World Trade Center, the Pentagon and rural Pennsylvania, all air traffic was temporarily grounded, nearly preventing newly named Austrian conductor Hans Graf from reaching Houston in time to begin the orchestra's fall season.[2]

In November of that year, the collapse of the Enron Corporation sent a terrible shock wave through the Houston economy, endangering the financial health of many performing arts organizations. Enron had been a major donor to the city's vibrant arts community and its sudden demise was a serious loss to all of them.[3]

Add in the following calamities and one can see that the early years of Graf's conductorship were hardly an easy time. That was equally true for Ann Kennedy, a 14-year board member who had been appointed the orchestra's first woman executive director three months before the flood.

In 2001, travertine marble tiles that had formed the decorative skin of Jones Hall's exterior walls began falling to the sidewalk below. Much of the sidewalk had to be blocked off, scaffolding had to be erected, and the 4,500 tiles covering the entire circular wall had to be re-cemented in place. The hall looked like a construction zone for several years and concert-going became a challenging experience for Houston Symphony audiences. The recession and "jobless recovery" that attended Graf's early years, plus the stock market crash and subsequent recession after 2007, left a nearly constant cloud over his efforts to rebuild the audience and provide stimulating repertoire for the orchestra and its listeners.

And heavy spending during the Eschenbach years had drained the Symphony Society's coffers, leaving another large deficit. Within a few seasons, negotiations with the musicians for a contract renewal broke down, orchestra members were leaving for positions elsewhere, and for the first time in its history, the orchestra voted to strike on March 9, 2003.

As the impasse hardened, Charles Nathan, a quiet, longtime symphony subscriber, contacted Houston real estate developer Ed Wulfe, who became special representative to solve the contract dispute. Wulfe asked prominent Houston attorney Alvin Zimmerman to join him in a mediation effort. They arranged a retreat, assembling the two parties in separate rooms, spelling out what needed to be done and coaxing them into an agreement over the weekend of March 29–30.[4] George Mitchell, a generous Houston arts patron, hosted the mediation process in the conference center at his real estate development, The Woodlands, 30 miles north of Houston.

As a result of the settlement, the musicians annually accepted three unpaid weeks of furlough for the next four seasons, while the Houston Symphony Society committed itself

to a $75 million capital campaign,[5] in still another effort to raise endowment funds and erase the long-term debt. The number of furlough weeks was gradually reduced to two weeks, then one week, finally ending in October 2011 after eight years. Wulfe was quickly appointed to the Symphony board, becoming vice-president for community affairs in December 2003, board president for two seasons beginning in the fall of 2004, board chairman for three seasons beginning in the fall of 2008 and a key advisor on the board's executive committee over an extraordinary ten-year period extending at least to the spring of 2013.

During his term, Wulfe also spearheaded the installation of video screens in Jones Hall, in a successful effort to attract more listeners for the Houston Symphony during a visually oriented era. While some concertgoers found them distracting, the screens brought soloists and individual members within the orchestra into closer contact with the audience, and enhanced the orchestra's performances in some major orchestral works: Richard Strauss' *Alpine Symphony*, Holst's *The Planets* and the film production of Leonard Bernstein's *West Side Story*. *The Planets–An HD Odyssey*, employing film producer Duncan Copp's NASA footage of the planets in our solar system, became a Houston Symphony spectacular that brought the orchestra major attention in Houston, at Carnegie Hall and during a week's tour of the United Kingdom in 2010.

Previous spread: **Hans Graf.** Top: **Graf and the Houston Symphony, 2011.** Bottom: **Graf's baton, fashioned with a wine cork from a 1928 bottle of Krug champagne. His love of wine inspired an annual fundraising event, the "Maestro's Wine Dinner."** Left: **In 2013 the City of Houston honored Graf, like his predecessor Eschenbach, with a star on the entry plaza to Jones Hall.**

When Graf became music director in the fall of 2001, there were still 97 members listed on the orchestra's roster, but that number dwindled to 94 musicians by the fall of 2003. Then it dropped sharply to 86 by the end of the 2003–04 season. It rose as high as 91 musicians by the end of the 2004–05 season, but it again dropped back and fluctuated between 86 and 88 members for the remaining eight seasons of his tenure. The losses were suffered throughout the string section, and they automatically threatened Graf's efforts to maintain the degree of tonal richness available to Eschenbach, let alone Comissiona, Foster, Previn, Barbirolli or Stokowski. Essentially, the orchestral complement shrank to the median number of musicians available to Kurtz during his last four seasons nearly 50 years earlier.[6]

Given straitened circumstances all around, which were common to the vast majority of American orchestras during those years, Graf had to be careful to program works that would attract audiences, not drive them away. There were liberal helpings of standard repertoire throughout his tenure, as had also been true of his predecessors. When it came to blending these works with less familiar repertoire, he was often careful to choose tonally accessible music.

For a time, he also favored thematic programming, tying several works in a season to particular themes. During the 2003–04 seasons, "Images in Music" brought forth works with some connection to the visual arts: Hindemith's *Mathis der Maler* Symphony; Martinů's *Frescoes of Piero della Francesca*, Dutilleux's *Timbres, espace, mouvement, ou La Nuit étoilée* and the Mussorgsky-Ravel *Pictures at an Exhibition*. During the 2004–05 season, he chose works based on fairytales: Zemlinsky's *The Mermaid*, Bartók's *Bluebeard's Castle* (sung in concert form) and *The Wooden Prince*, Tchaikovsky's *Nutcracker* suite, Mendelssohn's Overture to *The Fair Melusine*, Prokofiev's suite from *Cinderella*, the suite from Ravel's *Mother Goose* and lots of Stravinsky: the Divertimento from *The Fairy's Kiss*, the suite from *The Firebird* and *Pétrouchka*.[7, 8]

The Symphony board expressed its faith in Graf rather quickly. At the beginning of the 2004–05 season, it extended his initial five-year contract by another three years, through the end of the 2008–09 season. Graf had always felt eight years was long enough for a conductor with any orchestra—that orchestras and audiences grow restless for a change after that length of time. But in 2007, the board extended his contract for another three seasons, through the end of the 2011–12 season. At that point, he thought ahead and suggested one additional season, bringing his 12-year tenure right up to the orchestra's centennial and

Tropical Storm Allison

During Tropical Storm Allison in 2001, the Houston Symphony's offices were destroyed, including files, furniture and equipment. The orchestra lost instruments and the music library. All of the underground levels of Jones Hall, including the offices of Society for the Performing Arts, Houston Symphony and Jones Hall administration, were completely submerged. Fortunately, much of the Houston Symphony's equipment was saved from damage because it was at the offsite warehouse—to be used by the orchestra while finishing neighborhood Sounds Like Fun! concerts.

making him its longest-serving music director—one season beyond Hoffmann and Eschenbach.

As evidence of that support, certain board members stepped forward to provide financial assistance to sustain the orchestra. Notable among them were Mike S. Stude, representing the Houston Symphony's needs to the Brown Foundation, which had seen the orchestra through many a crisis for decades, and Bobby Tudor, who became Houston Symphony Society president in June 2009 and provided crucial support for the resumption of international touring activities.

Graf's talents began to unfold almost unobtrusively. At the second of his two audition concerts in March 2000, he turned out a refreshingly lyrical, captivating performance of Carl Orff's *Carmina Burana*. With each successive choral-orchestral performance, he proved to be the Houston Symphony's most communicative conductor of choral-orchestral works.

With ten seasons as director of the Salzburg Mozarteum, Graf could be expected to produce many fine Mozart performances. Those did come throughout his career, and they included several lesser-known symphonies and some exceptionally fine interpretations of Mozart concert arias. But other items from the standard repertoire also sparked attention. During a month devoted to music on Shakespearean themes, Canadian actress Maureen Thomas joined Graf, the orchestra and women choristers in a charming semi-staged performance of Mendelssohn's Incidental Music to *A Midsummer Night's Dream*. In February 2008, he brought Tchaikovsky's Fourth Symphony down to properly scaled volume levels in a beautifully phrased interpretation, free of all the hyperbole and screaming brass tone usually associated with that work. It was as though an era of exaggeration had suddenly been wiped away, revealing the true nature of the symphony.

The mention of Russian music brings up the subject of Graf's training with Arvid Jansons at the former Leningrad Conservatory. His personal acquaintance with Russian musical society seems to have been the source of his devotion to the music of Shostakovich. Over his 12-season term, he conducted eight Shostakovich symphonies, including most of the important ones, and welcomed guest conductor Claus Peter Flor to add his

mesmerizing interpretation of Shostakovich's Fifteenth Symphony. Graf was a major Shostakovich interpreter and imparted special importance to his 2008 performance of Shostakovich's Thirteenth Symphony by inviting poet Yevgeny Yevtushenko onto the Jones Hall stage to read his poems on the World War II massacre of the citizens of Babi Yar, which Shostakovich had set to music in the symphony. Graf filled out his survey of Shostakovich's music with performances of the first concertos for cello, piano/trumpet and violin; the song cycle *Michelangelo Sonnets*; and numerous smaller works, including the little parodistic musical play *Anti-formalist Rayok*, satirizing Soviet cultural functionaries.

Graf also kept pace with Eschenbach on the subject of Bruckner's music. Having grown up near the composer's hometown of Linz, he seemed to have a natural feeling for the craggy, rough-hewn character of Bruckner's music. Over his years in Houston, he conducted lively performances of the Third, Fourth, Sixth, Seventh, Eighth and Ninth Symphonies in Jones Hall, adding the incomplete sketches for the finale to the Ninth Symphony and Bruckner's *Te Deum*, which the composer had suggested as an alternate finale. As part of his special talent with choral music, he conducted the Mass in E minor. He also conducted a special concert performance of Bruckner's Seventh Symphony in the newly built Co-Cathedral of the Sacred Heart, feeling that its echoing acoustic properties simulated those of cathedrals in Bruckner's native Austria. Rather than conducting another complete cycle of the Mahler symphonies, Graf rounded out Houston's Mahler experience with a complete survey of Mahler's six song cycles. As to the symphonies, he limited himself to a few important ones: the Second, Fifth, Sixth and the Deryck Cooke-completed version of Mahler's incomplete Tenth Symphony.

Because of commitments elsewhere, Graf was not able to be physically present on the Jones Hall stage when his appointment was first announced. So, a videotaped acceptance speech was played, in which he spoke almost humbly about preserving what Eschenbach had achieved. Instead, the orchestra, Symphony Society and audience that Eschenbach left him were beset by one catastrophe and calamity after another, as outlined at the beginning of this chapter.

Above: **Concertmaster Frank Huang and retired concertmaster Uri Pianka.** Left: **Graf and the Houston Symphony, 2006.**

So, Graf was handed the task of rebuilding, rather than preserving and retaining, much of the orchestra, audience and patron support. He did that work patiently but firmly, wisely and with great resourcefulness. Because so many musicians from the Eschenbach orchestra left, he is credited with overseeing the appointment of 18 musicians—nearly one-fifth of what became a smaller orchestra, but one that was no less supple or expressive. They included five new, highly talented principal players: trumpeter Mark Hughes, cellist Brinton Averil Smith, oboist Jonathan Fischer, bassoonist Rian Craypo and concertmaster Frank Huang.

Toward the middle of his tenure, Graf expressed concern about neglecting American music,[9] but the record of his performances shows a quite decent attention to that segment of the repertoire. Over a period of several years, he revived eight of the 21 short fanfares that former composer-in-residence Tobias Picker had commissioned, mostly from living American composers, for the 1986–87 Texas Sesquicentennial. The musical scores and instrumental parts had been destroyed in the 2001 flood, and new copies, when available, were purchased with donations from Houston Symphony supporters.

Of far greater significance were more than a dozen works by living American composers, including eight concertos commissioned and given world or Houston premieres by Houston Symphony principal players during Graf's tenure. They included John Harbison's double bass concerto, a co-commission shared by 15 orchestras, performed in Houston by Timothy Pitts; Rice University composer Richard Lavenda's Clarinet Concerto, performed by David Peck; Larry Lipkis' *Pierrot*, premiered by

principal bassoonist Benjamin Kamins; Cindy McTee's trombone concerto, performed by Allen Barnhill; Augusta Read Thomas' *Absolute Ocean*, performed by harpist Paula Page and guest soprano Twyla Robinson; Gabriela Lena Frank's La Llorana for Viola and Orchestra, performed by Wayne Brooks; Damian Montano's Double Concerto for Piccolo and Contrabassoon, performed by Cynthia Meyers and Jeff Robinson; and John Williams' Horn Concerto (which was not a Houston Symphony commission), performed by William VerMeulen.

Among purely orchestral American works, Graf conducted Kevin Puts' First Symphony, John Adams' *Dr. Atomic* Symphony and his *Century Rolls*, two works by Christopher Rouse, three by Rice University composer Pierre Jalbert, Jennifer Higdon's *Blue Cathedral* and Aaron Kernis' *Musica Celestis*. He also devised novel ways of spotlighting the music of familiar composers. A day-long Jones Hall festival and exhibit of Beethoven's piano, chamber and orchestral music in 2007 was followed the next season by a Bach/Vivaldi festival in the recently built performing arts center at Houston Baptist University. During the 2011–12 season, he featured pianist Kirill Gerstein as soloist in a three-week festival of Rachmaninoff's piano concertos, plus symphonic as well as shorter orchestral works. And a three-week Brahms festival headlined his closing 2012–13 season, highlighted by a towering performance of the Fourth Symphony.

Graf had a thoughtfully planned method of leading his listeners into the typically audience-unfriendly area of the Second Viennese School of composers. In the 2007–08 season, he paired Alban Berg's Three Pieces from the *Lyric Suite* with Alexander

Above: **Roman Trekel and Anne Schwanewilms in the dress rehearsal for Alban Berg's *Wozzeck*, February 27, 2013.**
Right: **Music Director Designate Andrés Orozco-Estrada.**

Zemlinsky's *Lyric Symphony*, drawing upon thematic, stylistic and personal relationships involving the two works. At the end of the 2011–12 season, he honored newly named concertmaster Frank Huang with a gleaming performance of Berg's Violin Concerto. And he led the orchestra and a group of solo singers in a tonally lustrous account of Berg's *Wozzeck*, presented in two semi-staged concert performances in March 2013.

In 2005, Matthew VanBesien succeeded Kennedy as executive director of the Houston Symphony. A former member of the Louisiana Philharmonic horn section, he had undergone intensive training through the League of American Orchestras' management program and had risen up through several positions on the Houston Symphony's management team, including general manager prior to his executive appointment. When VanBesien's career path led to the Melbourne Symphony Orchestra (Australia) and the New York Philharmonic, he was succeeded by former Milwaukee Symphony Orchestra executive director Mark C. Hanson in 2010 who was also an alumnus of the LAO management program and an earlier position with the Houston Symphony. Both executive directors largely succeeded in achieving annual balanced budgets, while maintaining a smooth operation of the whole organization.

Because of the tight financial situation, there were no tours at all during the first half of Graf's tenure and a previously scheduled 2004 tour to Europe had to be canceled. But in 2006, the Houston Symphony Society self-presented the orchestra for a single concert in New York's Carnegie Hall. By a stroke of good luck, that unusual arrangement caught the attention of the *New York Times*, which devoted two articles to the Symphony's visit, with above-the-fold color photographs on the cover of its Arts section. Graf and the orchestra received the same treatment when they returned with their audio-visual production of *The Planets–An HD Odyssey* in 2010. They were enthusiastically welcomed on their aforementioned tour of the United Kingdom that fall. In 2012, during Graf's penultimate season, he led the Houston Symphony back to Carnegie Hall and then all the way to Moscow, accepting an invitation for two performances at the city's Festival of the World's Symphony Orchestras.

There were several instances during the Eschenbach years, and especially during the Graf years, when one could look over the announcement of a season's concerts by the New York Philharmonic and suddenly realize that more stimulating, novel orchestral repertoire was being performed right here by the Houston Symphony that season. So, the orchestra finished out its 99th season, not as the nation's largest or wealthiest orchestra, but as an orchestra that had survived the financial devastation that left some of its larger brethren crippled, bankrupt or silent in the early years of the 21st century. Graf and the orchestra also welcomed a core of younger, highly talented, fully confident players who provided their audiences a fresh, polished listening experience.

The Houston Symphony joined a small vanguard of American orchestras by looking southward for a new music director to open its second century. On January 16, 2013, Andrés Orozco-Estrada, a 35-year-old, Colombian-born, Viennese-trained conductor, was welcomed to the Jones Hall stage as the Houston Symphony's music director designate. With 11 years' experience leading orchestras in Graz, San Sebastian and, since 2009, Vienna's Tonkünstler Orchestra, Orozco-Estrada will begin a five-year contract as music director in September of the 2014–15 season.

CHAPTER
XII

THE MUSICIANS

The orchestra of the early years was diverse. A fair number of those whose backgrounds can be identified were first and second generation Germans, followed by Mexicans and French. Only eight of the hundred or so members who played in the first five years were women, but they were present from the very first season.

During the 1910s and 1920s, musicians in Houston found employment in theaters as accompanists for vaudeville shows and silent movies and with café orchestras. Full-time work as a musician was otherwise hard to find. Unemployment was rampant in the early years of the Depression, but by 1933–34 movie theaters once again presented musical reviews and hotels featured resident orchestras.[1]

Benjamin J. Steinfeldt was the concertmaster at the first Houston Symphony Orchestra concert in June 1913 and is listed as concertmaster in 1914–17 season programs. In 1911 he was a musician at the New Majestic Theatre. Steinfeldt was the conductor for the Prince Theatre in the 1910s and 1920s. Born in 1876 in Ohio to John Steinfeldt, who was a native of Germany, a music teacher and also a musician at the Cincinnati Opera House in 1910. City directories show him to have been in San Antonio as an orchestra leader in 1903, and in Dallas in 1922 as the concertmaster of the Palace Theatre.

Steinfeldt was followed by **E. D. Saunders** as concertmaster after November for the remainder of the 1917–18 season. Saunders was an expert violin maker and also a flutist.[2] These musicians were part of the early music community in Houston and belonged to chamber groups that performed around the city at elite restaurants and other venues.

Ten of the original 1913 group were members of the 1932 orchestra. "**Herman Wiess**, timpanist and flower grower, had moved to Houston from San Antonio in 1907 with Carl Beck's band. From 1919–22, he played for Julien Blitz in San Antonio and raised chickens. In 1922, he returned to play in theater orchestras at the Palace, Queen, Metropolitan, and Kirby theaters. Most other members of the orchestra also had other full-time day jobs."[3]

Ernest R. Hail, clarinetist, also worked as a manager for the orchestra and as a musician at the Majestic Theatre. As president of the Musician's Protective Association Local No. 65, American Federation of Musicians, he was on the 1921 committee to organize a new Houston Symphony.

Musicians in the early orchestra typically took many jobs. **Dr. Arthur J. H. Barbour**, "Joe", was in San Antonio from 1883 until at least 1899 as a music professor and also as organist of San Fernando Cathedral. He played at the Majestic Theatre in 1912; in 1913 he was the organist for First Methodist Episcopal Church and for the Isis theatre.

Except for the first concert in 1913, the Houston Symphony differed from many other orchestras in that women were included in the orchestra. The only two women in the original Houston Symphony Orchestra were violinists, **Marian Jenkins** and **Rosetta Hirsch**, both students of music educator Emil Lindenberg. The third and fourth seasons (1915–17) brought another violin student of Lindenberg, **Josephine Boudreaux**, as well as violinists **Iva Carpenter** (b. 1888) and **Miss F. Mobley**. The wife of violinist **Lee Smith** was also employed as harpist for a performance. Lindenberg's daughter **Grace Lindenberg Keller** (1881–1944) played viola in the Symphony's 1917–18 season and joined her friend Josephine as a member of the Boudreaux String Quartet in 1929. Keller had been a 1908 charter member and violinist of the Thursday Morning Musical Club. In the reorganized orchestra, she was principal viola for 1931–34. She was absent in 1935, but when she returned in early 1936, was second chair to principal Irving Wadler. Keller left the orchestra in 1937.

Maurice Derdeyn (1889–1990) played both violin and viola in the 1913 season. Derdeyn was born in Roules, Belgium, and studied piano and violin. He studied with Cesar Thompson at the Brussels Conservatory of Music and took classes at the Royal Conservatory. In Ghent he became friends with Paul Blitz. He was the orchestra's assistant director in 1915 and conducted the March 2, 1915 program, but he left after the 1916–17 season.

"Except for the first concert in 1913, the Houston Symphony differed from many other orchestras in that women were included in the orchestra."

One of the more remarkable families of Houston Symphony musicians was the Gutierrez family. **Jesus Gutierrez** emigrated from Zacatecas, Mexico, and had six children, three of whom also played in the Houston Symphony. One or more family members belonged to the orchestra from the orchestra's founding until 1948.

Originally a flutist, Jesus Gutierrez (1875–1940) immigrated to the United States in 1890. He lived and married in San Antonio, moving to Houston by 1910. He taught his children solfège, as he had been taught in Mexico. To supplement his musical career, Jesus ran a printing business. He learned to play bass and became a charter member of the orchestra, serving as principal bass both then and with the revitalized Houston Symphony until 1936. He took a lesser chair in the bass section until his death in 1940.

Previous spread: **String quartet: seated, Ray Fliegel; standing, Irving Wadler, Hank Hlavaty and Alfred Urbach.** Above: **The Blitz Quintette, with Julien Paul Blitz and Patricio Gutierrez on the right.** Left: **Detail from the wedding photo of Josie Hirsch and Jules Bloch in 1917. To the right is her sister and Houston Symphony violinist Rosetta Hirsch.**

Jesus' brother **José**, or Joe, was a trombonist who played French horn on several occasions with the Houston Symphony in 1915 and 1918. He was a jazz musician in the bands of Paul Whiteman, Jack Teagarden and Desi Arnaz, as well as a longtime member of the Xavier Cugat orchestra. José also co-wrote numerous works with Xavier Cugat.

Patricio "Pat" Gutierrez

(1896–1985) was born to Jesus and Frances Gutierrez in San Antonio. Although his primary instrument was the piano, he played cello in the first Houston Symphony concert in June 1913, having begun cello lessons with Julien Paul Blitz. Blitz deemed him a seasoned enough player to join others on the Majestic Theatre stage. The young Gutierrez had already joined the Houston Professional Musicians Association, Local 65, in 1907 at age 11. Patricio was the third instrumental soloist to perform with the Symphony, playing the Mendelssohn G minor Piano Concerto in 1915. As a pianist, he also was comfortable on the celesta and organ. In great demand as a soloist and accompanist, he was the pianist of choice for violinist Josephine Boudreaux in 1929, when giving her first public performance after returning from Europe.

In the 1930s, an uncredited clipping in Pat's scrapbook[4] notes: "He learned to play the French horn in a month. Conductor Hoffmann considers him, after one year with the horn, to be a virtuoso." When Hoffmann scheduled a performance of Saint-Saëns' *Carnival of the Animals*, two pianists were required. "When performance time came only Gutierrez appeared at one of the pianos. Hoffmann brought down his stick, dreading the consequences. The whole long composition went off perfectly. Gutierrez played both piano parts himself, something many of us say 'can't be done.' We are wondering now if Mr. Gutierrez can play more than one French horn at a time."

Along with his father, Pat was a charter member of the Houston Symphony and was part of the group for the first five seasons, as well as the first season of the reorganized orchestra. He was not listed on the roster again until 1935 and left the orchestra in 1938. Pat Gutierrez formed the Greenbriar Music Studios with his pianist wife, Edith, in 1951 and lined up other local musicians to teach there.

Josephine Boudreaux

A future concertmaster of the Houston Symphony, Josephine Boudreaux (1898–1993) moved to Houston with her family at the age of seven. She was born in Crowley, Louisiana, to Philippe Mozart Boudreaux and Margarite Octavine Clotiaux. In Houston, she studied violin with local Professor Emil S. Lindenberg.

As a teenager, she played with the Houston Symphony for the 1916–17 and 1917–18 seasons. She also was advertised as the featured soloist with the Isis Concert Orchestra at the Isis Theatre, part of the Saenger Amusement Company theater chain. The silent movies provided her a rich opportunity for performance and improvisation. After four years at the Isis, she raised enough money to study in Europe at the newly formed American Conservatory at Fountainebleau.* Before leaving for France, she was part of the 1921 musician committee urging musicians to join efforts to revive the Symphony under conductor William Reher.

Miss Boudreaux gave her notice to Saenger and departed Houston in June 1921 for Paris. Almost immediately she won first prize for violin, performing Edouard Lalo's *Symphonie espagnole*.† At the conservatory's inaugural ceremony, she heard speeches by Walter Damrosch, president of the American Friends of French Musicians and originator of the Fontainebleau Conservatory, and by composer Camille Saint-Saëns, who died later that year. Among the other students of that first class was the young American composer Aaron Copland.

After her first term, she won a scholarship for a second term at the conservatory. By February 1922, she was studying with Maurice Hewitt, a member of the Capet Quartet, as well as Lucien Capet. She also studied for two years under composer Jenö Hubay, director of the national conservatory at Budapest. She also studied ensemble with Adolph Schiffer, head of the cello department, playing in a string quartet with Schiffer.

Miss Boudreaux arranged to study with Otakar Ševčík in Pisek, Czechoslovakia, in 1924. Her concerts in the

Above: **Violinist Josephine Boudreaux, while studying in Europe in the 1920s.**
Right: **Fredell Lack as a young student of Miss Boudreaux.**

succeeding years were met with critical acclaim. "It was a great success for Josephine Boudreaux, the American violinist, at her concert in Salle Pleyel. Her technique places her in the very first rank violinistically [sic] and her interpretation evidences a deep musical and artistic sense. A brilliant future is opening for this young artist."‡ In 1926 she returned to Paris, and after six years of studying abroad, she returned to Texas in 1927.

She joined forces with former Houston Symphony musician and pianist Patricio Gutierrez, with whom she embarked on a number of public concerts beginning in March 1928.§ Boudreaux announced her availability to teach violin and for professional appearances in the fall of 1928. During that period, she was also forming her chamber ensemble, the Houston String Quartet. By 1929, the group was called the Boudreaux String Quartet; the other members included Octave Pimbert, second violin; Athelstan R. Charlton, cello; and Grace Keller, viola.

The Houston Symphony Orchestra Association engaged the Boudreaux String Quartet to perform a series of three chamber music concerts to be held in the homes of Association members for the 1929–30 season. This partnership continued for the 1930–31 season. These performances engendered a renewed interest in re-forming the Houston Symphony Orchestra, which had been disbanded in 1918. With Josephine Boudreaux as concertmaster, the Houston Symphony was reconstituted, performing two concerts in May 1931.

Miss Boudreaux was enlisted as concertmaster for the upcoming season, and Uriel Nespoli became the new conductor. She was featured soloist several times during her career with the Houston Symphony and widely praised for her part in the January 1936 performance of Saint-Saens' Prelude to *The Deluge*, Dr. Alfred Hertz conducting.

Other conductors she served as concertmaster were Frank St. Leger and Ernst Hoffmann, with whom she gave her last concert as concertmaster in January 1937. When her arm was injured in an accident, she left the orchestra and continued to teach generations of violinists, including Houston's acclaimed Fredell Lack. Miss Boudreaux died on August 11, 1993, in Houston.

Two more sons of Jesus Gutierrez belonged to the orchestra. Violinist **Federico** (1980–1985), or Fred, had the longest tenure of the Gutierrez clan as an orchestra member from 1931 to 1948, with the exception of the war years. He saw extensive military service in Patton's Second Army and earned seven bronze stars. **Joe Gutierrez** (1904–1982), nephew of José, was a clarinetist from 1931 to 1936 in the Houston Symphony and later played with the Long Beach Band in California.

Born in Wiesbaden, Germany, **Anton Diehl** (1867–1952) joined the original orchestra, playing violin all five years. In the 1890s, he had an office on Main Street where he taught music and hired out his services as the leader of an orchestra for receptions and other events. He served as the choir master for Christ Church Cathedral around 1893–96. During the Spanish American War, he joined the First Texas Cavalry as chief trumpeter. In 1908 he formed the Anton Diehl Conservatory of Music and in 1913 was listed in the city directory as operating the Anton Diehl Orchestra. His daughter, **Gabrielle "Soeurette" Diehl** (1906–1986), graduated in about 1930 from the New England Conservatory with highest honors and played in the reorganized orchestra for just one year.

As far as is known, brothers **William and Eugene Diehl** were no relation to Anton Diehl, but were also transplanted Germans. William (1860–1936) had a long career as a machinist and pattern maker, but added playing with his brother in the Herb & Lewis Band in the 1910s. He played French horn in the first year of the Houston Symphony. Eugene Diehl (1869–1938) was a violinist for all five years of the early Symphony.

Elmore Ewing "Joe" Stokes (1891–1966) was an original member of the Symphony, playing percussion for the first four years and rejoining the orchestra in 1932. During World War I, he organized and directed the original Ellington Field Band.[5] He retired from the orchestra in 1956, and for many years had been secretary and business manager of the musicians' local union and a vice president of the southwestern division of the national union.

When the Houston Symphony was reorganized in 1931, as centenarian orchestra member **George Illes** recently noted, the concertmaster (Josephine Boudreaux) was really very good, and his impression was that there were as many women as men. The women must have made their presence known, but in fact only a

* "Hopes Realized by Friends of Young Violinist," *Houston Post*, September 25, 1921.
† "Houston Girl Wins First Prize in French Conservatory Contest," *Houston Chronicle*, September 21, 1921.
‡ *Le Figaro*, Paris, May 25, 1927.
§ "Miss Boudreaux to Give Concert at Cathedral," *Houston Chronicle*, February 19, 1928.

quarter were female. George Illes (b. 1912) was a student at Rice University at the time and played violin for the new orchestra in 1931–33.[6] Josephine Boudreaux was the first concertmaster of the reorganized Houston Symphony Orchestra and served until 1937 under Nespoli, St. Leger and Hoffmann. By the late 1930s, the number of female musicians dropped to nine or ten. During the first year of the United States' entry into World War II, when many men went on active military service, only four women were added to the roll. The number of women in the orchestra doubled (23) by 1943, but dropped back to 16 for the 1945–46 season.

Father and son cellists joined the reorganized Symphony. **Mischel "Mike" De Rudder** (1892–1976) played for ten years with the Houston Symphony, beginning with the May 1931 concert for which he was listed as "solo" cello. He was a graduate of the Belgium Conservatory of Music and immigrated to the United States in 1919. **Louis DeRudder** (1913–1994) was born in Antwerp, Belgium. He studied music with his father, Mike De Rudder, and his uncle, professor Henri De Rudder, both of whom had studied at the Belgium Conservatory of Music. Louis was also a member of the San Antonio Symphony and principal cellist of the New Orleans Symphony. DeRudder had an intermittent tenure on the roster, playing in 1931–32, 1934–38, 1942–43, 1947–49 and 1950–78 for a total of 36 seasons.

Professor Henri, or Henry, De Rudder (b. 1890) was a violist who studied at the Belgium Conservatory of Music with his brother Mike and was a student of Belgian violinist, conductor and composer Eugène Ysaÿe. He played with Houston for four seasons, beginning in 1934, coming to work from San Antonio, where he taught and was employed by the W.P.A. Orchestra.[7]

Another notable musical family in the orchestra was the Fransees. **Dr. Waclav F. Fransee** (1872–1958) and his son and daughter all joined the orchestra in 1931. Born in Czechoslovakia, Dr. Fransee was a graduate of the Prague Conservatory of Music. His father was also a musician of note there. After coming to America, he married in Chicago in 1901. He and his wife, Margaret, came to Houston in 1921 as missionaries and teachers of English and music for members of the predominantly Czech congregation at Heights Presbyterian Church. The couple also established the Fransee Music School, where the multitalented Fransee taught piano, voice, all stringed instruments and brass. During the Depression, he and his family performed frequently on Houston radio station KXYZ as the Fransee Quartet, which included his wife, and the Fransee Trio. He spoke five languages: Czech, German, French, Italian, Spanish and English.[8] Dr. Fransee played viola with the Houston Symphony for six seasons.

The eldest child, **Vera Fransee** (1915–2002), was born in Illinois. Beginning her violin studies at the age of six, by age 11 she taught violin at the Fransee Music School. Four years later, in 1931, she accepted a position as a violinist with the Houston Symphony. For three years, she continued as the orchestra's youngest member. In 1933, she went to New York to study at the Juilliard School of Music. When family obligations forced her return to Houston, Vera rejoined the Symphony. In 1936, she married Paul Neal and continued in the orchestra's violin section for a dozen years.

The son, **Gabriel D. Fransee** (1917–2002), was a violinist in the orchestra and also substituted on viola when needed. In 1932, he was awarded a scholarship to Allen Academy in Bryan, where he also conducted the Academy Band. Having previously studied with his father, he also took lessons with conductor Frank St. Leger and played for six years with the Symphony. Gabriel held a 1941 bachelor's degree from the University of Houston and also a master's degree in political science. While pursuing postgraduate work at Louisiana State University, he held a teaching position. In the 1940s, he accepted the position of associate professor of music at Howard Payne University.

Henry "Hank" Hlavaty (1915–1991) was a member of the 1931 violin section, but in 1940 he switched to viola. During the war years, he was concertmaster of the Seabee's Radio Orchestra and a principal player with Meredith Wilson's armed forces network orchestra. He returned to Houston and stayed with the orchestra until 1953. Hlavaty also played in the Raphael String Quartet in the late 1940s with Ray Fliegel.

Leonard "Len" Manno (1915–1977) served 30 seasons in the orchestra as a bass player. Born in Galveston, he studied with Felix Stella and played in Galveston orchestras before moving to Houston and joining the Houston Symphony in 1936. Starting in 1949, he took a break from the Houston Symphony and played for ten years with accordion players Bill Hughes and Bill Palmer in The Concert Trio. Around 1957, he joined the Dixieland jazz group Delta Kings—with whom he occasionally played tuba—and made recordings, as he did with The Concert Trio. Manno also created a still-popular rosin for bass called Pop's Bass Rosin. He rejoined the Houston Symphony in 1958, where he played until the year before his death in 1977.

Irving W. Wadler (1912–2003) joined the orchestra in 1933 and did not retire until 1978. Wadler began in the violin section and was assistant concertmaster from 1933–35. He played as principal viola from the fall of 1935 until 1937. He continued as a violist until 1939, when he switched back to violin. He also taught at the Houston Conservatory of Music beginning in 1937, was co-owner of Wadler's Music Shop on South Main and served as director of music at the Jewish Community Center.

Following Josephine Boudreaux in 1937 as Houston Symphony Orchestra concertmaster was **Joseph Gallo**. Born in Italy, he first studied with his father, a member of the San Carlo Opera House in Naples. After coming to the United States, he continued his musical training at the New England Conservatory of Music. His teachers included Richard Burgin, Scipioni Guidi, and Otakar Ševčík, who had also taught Boudreaux. Gallo had performed in Boston for Houston's conductor Ernst Hoffmann at the Commonwealth Orchestra in Massachusetts before coming to Houston. He soloed with the orchestra in a *Scheherazade* performance in 1940 and was a member of the Houston Symphony Orchestra's string quartet, which gave chamber music concerts. In 1943 he left the orchestra and became head of the violin department at Incarnate Word College in San Antonio and its orchestra conductor. During the years before he rejoined the Houston Symphony, he served as concertmaster two years with the San Antonio Symphony, and in 1946–47 he played with the Cleveland Orchestra. He started a second term in 1953 with the Houston Symphony, in 1965 was assistant second violin and in 1969 retired with 22 years of service.

Raphael N. "Ray" Fliegel (1918–2005) first appeared as a soloist with the Houston Symphony in Mendelssohn's Violin Concerto—at the age of 13 under the baton of Frank St. Leger—a performance that garnered rave reviews. Late in life, he still recalled with chagrin that he was made to wear short pants for the occasion. He was born in Chicago, and at age four he began cello lessons. He switched to violin at six, his first teacher being Victor Young and later Herbert Butler. The family moved in 1930 to Houston, where he took lessons from J. Moody Dawson. He also studied at the Chicago Conservatory with Henry Ginsburg and with Sol Turner. In 1936, he began playing regularly with the Houston Symphony as the youngest orchestra member at that time in the nation. After

"Manno also created a still-popular rosin for bass called Pop's Bass Rosin."

Top left: **Wind principals in the 1990s. Front row, Ben Kamins and David Peck; back row, Bob Atherholt, Bill VerMeulen and Aralee Dorough.** Center left: **The viola section in the early 1980s. Standing, from left: Joy Plesner, Bernice Beckerman, Linda Goldstein, Kyla Bynum, Wayne Brooks, Wayne Crouse and Tom Molloy. Seated, from left: Fay Shapiro, Violeta Moncada, Hugh Gibson and Phyllis Herdliska.** Bottom left: **The Houston Symphony Brass Quintet, with Ralph Liese and Bill Rose, seated, and from left, John Moyes, James Austin and Kittrell Reid, circa 1959–65.**

high school graduation, he toured with the Carlos Moreno band. By 1939, he was again a regular member of the orchestra. He enlisted in the war effort in 1942 and was stationed at Ellington Field in Houston, still playing with the Symphony as duty allowed. Fliegel became concertmaster upon returning from service in World War II and held the post for 26 years, the Symphony's longest serving concertmaster. On the advice of his doctor, in 1972 he stepped aside as concertmaster to serve as principal of the second violin section until his retirement in 1995.

"During the years of World War II, men in uniform were admitted free to concerts."

In his earlier years in Houston, Fliegel was a popular music performer with his own dance band. Later, chamber music became an important part of his life; he started the Raphael String Quartet in the late 1940s, then the Music Guild Quartet and the Shepherd Quartet. In 1955, he joined with violinist Fredell Lack and Houston Symphony members Wayne Crouse and Shirley Trepel to form the Lyric Art Quartet. He served on the faculties of the University of Houston School of Music, Houston Baptist University and the Shepherd School of Music at Rice, where he was honored in 1989 with the title of professor emeritus. Ray Fliegel died in 2005 at

age 86, a well-beloved mentor to many of today's finest orchestral musicians. During his tenure, he played for most of the world's greatest conductors, appearing as soloist and recording with many.

Trombonist **Albert Lube** (1910–2001) had changed his name from Lubowski, as did his brother Joe Lube, who was principal trumpet in 1936. Albert played for one season for the Houston Symphony in 1940, and then toured the country with the George Olsen Orchestra, the Percy Faith Orchestra and the NBC Radio Orchestra in Chicago before moving to Houston in 1946. Lube became principal trombonist in 1966; he left the post to play second trombone in 1972 and served as a mentor to incoming musician Allen Barnhill. Lube taught for over a quarter century at the University of Houston, winning a 1993 teaching award from the International Trombone Association. He retired from the orchestra in 1977.

Born in Tennessee and adopted by German parents, **Joseph A. "Joe" Henkel, Jr.** (1890–1975) did his early studies in violin and piano in Europe. He studied violin in Germany with Joseph Joachim. In 1916, Henkel joined the faculty of Christian

Brothers High School in Memphis as band director. He became the concertmaster and then conductor of the Memphis Symphony. He also worked for the Memphis College of Music and was the first conductor of the W.P.A. Band in Memphis. Henkel conducted grand opera, light opera, vaudeville and movie theater orchestras. During his vaudeville days, he played for Jack Benny, Fred Allen and Walter Winchell.

In 1937, Joe Henkel joined the Houston Symphony. By 1939, he was the director of the Southern Music Camp in New Braunfels, in which conductor Ernst Hoffmann also participated. Henkel served as assistant conductor in 1940–41 and associate conductor in 1945. He was assistant concertmaster in 1944–45. In a switch of roles, on the staff he took care of publicity from 1942 to 1945.

The Houston Symphony's second female concertmaster was **Olga King Henkel** (1907–1977) during the war years, 1943–45, when many male members of the orchestra had been called to military service. She had taught violin at music schools in Memphis and, along with her husband and fellow orchestra member, Joe, was a faculty member at the University of Houston. They both played 11 seasons in the orchestra. During her tenure as concertmaster, one of her solo performances was in Saint-Saëns' Prelude to *The Deluge* on a special concert starring Oscar Levant.

During the years of World War II, men in uniform were admitted free to concerts. Many of the orchestra's men went off to war, but those who were stationed at Ellington Field and other regional bases were able to continue to play with the orchestra on occasion.

Verna McIntyre (1916–2005) was one of three in her family on the orchestra roster. She was raised in Louisiana with her siblings Mary Shelley McIntyre and Richard McIntyre. Verna studied violin at the New Orleans Conservatory and Juilliard, and musicology at Louisiana State University, and she attended Smith College. She also played for the New Orleans Symphony. She played with the Houston Symphony for 16 years over three periods from the early 1940s to the 1970s. She taught string classes in the Houston schools as well as privately.

Mary Shelley McIntyre (1912–1997), violinist in 1943–78, joined a year after her sister Verna. She also graduated from Juilliard in New York, with a year of post-graduate study. She played with the orchestras of Theatre Under the Stars and the Houston Ballet. Younger brother **Richard McIntyre** (b. 1915) was a member of the cello section for the 1946–47 season, when he offered his services with his sisters and Hank Hlavaty in the McIntyre String Quartet, "Distinctive Music for Formal Occasions."[9]

Left: **Concertmaster Joseph Gallo on left with an unidentified violinist and Franklin Washburn in 1940.** Center: **Timpanist Vladimir Nikiforoff, 1940.** Right: **Tuba player Roy Perry, 1940.**

Franklin Washburn (1911–1990) joined the Houston Symphony in 1933 and was principal second violin in 1939–42, after which he served in the military through the 1944 season. He left the orchestra in 1948. A Houston native, he had studied violin with Paul Bergé (1923–27), Samuel Gardner at Juilliard (1937), Edouard Dethier in Paris (1929–30) and in New York (1947). He was a founding member of the Houston Music Guild and violinist of the Music Guild Quartet. Washburn owned a music camp near Kerrville, Kamp Karankawa, in the 1950s and was a member of the San Antonio Symphony in the mid-50s. He moved in 1957 to Dallas, where he founded the Dallas Junior Honors Orchestra.[10]

Laila Storch (b. 1921) was hired by Efrem Kurtz to play oboe in 1948. She stayed for seven seasons and then won a Fulbright grant, spending two years in Austria. She went on to be principal oboe for the Mozarteum Orchester Salzburg and play with the Soni Ventorum Wind Quintet. She recently wrote a book about her teacher called *Marcel Tabuteau: How Do You Expect to Play the Oboe If You Can't Peel a Mushroom?* And she has another local connection: her daughter Aloysia Friedmann married concert pianist Jon Kimura Parker, who joined the Shepherd School faculty at Rice.

Juri Jelagin (1910–1987), a violinist who emigrated from Russia, came to the Houston Symphony in 1948. Three years later, he published *Taming of the Arts*, a rather scathing critique of the Communist regime's effect on music in the USSR. He had been in a German concentration camp in 1939 and was a former concertmaster for various state orchestras in Soviet Russia. He graduated from the state conservatory, organized the Soviet state jazz band and played for Stalin. He was also called to testify for the Committee on Un-American Activities in the 1950s. He taught Russian language classes at the Universities of Houston and St. Thomas. After 17 years with the Houston Symphony, he left in 1965 to work for the U.S. Information Agency.

Vera Jelagin (1921–2008) was born in Lodz, Poland, but received her musical education in Munich, Germany. After studying at the Akademie der Tonkunst in Munich, she played in several European orchestras. She joined the Houston Symphony's second violin section in 1948, while her husband, Juri, was among the first violins. She was naturalized as a United States citizen in 1953. She was divorced from Juri Jelagin, remarrying Eziaslav Harrin in 1989. She retired the next year, after 42 seasons with the orchestra.

Robinson Family

When one thinks of famous musical families, the family of Keith and Dorothe Robinson takes the leading role in Houston Symphony circles. Bassist Keith Robinson played in the orchestra from 1948 to 1975, and Dorothe Robinson was a member of the violin section from 1956 to 1993. All five of their children—cellist Sharon Robinson, bassist Harold "Hal" Robinson, violinist Erica Robinson and the twins, cellist Keith Robinson Jr. and violinist Kim Robinson—followed their parents into significant professional music careers.

Sharon is the cellist of the famed Kalichstein-Laredo-Robinson Trio and a resident faculty member at the Cleveland Institute of Music. Hal Robinson rose from principal or associate principal double bass positions with the symphony orchestras of Albuquerque, Houston and Washington, D.C., to become principal bassist of the Philadelphia Orchestra. He also teaches at Philadelphia's Curtis Institute of Music.

After studies with Houston violinist Fredell Lack, Erica won a summer slot at the famed Meadowmount School of Music in Westport, New York, followed by four years at the Curtis Institute. She married a Philadelphian and joined the Pennsylvania Ballet Orchestra, returning to Houston in 1986 as a member of the combined Houston Grand Opera/Houston Ballet orchestra. Erica spends her summers playing in the Chautauqua Symphony in cool, upstate New York. She counts herself fortunate to have all three branches of the orchestral literature at her fingertips.

Keith Robinson, Jr. began his studies with (now retired) Houston Symphony cellist Marian Wilson and progressed through Houston's High School for the Performing and Visual Arts, the North Carolina School of the Arts and the Curtis Institute to become a founding member of the Miami String Quartet. He has toured nationally with them for some 25 years. The ensemble is now in residence at Kent State University.

Violinist Kim Robinson also studied with Fredell Lack and joined her brother at the North Carolina School of the Arts. She joined Erica as a member of the Houston Ballet Orchestra for several years, but marriage to a man in the natural gas business took her to a part of Georgia where country music prevailed. Kim has relocated to Gallup, New Mexico, and is concertmaster of the symphony orchestra in Show Low, Arizona, and first violinist of the Red Rock String Quartet.

It was no easy task for Keith and Dorothe Robinson to educate five talented youngsters, provide them with expensive musical instruments and send them to major music conservatories throughout the nation. Several of them recall that their father was up and off to work at dawn, playing bass in a combo that provided background music to Channel 13's morning news show. Their mother was out the door by 7:30 to give violin lessons at countless public elementary schools before classes began.

"There was no daycare for us," Sharon remembered. "We went off to symphony rehearsals with our parents." When that was over, their father worked a day job downtown at Montgomery Ward. And at night, he often played at some nightclub until the wee hours of the morning.

But there were also fun times growing up in the middle of a symphony orchestra. "I used to love rolling down the hill in front of Miller Theatre, while my parents were rehearsing onstage," Sharon recalled. (She's glad to know the hill is still there.) "And I used to sell Girl Scout cookies to the musicians." Concertmaster Ray Fliegel and cellist Steve Gorisch were her best customers.

Erica and Hal went exploring one summer afternoon, while their father was rehearsing a Gilbert and Sullivan Society production in the University of Houston's Cullen Auditorium. "We wandered throughout all four floors of the Ezekiel Cullen Building—even out onto the fire escape," she said. "It was a more innocent time back then, when there was no danger lurking in the hallways."

And Kim remembers her mother plopping the twins in the front row of Jones Hall, so she could keep an eye on them from the stage during rehearsals. "When one rehearsal was over, we were told we had just slept through an entire performance of Stravinsky's *Rite of Spring*!"

Above all, there was constant chamber music in the Robinson home, with symphony musicians stopping by to fill in an instrumental part that wasn't in the family ensemble. And there were serenades for all the neighbors when it was time for Christmas carols.

Violist **William "Billy" Welch** (1928–1988) was also a 40-year member of the orchestra. A native of Port Arthur, he studied at the Curtis Institute of Music in Philadelphia and taught violin and viola privately in Houston. He was the business manager for the Houston Musicians Union for several years.

Jimmy Simon won a spot in the orchestra in 1951, serving as principal percussionist by 1955. Simon married violinist Nancy Heaton, who played nine years to his 35 years. On the side, he played for Tony Martin's band and she sang in local bistros. He also had a dance orchestra and played with the André Previn Trio. He was even the personal drummer for Eleanor Powell and Dinah Shore.[11] Simon invented and sold a successful cymbal polish called Allegro Rouge. He was also something of a prankster and could do a great imitation of Sir John Barbirolli, which Sir John enjoyed tremendously.

Stokowski hired **Wayne Crouse** in 1951 as principal violist, and Crouse retired in that post after 32 years in 1983. Crouse had studied with William Primrose and at Juilliard with Ivan Galamian and Milton Katims. He was a featured soloist in the Central and East Coast U.S. tour led by Sir John Barbirolli in 1965 and was a frequent soloist with the orchestra's classical series, playing nine times from 1962 to 1980, most often in Berlioz' *Harold in Italy* and Strauss' *Don Quixote*. After Crouse was artist-in-residence at the University of Houston, Samuel Jones invited Crouse to become a charter faculty member of the Shepherd School of Music at Rice University and play in the Shepherd String Quartet.

Since so many of the musicians also teach, they have written about method for various instruments. **Dall Fields**, who played bassoon from 1915–17, later wrote *Bassoon method, Volume 1*, published by M.M. Cole in 1937. He went on to play with Minneapolis, Cincinnati and Chicago. **Bill Rose**, who was principal tuba for 26 years, taught at the University of Houston and wrote a popular text *Studio Class Manual for Tuba and Euphonium* in 1980.

Over the years, several of the musicians also contributed by writing the notes for the concert programs: **Dr. H. Leigh Bartlett** only played violin for the orchestra in 1931, but wrote the program notes from 1938–41; violinist **Betty Barney** wrote in the 1940s; and **Marjorie Bourne**, harpist from 1937–44, wrote program notes for the student concerts. She was the daughter of bass player and manager **Harry Bourne**. **Jack Ossewaarde**, organist at Houston's Christ Church Cathedral, occasionally played for the orchestra and wrote program notes from 1955 to 1958.

Forty-year orchestra member **David Wuliger** (1912–1998) was born in Cleveland, Ohio, where he studied at the Cleveland School of Music. Among his teachers were Karl Glassman, timpanist of the NBC Symphony, and Saul Goodman, timpanist of the New York Philharmonic. Wuliger played as timpanist at the Cleveland Orchestra during the summer season of 1942. In World War II, he served from 1942–46 in the 386th Army Service Forces Band. From 1946 to 1986, he was principal timpanist of the Houston Symphony. He appeared as soloist with the orchestra several times during his 40-year tenure. In 1949, he became the head of the Percussion Studio at the University of Houston School of Music, retiring from the university in 1984.

Alfred Urbach (1914–1988) joined the orchestra as principal cellist in 1946 and founded the Houston Chorale, a volunteer organization that was formally affiliated with the Houston Symphony in 1949 and is now known as the Houston Symphony Chorus. Urbach also played in the Raphael String Quartet with Ray Fliegel.

Cellist **Dorothy Moyes** (1922–2007) was born Dorothy Louise Kautzman. She studied at the Mannes Music School in New York. She also taught at Sam Houston State University. After 40 years with the Houston Symphony, she retired in 1987. She was married to **John Moyes** (1915–1971), Houston Symphony horn player. Moyes was born in Boston, where he studied with the first horn in the Boston Symphony. He retired in 1966 with 20 years of service.

Among the violins from 1949 to 1953 was **Joseph Silverstein**, who went on to be concertmaster of the Boston Symphony and its assistant conductor. He organized the Boston Chamber Players in 1962 and became the music director of the Utah Symphony Orchestra and the Chautauqua Symphony. He was also a professor of violin at the Curtis Institute of Music.

Arlene Weiss was a bass clarinet player for just one season in the 1950s. She married actor Alan Alda and went on to a successful career as a writer of children's books and as a photographer.

Flutist **David Colvig** studied music at San Francisco State College and graduated from the Curtis Institute of Music. He was part of the 1948 class of musicians engaged by Efrem Kurtz, retiring in 1985. He was much sought after as a flute repairman and technician by professional flutists all over the country.

Barbara Hester was a 39-year member of the orchestra, joining in 1955. She was the student of longtime principal oboist Ray Weaver. For most of her tenure, she was second oboist, retiring in 1994. She was married to principal flutist **Byron Hester**, who belonged to the orchestra from 1953 to 1990. Byron had attended Juilliard and Curtis and was professor of flute at the University of Houston from 1954 to 1994, retiring as professor emeritus.

Philadelphian **Bill Black** (d. 2004) graduated from the Curtis Institute of Music in 1956, when he joined Houston's bass section. Black was a member of the contract negotiating committee that obtained the first 52-week contract in 1971, and from 1971 to 1976 he was principal bass. He is credited with the concept of the first Sounds Like Fun! summer concert series. Black was a member of the four-member ensemble Air Mail Special, which performed in 320 in-school concerts over a 16-year span. His dance band was the Bill Black Ensemble, and he was a member of the Best Little Klezmer Band in Texas. Among his other talents was music calligraphy. He served as a principal copyist for the noted American composer Carlisle Floyd on operas that included *Bilby's Doll, Willie Stark* and *Cold Sassy Tree*.

Another legacy of the Stokowski years was viola player **Violeta Moncada** (1925–2011), born in Cuba. In 1956 she started her 36-year service and was the assistant or associate principal viola from 1965 to 1976. Her sister, Elena Diaz (d. 2010), was born in Madrid, Spain, and played violin with the Orquestra de Camara in Madrid before coming to Houston in 1959. Diaz retired in 1991.

Assistant principal clarinetist **Herman Randolph** (1931–2007) attended the University of Houston and was recruited by Leopold Stokowski. He served as an unofficial Houston Symphony photographer, taking photos of rehearsals and tours. Although he only played with the Houston Symphony for six years before he left, Randolph continued to teach in Houston and played with the Galveston Symphony Orchestra and the Houston Symphonic Band. He is remembered for his sense of humor.

Richard Pickar, who played in the clarinet section with Randolph, recalled that once they sneaked out during the intermission to see part of a boxing match next door. The two almost missed rejoining the Symphony for the second half because Randolph kept waiting for a knockout.[12]

> "Alfred Urbach (1914–1988) joined the orchestra as principal cellist in 1946 and founded the Houston Chorale, a volunteer organization which was formally affiliated with the Houston Symphony in 1949 and is now known as the Houston Symphony Chorus."

LEOPOLD STOKOWSKI

Mr. David Wulliger   22 Dec 60
1619 Walker
Houston 3, Texas

Dear Mr. Wulliger

     I am very touched by your frank and warm letter. The only
reason I am not returning is that I am having increasing difficulty,
legal and personal, regarding my sons and my presence in New York
is necessary to meet these difficulties. All the same, General Hirsch,
the President of the orchestra, has invited me to return to Houston
next season to conduct the "Gurrelieder" of Schoenberg which I am
confident you will enjoy; so will I.

     I hope that in the future somewhere and some time you and I
can make music together again, because for me you are the greatest
tympanist, not only of the United States, but of the world. This is
not a compliment, but just the truth.

Sincerely

Top: **Houston Symphony musicians in 2007.** Center:
Leopold Stokowski sent many typed notes on this memo
size paper. This one was to principal timpanist David
Wulliger. Bottom: **Timpanist David Wuliger, April 1960.**

Starting in 1959, Richard Pickar played with the orchestra for 31 years, retiring as principal clarinetist in 1990. Pickar was on the faculty of the University of Houston and is retired from Rice's Shepherd School of Music. He was the conductor of the Galveston Symphony Orchestra since its founding in 1979, leaving after the 2011–12 season. He is currently its conductor emeritus.

Cellist **Marian Webb Wilson** (b. 1935) is the daughter of clarinetist and pianist Howard Webb, founder and conductor of the Houston Youth Symphony, and of cellist Elizabeth Webb. In 1954, she won the Women's Committee Student Auditions with the Boccherini Cello Concerto, receiving a prize of $50 and a performance with the orchestra. She joined the orchestra in 1959, when the orchestra had a 25-week contract and earned $90 per week. She noted that "we supplemented our income by delivering yellow pages or anything else we could find."[13] Wilson was an original member of the "Bad Boys of Cello," as the cello section called itself, and she retired following the orchestra's European tour in 2000.

Joy Hine Plesner joined the Houston Symphony viola section in 1961. She had been a member of the first violin section of the Honolulu Symphony at age 15. She attended Oberlin College Conservatory of Music and graduated with degrees in both violin and piano. Her studies took her to the Mozarteum in Salzburg, Austria. In Houston, she also played the keyboard as needed. Plesner taught at the High School for the Performing and Visual Arts and at Sam Houston State University. Her stand partner was Hugh Gibson. Now living in San Luis, Colorado, she teaches violin and viola at Adams State College in Alamosa, Colorado.

Thirty-three-year veteran **James Austin** was principal trumpet from 1962 to 1977. A graduate of the Eastman School of Music, he played with the Eastman and Rochester Philharmonic Orchestras. He had joined the Houston Symphony in 1959 and taught privately and at the University of Houston.

Hugh Gibson joined the viola section in 1963 and retired in 1994. Also a talented artist, he exhibited paintings at the Museum of Fine Arts, Houston and in New Orleans, San Antonio, Taos and San Francisco. Gibson received degrees in art from the University of Oklahoma and University of Illinois. He also played for the Santa Fe Opera in the mid-1960s.

Horn player **Jay Andrus** belonged to the orchestra from 1963 to 1995. Joining just after college graduation, he was chairman of the musicians' contract negotiation committee during the work stoppage of the 1970s. He had attended the University of Houston, studying there with Caesar LaMonaca, and later also served on the faculty there for ten years. Andrus was a student of martial arts and earned a black belt in judo.

Bass player **Robert "Red" Pastorek** joined the Houston Symphony in 1964. His father was an accountant, and his mother was an untrained, but very talented singer. She performed on Polish radio in Chicago. Born in Chicago, he began his musical career as a percussionist. He switched to double bass in high school. While he continued his studies at DePaul University in Chicago, Pastorek was selected to be a member of the Chicago Civic Orchestra, a training branch of the Chicago Symphony. He then played with dance bands and toured with the Mantovani Orchestra. In 1961, Pastorek became principal bass with the Florida Symphony. In Houston, he also worked as a sail maker. In 2001's Tropical Storm Allison, his 1800 Justin Maucote bass viol was stored in Jones Hall and was destroyed by floodwaters.

Red Pastorek met his future wife, **Christine Louis,** when she joined the second violin section in 1969. Beginning in 1986, she also served on the staff for over 20 years as orchestra personnel manager and, in the 1990s, community outreach manager. Both husband and wife continue in the orchestra, with 49 and 44 years of service, respectively.

Violist **Tom Molloy** came to the Houston Symphony the same year as Red Pastorek, in the fall of 1964, just after Sir John Barbirolli's first East Coast tour with the orchestra. The New Jersey native attended the Mannes College of Music. In Houston, he took on extra duties as a radio announcer for classical station KLEF FM. After the station closed, he became a part-time employee of Houston Public Radio. From at least 1991 to 2013, he has hosted the Sunday Morning Music show on KUHF-FM (now KUHA-FM). During his 48 years with the orchestra, he also spent four years as a stage librarian.

Native Houstonian **Newell Dixon** (1945–1995) was 20 when he began playing bass in 1965 and was on medical leave when he passed away in 1995. **Barbara Shook-Cleghorn** joined the violin section in 1966 and also played for 30 years.

David Waters (1940–2010) was a Houston native who graduated from Austin High School and received a bachelor's degree in music education from the University of Houston and a master's of music from the University of Texas. He played bass trombone and trombone with the Houston Symphony for 41 seasons, beginning in 1966. He was a founding faculty member of the Shepherd School of Music at Rice University, and played with a number of show orchestras, stage bands and jazz ensembles.

Larry Thompson (1937–2010) got his B.A. degree from Fredonia State University School of Music, and then went on to graduate school at Eastman School of Music. He played oboe and English horn with the Dallas Symphony for seven years, and then joined the Houston Symphony in 1967. An enthusiastic pilot, he built his own airplane. He retired in 2003 after 36 years.

Richard "Dick" Schaffer played trumpet for 34 seasons, 1967–2001. Schaffer played with Bill Black, Richard Nunemaker and Brian Del Signore in Air Mail Special. Serving from time to time as assistant principal trumpet, he also spent time as the assistant personnel manager in 1980–85.

Percussionist **Fraya Fineberg** was the percussion keyboard specialist for 30 years, beginning in 1967. A native of New York, she graduated from Juilliard and studied with Saul Goodman. A great dog lover, she has done animal volunteer work since her retirement in 1997.

Retired clarinetist **Richard Nunemaker** (b. 1942) has published several books: *Scales and Chords (A New Approach for all Instrumentalists); If the Shoe Fits; The Effortless Clarinet;* and *The Effortless Saxophone.* Over his 40 years in the Houston Symphony, he played clarinet, bass clarinet and saxophone, retiring in 2008. Nunemaker was the leader of the four-member group Air Mail Special, which gave highly successful educational performances in schools for many years. He has also had several compact disk releases, *Golden Petals* and *Multiplicities.*

Polish violinist **Jan Karon** (1919–2008) joined the orchestra in 1968. Born in Cluzec, Poland, he studied at the Music Academy of Warsaw in Poland and played with the National Philharmonic Orchestra of Warsaw. Karon studied violin-making as well as playing with his uncle, and in Houston he made and repaired fine violins at his own violin shop. His international reputation gained him such customers as Henryk Szeryng and Yehudi Menuhin. Also a poet and an author, Karon wrote *Know Your Violin.*

The youthful **Ronald Patterson** (b. 1944) became concertmaster of the Houston Symphony in 1972 at the age of 28, coming from the Denver Symphony. He was a student of Jascha Heifetz, Eudice Shapiro and Manuel Compinsky. While in Houston, he taught at the Shepherd School of Music at Rice University and played with Ray Fliegel, Wayne Crouse and Shirley Trepel in the Shepherd Quartet. He left Houston in 1979 to go to Monte Carlo, joining former music director Lawrence Foster. He has had a prolific recording career and is chairman of the strings division of the University of Washington School of Music.

Horn player **Philip Stanton** spent 36 years with the orchestra, beginning in 1975. He has music degrees from Michigan State and Catholic University of America. Before 1975 he played with the U.S. Navy Band and the Grand Rapids Symphony. He has taught at Huntsville State University and the University of Houston, and was a visiting professor at Michigan State. He has also been president of the Houston Musicians Federal Credit Union.

Charles Tabony studied violin with Houstonian Fredell Lack and won the Women's Committee Student Auditions in 1961. He studied with Louis Persinger at the Juilliard School, graduating with a bachelor's and master's degree in music. From 1977 to 2012, Tabony was in the second violin section, becoming acting principal second in 1995; he was named associate principal second in 1998 and retired in 2012. Tabony's stand partner for 13 years was Ray Fliegel. His wife, Peggy, was also a Houston Symphony violinist who was previously married to Houston Symphony oboist Louis Ruttenberg. She retired in 1995, after 23 years.

Cellist **Robert "Bob" Deutsch** retired in 2007 after 30 years of service with the Houston Symphony. He grew up in Florida and studied with cellist Alfred Hillman. Deutsch was awarded a full scholarship to the New England Conservatory of Music and earned a master's degree at Yale. He had been a pick-up musician with the Barry White Band when the band got to Houston, and he called the Houston Symphony to see if there were any openings—his audition won him the position. At his Heights area home, he repaired and made violins and cellos.[14] He still teaches privately and devotes his time to the collection, restoration, maintenance, adjustment and sale of fine string instruments.

Alan Traverse (1938–2006), British-born, joined the Houston Symphony in 1978 as co-concertmaster and for the 1979–80 season served as acting concertmaster. He had been concertmaster or assistant concertmaster of the Royal Liverpool Philharmonic, the London Royal Philharmonic, the Royal Opera House in Covent Garden, and principal of the English Chamber Orchestra before coming to Houston. He had received a scholarship to the Royal Academy of Music at age ten and studied with David Martin. He was also an active chamber music musician and composer. Ill health forced him to retire from the Houston Symphony in 1997. His daughter Eleanor Traverse Herrera, a cellist, was a contracted substitute with the Houston Symphony in 2006–07.

Eight members of the current orchestra were added under the aegis of Lawrence Foster. Bassoonist **Eric Arbiter** is a 41-year orchestra member who is now the associate principal. By avocation he is a talented photographer, who has just completed a series of portraits of Houston Symphony musicians for the orchestra's centennial. Another long-serving musician is 42-year violist **Phyllis Herdliska**. **Myung Soon Lee** joined the orchestra in 1976 as Margaret Deutsch, wife of cellist Bob Deutsch. Except for two years of leave in 1988–89, she has remained an orchestra member for

Above: **Bassist John Gottwald, 1936.**

Top left: **Paul Burke, principal cello in September 1936.**

Bottom left: **Bass player Red Pastorek in 2007.**

34 years. **Kevin Kelly** has been part of the orchestra's second violin section since 1977. His wife, Kristen, was an occasional contracted violin substitute from 1992 to 2001. Current principal trombonist **Allen Barnhill** and principal violist **Wayne Brooks** both joined the orchestra in 1977. Cellist **Kevin Dvorak** was in the last class of musicians from 1978, along with acting bass principal **David Malone**. In 2001's Tropical Storm Allison, Malone's 1692 Testore double bass was lost (valued at $100,000.)

Margaret Bragg joined the second violin section in 1974 and retired in 2013, after 39 seasons. Coming from a family of string players, she attended Oberlin Conservatory and the University of Illinois. Also retiring in 2013 was principal clarinetist **David Peck**, who had joined the orchestra in 1975 as associate principal. He left in 1986 to play principal clarinet for the San Diego Symphony, but returned to Houston in 1991 as principal clarinetist.

Violinist **Ruth Zeger** was hired in 1981 before which she had played with the Kansas City Philharmonic in the first violin section. Her musical studies began on piano and then the violin at the age of nine. While attending California State University, Northridge, she played in seven community orchestras in the Los Angeles area, including the Pasadena Symphony and the American Youth Orchestra. While still in college, she had many opportunities to record for movie soundtracks, albums and commercials. She also studied with Hungarian violinist Kato Havas.

A native of Argentina, **Ruben Gonzalez** (b. 1939) studied in Buenos Aires with Osvaldo Pessina and later in France with Salomon Baron and in Italy with Riccardo Brengola. He was a member of several European groups and associate concertmaster of the Minnesota Orchestra before coming to Houston as guest concertmaster in 1980 (earning the title of concertmaster the next year). While here, he also served on the faculty of Rice University's Shepherd School of Music. He left Houston in 1987 to become concertmaster of the Chicago Symphony, from which he has retired. He is also a conductor and composer.

Eric Halen (b. 1957) joined the Houston Symphony on New Year's Eve 1986 as assistant concertmaster, sharing the stand with his brother David, also an assistant concertmaster. He subsequently became the associate concertmaster and served as acting concertmaster for 2005–06 and 2008–10, and is currently associate concertmaster. Halen is from a musical family and began his violin studies at six with his father, who taught at the Central Missouri State University, and his mother, a violinist with the Kansas City Philharmonic. He received his master's degree from the University of Illinois, studying with Sergiu Luca. Halen has appeared as a soloist with the St. Louis Symphony and many times with the Houston Symphony. He toured with the Houston Symphony Chamber Players and has been a frequent guest with Da Camera of Houston and Context.

Radio Marathon

Musicians typically have a uniform anonymity for audience members and are known to most only by the instruments they play or their position on stage. However, during the late 1970s and early 1980s, the Houston Symphony League staged an annual radio marathon fundraiser during which premiums were sold over the air and the musicians were asked to make donations that could reflect not just their musical talents, but their other interests as well. Some intriguing personalities emerged. Of course, many did donate music lessons, musical instruments or musical performances. One could buy a lesson on every orchestral instrument plus mandolin, the last being donated by Irving Wadler, violinist, who also threw in the mandolin and a case for it. Performances could be bought ranging from a harp and piccolo duo (Bea Rose and Carol Slocomb, respectively) to the whole bassoon or trombone/tuba section. Sometimes the musicians added a meal as well.

These bonus meals were legendary: Korean by the Deutches, spaghetti by Allen Barnhill, Russian by Vera Jelagin, barbecue by David Waters, Japanese by Toshi Shimada (assistant conductor, who would also include a Japanese lesson), Chinese by David Malone, gourmet Italian by Benjamin Kamins, kosher by the Ruttenbergs, gourmet vegetarian by Eric Arbiter and health food by Shirley Trepel. Shirley also offered a poker game with beer in her home. Thomas Bacon would teach you how to properly debone a chicken and cook it, and help you eat it.

Sports were very well represented. One could avail oneself of racquet ball (Eric Arbiter and Gregg Henegar), sailing (Larry Thompson or Red Pastorek), canoeing (David Waters or Paul Ellison), flying (Raymond Weaver) and fishing (Ralph Liese). One could play tennis with violinists Irving Wadler and George Bennett or with Mack Guderian

or with the Hesters; or golf with Newell Dixon, Larry Thompson, Alan Traverse or stage manager Don Jackson. For the more physically fit, there was a 50-mile bicycle ride with Richard Pickar or a 3.5-mile run with Ruben Gonzalez or a jump rope lesson from Richard Nunemaker. The less athletically inclined had a choice of bridge players: Paul Tucci, Mack Guderian or David Chausow. Kyla Bynum would give you a yoga lesson, Deborah Moran would treat you to an all-night star-gazing picnic (she belonged to the Houston Astronomical Society), or—even easier—David Kirk would give you breathing lessons to help you relax.

Some musicians offered gift items. Noted painter and violist, Hugh Gibson, donated a painting each year; Jimmy Simon invented his own cymbal polish called Allegro Rouge and donated a case every year; Marian Wilson made handwoven belts; and Fay Shapiro knitted sweaters. Nancy Goodearl needlepointed, and Linda Goldstein baked bread in musical shapes. You could buy a handmade canoe paddle from Kendrick Wauchope or a load of horse manure fertilizer from Richard Schaffer. He would deliver it, too. Of course, there was the classy autographed baton from Maestro Comissiona and, not to be outdone, old autographed timpani heads from David Wuliger.

A few very unusual services were also offered by our multifaceted musicians. While there was the obvious— David Colvig offered an expert flute overhaul, and both Bob Deutsch and Tom Molloy would give you advice in stereo shopping and building a record library—others were more unexpected. Josephine McAndrew would take a gentleman shopping for his lady; Warren Deck would overhaul your bike; George Bennett would recite poetry at your party; Eric Arbiter (also a professional photographer) would produce a portrait for you; Fraya Fineberg would take you plant shopping at a nursery; Barbara Shook-Cleghorn would analyze your handwriting; and George Womack would change the oil in your car and give it a lube job, and Richard Schaffer would tune it up. And Allen Barnhill offered a day of work as a handyman. He'd paint, do plumbing and even repair your roof.

Top left: **Alan Traverse looks on as Bob Deutsch tries a new bowing technique with Jeff Butler.** Center left: **Jimmy Simon in the percussion section, 1958. The City Auditorium proscenium is visible in the background.** Bottom left: **Barbara Hester, Ray Weaver and Paul Tucci on a break, 1958.**

Before becoming Houston's concertmaster in 1987, **Uri Pianka** (b. 1937) had held that post in the Israel Philharmonic for 20 years, where he also appeared every year as soloist. He was born in Tel Aviv and at age 16 was awarded a scholarship to the Juilliard School of Music, where he studied with Ivan Galamian and Dorothy Delay. Pianka retired in 2005, and during his 18-year career with the Houston Symphony (the second longest tenure of any concertmaster, second only to Ray Fliegel), he made several recordings and appeared many times as a soloist. An active chamber music musician, he founded the critically acclaimed Yuval Trio and played and toured internationally with the Houston Symphony Chamber Players.

Angela Fuller (b. 1977) was the third woman to hold the concertmaster position for the Houston Symphony, but remained only two years. She came to Houston from the Minnesota Orchestra, where she was a first violinist for six years.

Many of the orchestra's members over the years have found that working together brought them together personally. Among these married couples, other than those already mentioned, were bassist Alexander Boffa and violinist Marcella Conforto, cellist Stephen and violinist Eunice Gorisch, trombonist Kauko and bassoonist Frances Kahila, principal horn player Tom and violist Louise Newell, principal bassist Bill Rose and principal harpist Beatrice Schroeder, E-flat clarinetist Don and flutist Carol Slocomb, violinists James and Betty Stephenson, trumpeter Dan and cellist Jane Tetzlaff, horn player Bruce Henniss and bassoonist Karrie Pierson, oboist Colin Gatwood and principal flutist Aralee Dorough, bassoonist Herbert and flutist Patricia Fawcett, violinists Richard and Margo Collins, horn player Caesar and violinist Mary LaMonaca, cellist Lucien and violinist Helen DeGroote, and oboist and English horn player Modesto and violinist Mary DeSantis.

Current orchestra members brought in during the Comissiona era, who continue with 30 or more years of service, are: violinists Martha Chapman, Mi-Hee Chung, Ruth Zeger and Amy Teare; bassist and assistant librarian Mike McMurray; bassist Mark Shapiro; violists Fay Barkley Shapiro and Linda Goldstein; principal tuba David Kirk; associate principal trumpet John DeWitt; horn player Nancy Goodearl; and harpist Paula Page. Page has announced her intention to retire in late 2013. The Shapiros are married, and Teare married John DeWitt. Those with over 20 years of service are: assistant principal trumpet Bob Walp; violinists Hitai Lee and Eric Halen; principal flutist Aralee Dorough; cellists Jeffrey Butler and Jim Denton; associate principal cellist Chris French; associate principal clarinetist Thomas LeGrand; principal keyboardist Scott Holshouser; principal timpanist Ronald Holdman; and principal percussionist Brian Del Signore.

Twenty-four players hired in the Eschenbach era still play in the orchestra. With service of 12 to 24 years, these are: violinists Marina Brubaker, Rodica Weber Gonzalez, Ferenc Illenyi, Sophia Silivos, Qi Ming, Sergei Galperin, Mihaela Frusina (sister to Rodica Gonzalez), Si-Yang Lao, principal second Jennifer Owen and Alexandra Adkins; associate principal violist Joan DerHovsepian, assistant principal violist George Pascal, Dan Strba and Wei Jiang; cellist Xiao Wong; principal horn player Bill VerMeulen and hornist Brian Thomas; oboist Colin Gatwood and associate principal oboist Anne Leek; associate principal flutist Judy Dines; contrabassoonist Jeff Robinson; clarinetist Chris Schubert; and bassists Donald Howey, Eric Larson and Burke Shaw. Associate principal flutist John Thorne, who was hired in 1992, resigned in 2013 to be a professor at Northwestern University.

Hired during the Graf era, 21 players continue in the centennial year. This group includes: violinists Christopher Neal, Kurt Johnson, Kiju Joh, assistant concertmaster Assia Dulgerska and concertmaster Frank Huang; violist Sheldon Person; cellist Tony Kitai and principal cellist Brinton Averil Smith; associate principal trombonist Bradley White and trombonist Philip Freeman; trumpeter Tony Prisk and principal trumpeter Mark Hughes; principal bassoon Rian Craypo and bassoonist Elise Wagner; English horn player Adam Dinitz and principal oboist Jonathan Fischer; associate principal hornist Robert Johnson; and percussionists Matt Strauss and Mark Griffith.

Current concertmaster **Frank Huang** was born in China, raised in Houston and at the age of 11 performed with the Houston Symphony in a nationally broadcast concert. He won honors in both the Houston Symphony League Concerto Competition and the Ima Hogg Young Artist Competition. He studied with Fredell Lack, Donald Weilerstein and Robert Mann, and graduated from the Cleveland Institute of Music. Before joining the Houston Symphony in 2010, Huang held the position of first violinist of the Grammy Award-winning Ying Quartet and was a faculty member at the Eastman School of Music. He is also on the faculty at Rice University and the University of Houston and serves as concertmaster of the Sejong Soloists, a chamber orchestra based in New York.

Huang's musical lineage is one that spans the first century of the orchestra—he might be considered the musical great-grandson of Emil Lindenberg. Lindenberg, whose daughter Grace Lindenberg Keller played violin in the orchestra, was teacher to concertmaster Josephine Boudreaux. Boudreaux taught Houston concert violinist Fredell Lack, who in turn was one of Huang's teachers.

Above: **Concertmaster Frank Huang in 2009.** Right: **Horns and trombones in 1963–64. Seated: Jay Andrus, Nancy Fako, Caesar LaMonaca and Jim Tankersley. Standing: David Bean, Al Lube and Ralph Liese.**

XIII

HOUSTON SYMPHONY CHORUS

The Houston Symphony Chorus has had seven directors throughout its history, beginning with conductor Alfred Urbach, former principal cellist and personnel manager of the orchestra. He established it as the Houston Chorale in 1946 and directed it for two decades. Highlights of his tenure included Leopold Stokowski's acclaimed performance and recording of Carl Orff's *Carmina Burana* in the 1950s and Sir John Barbirolli's legendary performance of Sir Edward Elgar's oratorio *The Dream of Gerontius* in the 1960s.

Resident conductor A. Clyde Roller and Wayne Bedford each conducted the chorus for one season following Urbach's retirement, but the late Donald Strong is credited as the next choral builder during his eight-year tenure (1969–77). These years largely coincided with Lawrence Foster's term as music director, and they included his riveting performance of Prokofiev's *Alexander Nevsky*, such challenging works as Stravinsky's *Persephone* and *Oedipus Rex*, a concert performance of Wagner's *The Flying Dutchman*, Bach's *St. Matthew Passion* and a long-remembered performance of Brahms' *A German Requiem* by guest conductor Erich Bergel. There was also an electrifying 1970 performance of Beethoven's *Missa Solemnis* marking famed choral conductor Robert Shaw's debut with the ensemble.

Virginia Babikian, who had built a notable career as a concert soprano and voice teacher, directed the choir for the next decade (1977–86), bridging several seasons of Houston Symphony guest conductors and most of the tenure of former music director Sergiu Comissiona. Her term was highlighted by the chorus' performances of numerous works of Berlioz, including the dramatic symphony *Romeo and Juliet*, and the melodrama *Lélio*, and the first Houston Symphony performances of Arnold Schoenberg's post-romantic choral song cycle *Gurrelieder*. The 1980s also saw the rise of the annual Houston Symphony Summer Festival, with the chorus participating in a memorable performance of a Haydn mass in the summer of 1982.

In the summer of 1986, Edward Polochick, director of the Baltimore Symphony Chorus, was appointed to succeed Babikian in a dual appointment with both choruses, but his tenure was cut short by a serious automobile accident that prevented him from commuting between the two cities. Charles Hausmann, director of choral activities at the University of Houston, replaced him in October of that year.

Hausmann's 27 seasons with the chorus have exceeded those of any other director, spanning the last years of Comissiona's tenure and the entire tenures of Christoph Eschenbach and Hans

Graf. Unquestionably, he has maintained the chorus at its highest level of discipline during its busiest and most ambitious seasons. These years have included not only the standard choral-orchestral masterworks of the last four centuries, but such rare and adventurous works as Mahler's monumental Eighth Symphony, Dvořák's *Stabat Mater*, Hindemith's *When Lilacs Last in Dooryard Bloom'd*, Roberto Sierra's *Missa Latina*, Samuel Barber's *Prayers of Kirkegaard*, John Adams' *Harmonium*, Mendelssohn's *The First Walpurgis Night*, Britten's *War Requiem*, Gunther Schuller's *The Power Within Us*, the *Te Deum* settings of Bruckner, Dvořák and Kodály, and Rachmaninoff's *The Bells*.

It also included a revelatory interpretation of an old favorite, the inspired 2001 performance of Carl Orff's *Carmina Burana* that introduced audiences to the very sensitive choral conducting of Hans Graf. It was the Houston Symphony Chorus' 30th set of performances of the Orff work. For the chorus' 33rd singing of *Carmina Burana* in 2012, Graf encored that memorable first performance with a much bolder, lustier interpretation, generously laced with comic touches. It was a convincing sign that this huge 205-member ensemble has matured into a supple, highly expressive unit of the Houston Symphony organization.

Previous spread: **The Houston Symphony Chorus in its 60th year, 2007.** Above: **Virginia Babikian.** Top right: **The Houston Chorale at South Main Baptist Church, 1950.** Center right: **Houston Symphony and Chorale in the mid-1950s.** Bottom right: **Houston Symphony Chorale, 1966.**

To Howard & Beth Webb — in affectionate 11/10/66
remembrance of your loyal friendship —
Jeanne & Al Urbach

CHAPTER
XIV

THE STAFF

Ernest Hail, who also played clarinet for the first five seasons, served concurrently as the manager. The board of directors did what they could to sell tickets and pick up many of the mundane details needed for the orchestra to function. This was a relatively easy task when the group played only three concerts a year. The 1930s seasons started with six concerts a year, and the board created an auxiliary committee whose function it was to sell tickets. During the early to mid-1930s Ima Hogg was consulting on, or making, many management decisions for the orchestra, including discussing repertoire with the conductors and finding soloists.

Like Hail, other musicians were also on staff. The orchestra's music librarian was usually a musician in the orchestra, beginning with violinist **Louis Arnouts** in 1913. Thirty years later, bass player **Ray Moore** became librarian and stayed until 1972. Two years after that, James Medvitz was the first full-time librarian to be hired, and he was followed by **Lynn Barney**, **Peter Conover** and **Tom Takaro**. Takaro's current assistant librarian, bass player Mike McMurray, has worked in the music library since 1981.

In 1948 **Tom Johnson** was brought in to replace the ailing **Frank Deering**, at Deering's suggestion, as general manager of the Symphony. It was fortunate that Johnson was also a performing violinist, played the trumpet and had studied conducting at Juilliard. He had served on the faculties of Southwestern University and Southern Methodist University before organizing and conducting the G.I. Symphony in Germany during World War II. Johnson worked with conductors from Kurtz to Foster and Symphony Society presidents Ima Hogg and Maurice Hirsch before finally retiring in 1974.

In 1955 Johnson hired **Carl Fasshauer** as his assistant, who stayed for 19 years before going to the Chicago Symphony. In 1963 Virginia Raines became executive secretary to Tom Johnson, not leaving until 1976.

James Wright was general manager for one brief year, and then **Michael Woolcock** filled the role for five years before acquiring the new title of executive director. Woolcock remained for two more years, leaving in 1981. His replacement as executive director was **Gideon Toeplitz**, who arrived in 1981 just as the overheated economy began a bust cycle. He persevered until 1987.

David Wax arrived in 1989 and spent 11 years with the orchestra, spanning the majority of Eschenbach's tenure. After Wax left, the Society hired former board member and consultant **Ann Kennedy** to the post in 2001. A few months later, the offices were destroyed by Tropical Storm Allison, and opening night almost did not happen because of travel restrictions from the attacks of September 11. Kennedy weathered the other storm of contract disputes and a strike in 2003, and resigned in 2005.

Kennedy's successor was **Matthew VanBesien**, a former New Orleans Symphony member who had been on staff at the Houston Symphony as a Fellow of the American Symphony Orchestra League (now the League of American Orchestras) management fellowship program; he served four years. **Mark C. Hanson**, also a product of the management fellowship program, became the current executive director in 2010.

While Toeplitz was executive director, the operations manager became the second-in-command position at the symphony. **Tom Fay** filled this spot beginning in 1984 for seven years and doubled as interim executive director until Wax was hired. He was succeeded as general manager by **Jim Berdahl** (1991–2001), **Jeff Woodruff** (2002–03), **Matthew VanBesien** (2003–05) and **Steven Brosvik** (2005–13).

Mrs. Guy Rall joined the staff as a bookkeeper in 1939 and held the title of auditor. Anita, known as "Grandma" Rall, retired in 1974 after 35 years. Joining the same year was **Winifred Safford**, who worked in the box office. In 1941, she married McClelland Wallace and left the staff the next year, although she remained a lifelong supporter of the Symphony.

In the box office area, in 1982 **Michael Clements** began work as customer services manager, serving a dozen years before his death in 1993. Since 1997, **Melissa Lopez** has held numerous positions in the areas of audience development, group sales and family concerts, and she is currently the director of marketing/single ticket and group sales. **Glenn Taylor** was hired in 2004 as assistant marketing manager. By 2010, he was the senior director, marketing, and in 2013, he was promoted to chief marketing officer, with responsibility for both marketing and communications.

Previous spread: **Houston Symphony Manager Tom Johnson.** Above: **On left, Librarian Tom Takaro with Mike McMurray, assistant librarian and bass player.** Right, top to bottom: **Symphony Executive Directors David Wax, Matthew VanBesien and Mark C. Hanson.**

In the finance area, **Lee Clark** was the director of business affairs from 1982 to 1991 and was key in helping **Tom Fay** and other senior staff members manage the orchestra during the years in which there was no executive director. In 1995, **Chris Westerfelt** joined the finance department and continues as manager, accounts payable and special projects. Another long-serving department head was **Mike Pawson**, hired in 2003 as senior director of financial planning, technology and administration. He left the staff in 2013 as chief financial officer. **Sally Brassow** joined the Symphony in 1998 as director of accounting. She continues to serve as controller.

With only a few years interruption, cellist **Alfred Urbach**, who also directed the Houston Chorale, was the personnel manager from 1948 to 1964, retiring as an active orchestra musician in 1957. Orchestra member **Ralph Liese** added his talents as orchestra personnel manager from 1969 to 1979 and also held the position of touring consultant. In 1986, violinist **Chris Pastorek** added to her orchestra duties those of personnel manager of the orchestra, which, with the exception of one year, she performed for 22 years. **Steve Wenig** began in 2004 as assistant personnel manager and was later promoted to orchestra personnel manager. In 2013 he was named to the new position of director, community partnerships.

Alice Bruce Currlin was the Symphony's public relations manager from 1955 to 1970. Her 16 years spanned the eras of Stokowski, Barbirolli, Previn and de Almeida. She was followed as director of public affairs by **Mary Buxton**, **Jim Benfield**, **Toby Mattox** and **Frances Carter Stephens**. **Art Kent**, a former NBC news correspondent, served as director of public affairs from 1997 to 2008.

From at least the 1940s, the Women's Committee maintained donor and subscriber address lists, names of prospective subscribers and related annual fund files. By the 1950s, a staff secretary was added to work with the committee. One of these, **Thalia Seay**, began in 1956 as maintenance fund secretary. She left the staff in 1958, but returned in 1963 for another nine years. She was followed by **Mildred "Tuffy" Simmons** as the annual fund coordinator in 1972–81.

The development department added staff to coordinate the many activities of the Houston Symphony League, and **Madeline Demel** filled the role of League activities coordinator for a dozen years, starting in 1970.

Nancy Giles joined the development staff in 1995. She was associate director of individual giving, then director of corporate and foundation giving before leaving in 2000. After several years, she returned as director of individual giving, leaving in 2007. **David Rockoff** initially held the title of director of development in 1980-81 and returned to the Symphony in 2005, ending his association as senior director of development in 2010. **David Chambers** was hired in 2011 as chief development officer.

Miller Outdoor Theatre, the Fourth of July and the 1812 Overture

Former stage manager Don Jackson reminisces about Miller Outdoor Theatre concerts in a 2006 interview with Houston Symphony archivists. Excerpts from that conversation follow:

Jackson: "Well, going back to the 1812 Overture, before the cannons we started using later, Tom Johnson (general manager) used to shoot a shotgun backstage at Jones Hall. That's how it started. Then we got out to Miller Theatre and I got two or three shotguns and we did it in the pit. Just shot the guns. And the stagehands always got it wrong! … It was just not right, the timing was all wrong. So I went and had 16 cannons built. Then I wired them up to a box that we still use and we got switches. So now we could take a score and fire right with that score. So then I got the bright idea, 'what if I got some boys to shoot the cannons?' So my son was in the Coast Guard at the time and he was stationed at Vicksburg. So I went up to visit him and went in that park, looked at all those cannons, and took some pictures. Then I came back here and designed a cannon that we could take apart and use. I built sixteen cannons and we are still using them today."

Interviewer: "If you have cannons, then you have to have cannoneers."

Jackson: "We decided to have people dress up in black pants and white shirts and then one of the stagehands' wives got some red sashes and I bought some hats and we put hats on them."

Interviewer: "And every year they have to scrape up volunteers to wear the costumes.* So tell us about how cooking for the orchestra started in."

Jackson: "It got cranked up because of Miller Theatre. Everybody went out there for rehearsal, but you couldn't leave between rehearsal and the show because of traffic. So, I had this pit—eight feet long—and could cook twenty briskets at one time. So we started cooking for the orchestra and put chairs and tables under the trees and everyone would eat out there. We fed 100 chorus, 100 orchestra, 50 policemen, stagehands—about 300 people in all. So that's how we started cooking for the orchestra. Later, any time a visiting orchestra would come in, we would cook for them in the rehearsal room."

* For many years members of the Houston Symphony Chorus volunteered as cannoneers.

Hired in 1982 as a records coordinator in the development department, **Kay Middleton** is one of the three longest-serving Houston Symphony employees still on staff. Her official title is receptionist, as hers is the first face seen on entry at the main office. She also assists with some accounting duties, handles the switchboard and serves as an invaluable source of information and institutional memory.

Alfred R. Neumann wrote program notes for 15 years, beginning in 1960. Neumann was the founding president in 1974 of the University of Houston Clear Lake and was married to Houston Symphony Society board member Selma Neumann, who was the second president of the Houston Symphony League Bay Area. **Elmer Schoettle** also wrote for the concert programs as co–program annotator with Neumann from 1960 to 1973.

Long-serving stage staff included **Noel Crenshaw**, who retired in 1998 after 37 years. Stage manager **Don Jackson** began in 1967 and topped Crenshaw by one year, retiring in 2005. He was succeeded in the position by his son, **Donald Ray Jackson**, who, you might say, was raised in the business. After 20 years, stage technician **Zoltan Fabry** is still on staff.

Ginny Cade had been a regular substitute percussionist since 1958, but came on staff as educational coordinator in 1980. Her title changed to the educational director until 1990, then to director, education and community relations. Her name changed, too, and she retired in 2001 as **Ginny Garrett**. In 1995, volunteer **Carol Wilson** was hired as an education assistant, leaving in 2012. **Roger Daily** came in 2001 from the Rochester Symphony as director, Music Matters.

Jan LaRocque, who is now manager of the patron database, started as a computer services coordinator in 1984. **Jo Davenport** worked 11 years, 1985–95, as a computer services assistant.

Philip Gulla came in 2003 as network systems engineer. In his current role as director, technology, he oversees all computer systems at the Symphony, both hardware and software. **A. J. Salge** has been on staff for ten years as a network systems engineer.

Publications manager **Connie Juvan-Savoy** also came on staff in 1986. Her job was to put together the concert programs and, quite often, to serve as a staff photographer.

Stephen Aechertnacht was named the first director of artistic operations and served from 1982 to 86; he was followed by **Doug Merilatt**, who began in 1987. He assisted the music director and management in designing the season offerings and tended to contract negotiations with guest artists. Merilatt left in 1995 and was followed by **Aurelie Desmarais**, who is the current senior director of artistic planning with 17 years in that role.

Merle Bratlie started his career at the Symphony in 1989 as a marketing secretary. In 1990, he was appointed acting operations manager and then the artistic services coordinator. Today Bratlie is director, artist services, handling the myriad of details for visiting artists. Bratlie and LaRocque join Middleton as the three longest-serving office staff.

Top left: **Houston Symphony staff pose for a photo following a team-building retreat on March 26, 2012.**

134

Esperson Chimes

In a 2006 interview, Don Jackson told the story of moving the chimes from the Neils Esperson Building for a performance.

"Brian (Del Signore, principal percussionist) decided he wanted to use these huge chimes... Some of them were roughly 11 feet long and weighed about 500 pounds, the big ones. Brass, solid brass... So I took about ten guys over to the building and up into the roof. The big chimes wouldn't fit in the elevator—that is, the elevator they would fit in wouldn't go up that high. So we had to take them down the steps about ten floors. So the only way we could get them down was, you know, some guys would get down below and others would go over the rail with a rope and let each one down one at a time."

Interviewer: "For ten floors?"

Jackson: "Five hundred pounds... we had about ten of these chimes."

Brian Del Signore remembers: "I think Don Jackson remembered it well. To clarify: We took them down the ten flights of steps by hand. We had half a dozen stagehands, and we had to hug (the chimes) and maneuver them around the spiraling steps one at a time. They had been lifted into the rooftop gazebo by a huge crane back in the 1920s. Five hundred pounds with six or seven guys holding on is a big weight for each guy. And if a bell got away from us on the stairs (the bells are tubular), it would have been like a missile, possibly crashing through a window way up there. There were five bells. Those guys always remind me that they'll never forget that crew call!"

Then, further in the conversation with Jackson:

Jackson: "So Brian heard that there was a set of them (chimes) for sale up in Ohio or somewhere in a junkyard. So he went up there. They came out of a theater somewhere and the junkman got them. He wanted a lot of money for them. Brian had flown up there and the guy wouldn't sell them for what he wanted to pay, so Brian flew home. A few months later, he flew back up there, offered the guy, I don't know what it was. And he told the guy, I'm at the hotel; I've got a flight at a certain time. Call me, and if you want this money, I'll give it to you, and I'm going to put the chimes in a rental truck and bring them back." The guy called him; he loaded those things on a Ryder truck and brought them home... so now we've got our own set here... And they're stored at the warehouse."

Interviewer: "So do those belong to Brian, or do they belong to the Symphony?"

Jackson: "To Brian, he paid for them, went to all the trouble of getting them."

Interviewer: "That's not so unusual. A lot of percussion players do own a lot of their own stuff."

Jackson: "So now Brian came to me and said, 'Do we have a stand that we can put 2,000 pounds of chimes on?'...So then I had to go to the welding shop and work with my welder, who's really good. We had to design a stand that'd come apart, that we could safely hang these—some of them were 500, some of them were 300—these chimes on. Now when you've got an 11 foot chime, you've got to get to the top of it to play it. You've got to use a stepladder. George (Womack, percussionist) used to go up the stepladder. Then, when you get up there, you don't have a music stand, so I had to design a stand for the music."

CHAPTER
XV

THE BOARD

Over the last century, in excess of 1,700 individuals have served as directors of the Houston Symphony, a moving testament to the worth of symphonic music in the lives of Houstonians. The earliest board members of the Houston Symphony Orchestra Association were drawn from leaders of Houston musical organizations and businesses, as well as other musically educated social leaders. Often credited as the founder of the Houston Symphony, Miss Ima Hogg always insisted she was just one of many founders.

Among those who helped her garner support for the orchestra were leaders in the 12-year-old Women's Choral Club—Katherine Parker, Hettie Garwood, Mary Campbell Abbey, Corinne Waldo and Theresa Hirsch.

Even so, the founders were certainly not all women—Miss Ima had recruited ten men to join the ranks of 15 female directors for election in the fall of 1913.

Mrs. Edwin B. (Katherine Blunt) Parker, whose husband worked for the law firm of Baker & Botts, had been a charter member and the chairman of the board of examiners of the Thursday Morning Musical Club in 1908. She was also a member and the director of the Women's Choral Club. After the Houston Symphony's first concert in June, Mrs. Parker visited Europe from July to September, returning in time to be elected the first president of the Houston Symphony Orchestra Association and be a signer of the charter application. When Mr. Parker joined the Woodrow Wilson administration in 1918 in Washington, D.C., Katherine Parker transferred her efforts to organizing, supporting and raising funds with the women's committee for the fledgling National Symphony.

Miss Ima Hogg had returned from her piano studies in Europe and taken up teaching piano by 1909. As the daughter of Governor James S. Hogg, she was an experienced campaigner and knew how to gather support for her cause, which in this case was to start a local symphony orchestra. She declined the position of president in favor of that of first vice president of the newly formed Association. She continued to be active and persuaded Paul Bergé to lead the orchestra after Blitz left the group in 1916. In 1917, she followed Mrs. Parker in her first term as president, but in the spring of 1918, when men were leaving to fight in World War I, the

Association voted not to attempt the next season. She served as president until 1921, when William Reher conducted an April concert for schoolchildren.

In 1925, Miss Ima had worked with the Association and the musicians' union to try once again to reorganize the orchestra, unsuccessfully. During the 1920s, her focus was mostly on other things, including the building of Bayou Bend, home for her and her brothers. In 1929, she headed the committee to find a conductor, visiting orchestra managers in St. Louis and Cleveland. In October 1929, Miss Ima chaired a series of musicales for the Association featuring the Josephine Boudreaux Quartet, one of which was held at Bayou Bend. She was content to keep a lesser public role and was again elected second vice president of the Symphony Association in 1930.

No detail concerning the Symphony was too small for her attention—her correspondence from the early 1930s is breathtaking in its scope. She sold ads, made suggestions for musical programming, recruited board members and made inquiries around the country for players and conductors. Although Dr. Joseph Mullen was president, they heavily relied on her expertise. In 1932, business manager Bernard Epstein wrote to her: "With regard to the violinist for the Bruch concerto, we really are at sea. You will have to make some decision about this…" "Regarding the sixth program, do you think St. Leger has in mind doing without a soloist?" He went on for four typewritten pages about programming, soloists, budgets, publicity and subscriptions.[1] And Miss Hogg made sure that tickets were sent to music students, public school music teachers, nurses and school bands—and she picked up the tab for it. When Frank St. Leger was hired as conductor in 1932, Miss Hogg installed him and his wife, Kay, in her guesthouse at Bayou Bend.

In the summer of 1933, Miss Hogg was in New York and underwent an operation for phlebitis; she was still suffering from depression. While still recovering, she was asked to assume the presidency of the Symphony for the 1933–34 season, but felt obliged to decline.[2] She accepted a second presidency in 1946, continuing until 1956. She continued on the executive committee until her death in 1975 as past president.

Given the paucity of records before 1929, it is not certain who served on the Houston Symphony Orchestra Association board during each of those years. If those records were complete, it might sustain the notion that Ima Hogg's board service was augmented by six years, adding to the 53 years that are confirmed.

Frantz Brogniez was the Association's second vice president. Born in Belgium, he moved to Houston in 1910. In Belgium, he had been director of the Zwane Music Academy and was awarded a gold medal by the King of Belgium for his music composition "Jaire." He led the Sint Cecilian Band in the 1880s and 1890s. Brogniez was a master brewer with the Houston Ice and Brewing Company (Magnolia Brewery). Southern Select, a beer brewed by Frantz at the Houston Ice and Brewing Company, won the Grand Prix of the Exposition Universelle de Belgique in Ghent. After Prohibition began, he accepted a job with a brewery in Juárez, Mexico. Using plans designed by Brogniez, Howard Hughes built the Gulf Brewing Company, for which Brogniez became master brewer in 1931. His Grand Prize beer was popular for more than 30 years.

Recording secretary **Mrs. Z. F. (Carrie Holland) Lillard** was married to Dr. Zachariah Ford Lillard, a member of the Board of Health of Houston who died in 1915. She was one of the singers in the May 1914 Houston Symphony Orchestra performance of Donizetti's Sextette from *Lucia di Lamermoor*. Living in New York in the 1930s, she supervised a candy manufacturing firm, which produced confections based on her recipes.

Henry Frederick MacGregor, who took on duties as the group's treasurer, had been a director of the Houston Quartette Society for the season of 1911–12. MacGregor was vice president and general manager of the Houston Electric Street Railway Company.

"Miss Hogg made sure that tickets were sent to music students, public school music teachers, nurses, and school bands— and she picked up the tab for it."

Mrs. William Abbey, née Mary Norwood Campbell, was the first corresponding secretary for the Association. She attended the Cincinnati Conservatory of Music, studying singing and piano, and was a member of the Women's Choral Club. Her father, William T. Campbell, was one of the original partners of Texas Company (later Texaco) and a member of the Hogg-Swayne Syndicate. Mrs. Abbey was sister to Sarah Campbell Blaffer, whose husband, Robert Lee Blaffer, was also an original guarantor. Sarah Blaffer filled seven terms on the board; her daughter Titi Hudson (Mrs. Edward J. Hudson), 13 terms; and her daughter-in-law Camilla Davis (Mrs. John H. Blaffer), five terms.

Families of the original board and guarantors have continued to be active in their support of the Houston Symphony. Organizer and original board member **Mrs. Jules (Theresa Meyer) Hirsch** was a singer and member of the Women's Choral Club. Her daughter Rosetta was one of two female violinists in the original orchestra, and her son Maurice went on in later years to lead the Houston Symphony Society as its president. Her other daughter Josie Hirsch Bloch helped organize Oklahoma City's first symphony orchestra.

Maurice S. Hirsch was born in 1890 and began practicing law in 1914, forming Hirsch and Westheimer. During World War I, he was chairman of Houston's Civil Service Commission and secretary of the Priorities Committee of the War Industries Board. In World War II, he volunteered and was promoted to Brigadier General as chairman of various war price adjustment boards. Hirsch had first served briefly on the Symphony's board in 1937, and then rejoined in 1950. He followed Ima Hogg as president in 1956, working with music directors Leopold Stokowski, Sir John Barbirolli and André Previn. In 1970, he was named president emeritus and was awarded a Houston Symphony Gold Baton Award for Exemplary Service in 1972. His wife, Winifred, was also an active member of the board beginning in 1959, and she stayed on the board for 26 years.

Judge Hiram M. Garwood, whose wife, Hettie, had died in 1917, remarried in 1921 to **Huberta Nunn Garwood**. Mrs. Garwood made herself useful to the Symphony Association as president, following Ima Hogg's term in 1921, until 1929. She presided over efforts throughout the 1920s to restart the orchestra and worked with the city Department of Recreation and Community Service to sponsor a free concert. The well-received December 1921 concert was led by William Reher, but the Association was unable to meet the union's salary demands. In 1925, another attempt to start up failed, but in the spring of that year the Association sponsored the visit of the Kansas City Orchestra. At the beginning of 1929, discussions were renewed about forming the orchestra, and Mrs. Garwood appointed Ima Hogg as chair of the investigative committee.

Top: **Mary Norwood Campbell Abbey, an officer of the 1913 board.** Bottom: **General Maurice Hirsch, Houston Symphony Society president, 1956–70.** Right: **Retirement party for Houston Symphony Society president Walter Walne on June 18, 1942, at River Oaks Country Club: Leopold Meyer and John Green, standing; Ernst Hoffmann, Walter Walne and Joseph Smith, seated.**

Mrs. Gentry (Corinne Abercrombie) Waldo was on the first board and signed the charter application. A member of the Women's Choral Club, she was also a charter member of the Houston Public School Art League and the founder of the Girls Musical Club.

Early board member **Blanche Foley** was the vocal soloist for the Houston Symphony in June 1913. Miss Foley was educated in Montreal at Sacred Heart Convent in Sault-au-Récollet, and then studied music and language in Paris for three years. Subsequently she was president of the Girls Musical Club (now Tuesday Musical Club), in 1921–23. Her father, William L. Foley, operated a dry goods store. Blanche Foley's cousins began Foley Brothers department store, which was the only company listed in 1913 as an original guarantor.

Mrs. Will Jones (Mary Gibbs) served on the first board, as did her future husband, Jesse H. Jones. Her term lasted 15 years, and her son John T. Jones served 11 years. With his urging, the Houston Endowment formed by Jesse Jones gave the funds to build Jesse H. Jones Hall for the Performing Arts and continues to support the activities of the Houston Symphony.

Mrs. Walter Benona Sharp, Sr. (Estelle Boughton) served for seven years in the 1910s and 1940s. Her son W. Bedford Sharp served three years; his wife, Patty (Lummis), five years; and daughter-in-law Mrs. Dudley C. Sharp (Tina Cleveland), seven years.

Among the first board members was **Joseph Stephen Cullinan**, who organized the J. S. Cullinan Company that later became Magnolia Petroleum Company; he was also a founder of the Texas Company in 1902. From 1913 until 1919 he was president of the Houston Chamber of Commerce. His daughter Mary Catherine, who married Rorick Cravens, served on the board from 1929 to 1931. Daughter Nina Cullinan took her turn on the board for 22 years, and grandson Craig F. Cullinan, Jr. served for six terms.

One 1913 board member was **Miss Agnese Carter**, the daughter of William T. and Maude Holley Carter. She married Haywood Nelms and served another four years. Her brother's wife, **Marjorie Leachman (Mrs. Aubrey Leon) Carter**, served 13 terms beginning in the 1940s. William T. Carter's grandson Victor Neuhaus Carter did a three-year stint in the 1950s, as did Victor's wife, Betty, in the 1960s and 1970s.

William E. Kendall joined the first board and also served as the business manager from 1915 to 1917. Kendall was a grandson of General Sidney Sherman.

A number of educators were on the board. One was the president of the newly formed Rice Institute, **Dr. Edgar Odell Lovett**, who was a mathematics professor and a member of the Symphony's original board. He served at least 11 terms, ending in 1936. His daughter-in-law **Martha Wicks Lovett** co-chaired the 1939 Symphony ball.

Mrs. Joseph Mullen, née Ida Kirkland, was on the board for five years and was the wife of future Houston Symphony Society president **Dr. Joseph Mullen**. Their son Joe married Joanna Nazro and later provided endowment funds to establish the annual Nazro Memorial Concert.

Mrs. E. A. Peden (Cora V. Root) was elected to the Symphony Association board in 1916 and served at least 25 years on the board between then and 1963. Born in Galveston, Mrs. Peden was the primary organizer of the Women's Choral Club and was noted for her beautiful singing voice. Her husband, Edward, was appointed by President Herbert Hoover as the federal food administrator for Texas in 1917, and in 1919 he was sent by Hoover to Europe to assist with food relief efforts.

One of the longer serving board members was **Homoiselle Davenport Randall**, who married John F. Grant. She grew up in Galveston and studied music in Berlin and New York City. She was featured in Liszt's Piano Concerto in E-flat for the final concert of the 1916–17 season. Her first board service was in 1917, and she was on the board for a total of 25 years, until 1964. She was president of the Women's Committee from 1939 to 1941.

Mrs. Walter H. Walne (Margaret Butler) joined the Houston Symphony Orchestra Association as its second vice president in 1925 and remained on the board until 1961. She served as chairman of the box seats committee for years. In 1936, her husband joined the board as president for the year after St. Leger departed and guest conductors filled the podium. This was also the year that the Houston Symphony Orchestra Association changed its name to the Houston Symphony Society and adopted a new charter. Walne was president until Hugh Roy Cullen assumed the post in 1942. Walne had served as managing partner of the law firm Baker & Botts from 1926 to 1933. He served a total of nine years on the Symphony board.

Oveta Culp Hobby was 28 years old when she was elected to the board in 1933, serving as parliamentarian until 1937. She was the first Popular Concerts committee chairman for Hoffmann's experimental series in 1937. Like Miss Hogg, her father was involved in state government, serving as a legislator from Killeen. She had already been the legislative parliamentarian for the Texas House of Representatives from 1925 to 1931. In 1931, she and former Texas Governor William P. Hobby married and she involved herself in his newspaper, the *Houston Post*. Governor Hobby also served on the board from 1934 to 1936. In 1940, she was corresponding secretary for the Society. The next year, she was asked to be the first commanding officer of the Women's Army Corps during World War II. After the war, she returned home as director of KPRC radio and KPRC-TV and executive vice president of the *Houston Post*. She rejoined the Symphony board and by 1948 was vice president, serving in that spot for the next five years. In 1953, President Eisenhower named her the first secretary of the new Department of Health, Education and Welfare. She remained on the board until 1980, having served 42 years. Mrs. Hobby's son, Texas Lieutenant Governor William P. Hobby, Jr., joined the board in 1960, serving for 11 years.

Mrs. Ray Lofton (Mary Fredrica Gross) Dudley was a 41-year board member. Her husband was the general manager of the *Post-Dispatch*, and they became the owners and publishers of the Gulf Publishing Company. She graduated from Baylor in 1915 with two degrees. Her first year on the board was 1933, and by 1936 she was corresponding secretary. She chaired the children's concerts committee in 1937 and 1940, then served another four years as corresponding secretary, beginning in 1946. She was on the executive committee for nearly 30 years and served as vice president from 1950 to 1970. Her husband, Ray L. Dudley, also joined the board for seven years.

Top: **Oveta Culp Hobby was a vice president of the Houston Symphony Society.** Bottom: **Fredrica Gross Dudley was on the board for 41 years.** Right: **Hugh Roy Cullen, Houston Symphony Society president in 1942–46.**

Hugh Roy Cullen, founder of Quintana Petroleum, joined the board in 1934. His wife, Lillie Cranz Cullen, became a board member two years later, serving as the Serenade Concerts committee chairman in 1937, and remained on the board until 1959. In 1940, H. R. Cullen was elected a vice president of the Houston Symphony Society, and in 1942 he was elected president, overseeing the wartime activities of the Symphony. He remained in office until 1945. His grandson Roy Cullen continued the family tradition in 1961 by joining the board for 20 years.

Gus S. Wortham, a founder of American General Insurance Company, was elected to the board in 1945. The next year, he was named the first chairman of the board in 1946, serving in that capacity until 1948. For those two years he was also chairman of the Maintenance Fund campaign, being the first to raise $100,000 in a year. For most of the 1960s, he chaired the finance committee. He remained on the executive committee until 1972. His wife, Lyndall Finley Wortham, joined the board in 1962 and served 17 years.

One of the founders of Brown & Root, **George R. Brown** first joined the board in 1945, but was absent when his brother Herman served two terms in 1946–48. George Brown rejoined in 1948 until leaving the board in 1981, having served 34 years. His daughter Isabel, Mrs. Wallace S. Wilson, was a 12-year board member starting in 1970. Between 1974 and 2003, her husband, Wallace Wilson of Wilson Industries, served 12 years.

Mrs. Herman Brown (Margarett Root) was elected in 1958, serving until 1962. The Herman Browns had adopted the children of Stokes and Lucy Stude, Louisa and Mike. Mike S. Stude is the nephew of original 1913 board member Henry W. Stude. (The Stude family established a bakery managed by Henry Stude, who served as president of the National Association of Master Bakers, the American Bakers Association and the American Institute for Baking.) **Mike S. Stude** has chaired two capital campaigns for the Symphony, in 1990–92 and 2003–05. His classical radio station KRTS 92.1 FM to Houston was the weekly broadcast sponsor of Houston Symphony performances from 1992 to 1995. Now a life trustee and chairman emeritus of the Houston Symphony Society, he was chairman of the board in 2001–08. His wife, Anita, was also on the board for three years. His brother-in-law, investment manager **Fayez Sarofim**, was president of the Society from 1975 to 1978.

Judge James A. Elkins, Sr., a founder of the law firm Vinson, Elkins, Weems & Searls, was a board member for 27 years, beginning by helping with the Maintenance Fund campaign in 1945. He served on the Houston Symphony Endowment board in 1962. His son James A. Elkins, Jr., who was president of First City National Bank, served concurrently on the board with his father, having joined the board in 1945. James, Jr. was the executive vice president of the Houston Symphony Society from 1946–49 and vice president from 1949–51. He also worked on the Maintenance Fund and gave 36 years as a board member.

Seven members of the **Farish family** have been members of the board during the century. The first two joined in 1945: Mrs. William Stamps Farish, Sr. (Libbie Rice), a 23-year member, and Stephen P. Farish, first cousin to her husband, serving three years. In 1946, Mrs. William Stamps Farish, Jr. (Mary Wood) briefly was a member, then in 1948, Mrs. Stephen P. Farish (Lottie Rice), who was a first cousin to Libbie Rice Farish, began a 21-year tenure. William S. Farish III began a 12-year stint in 1961, with his wife, Sarah, joining briefly in 1969. In 1990, Stephen P. Farish III was a board of advisors member for four years.

The closest rival to Miss Hogg in length of board service was **Mrs. Ben A. (Katherine Hume) Calhoun**. The daughter of Fredrick H. Seymour and Kate Hume, she debuted as a soprano in 1927 in *La Bohème* at the San Francisco Opera. She joined the board in 1948 and became president of the Women's Committee for 1951–53. Her engraved gavel is still passed down to each Houston Symphony League president. She continued on the board until 2003, compiling a record of 56 years.

Lloyd H. Smith served an unbroken term of 32 years on the board, beginning in 1949. He was married to Elizabeth Wiess, whose sister Caroline was on the board in 1945. Caroline was on the board a total of five terms, in 1946–48 as Mrs. William H. Francis, Jr., and in 1979–81 as **Mrs. Theodore N. Law**. These two daughters of Harry and Olga Wiess were sisters to Margaret, Mrs. James A. Elkins, Jr.

Mrs. Charles L. Bybee, née Faith Poorman, joined the board in 1946 and was recording secretary from 1949–1951. She served continuously on the board until 1982. Her husband, Charles, followed her as recording secretary in 1951 and was the Maintenance Fund chairman for three years in the 1950s and six years in the 1960s. He was the chair for the Houston Symphony Endowment from 1960 to 1966 and treasurer and vice president from 1956 to 1972. In 1972, he was one of a select group of individuals awarded the Houston Symphony's Gold Baton Award for Exemplary Service. Their combined years of service totaled 75.

> "Her engraved gavel is still passed down to each Houston Symphony League president."

Mrs. Elva Kalb Dumas spent 36 years on the board, first joining in 1946. During World War II, she joined the Symphony in opera selections at the 1942 Camp Wallace army camp concert. In 1943, she joined other singers to present Act 3 of *Aida* with the Symphony at City Auditorium. In April 1944, she sang the title role in a Houston Symphony production of Puccini's opera *Tosca*. A year later, she joined the Symphony cast for a production of *La Bohème*. She attended Rice University and Columbia University and studied voice in New York City, where she had a weekly radio program.

Mrs. Albert P. (Nettie Lewis) Jones was an accomplished pianist who studied at the Chicago Musical College. Having served as president of the Women's Committee from 1949 to 1951, Mrs. Jones joined the Association of Women's Committees board from 1951 to 1955 and served as chair for the March 1953 conference held in Houston. She was elected president for the succeeding two years. She served on the Houston Symphony Society board from 1946 to 1972, 1980 to 1981, and was on the advisory board from 1981 until her death in 1990. In the 1960s, she moved to Austin, where her husband, a former president of the State Bar of Texas, became a professor at the University of Texas Law School. In Austin, she served on the Honorary Advisory Council of the Austin Symphony Orchestra Society.

Beginning in 1946, Foley's Department Store's **Max Levine** began as a board member and worked on the Symphony's Maintenance Fund drive, becoming chairman in 1951 and again in 1969–71. Foley's was absorbed by Federated Department Stores in 1947, but continued to support the orchestra. Levine was elected treasurer of the Society for 1950–52 and then a vice president for 1952–77, serving as vice president of finance from 1969 to 1973. Under his leadership, Foley's sponsored a pops series, Sounds of the 70s, as well as a summer pops series. He became president of the Houston Symphony Endowment in 1981–82, chaired the foundations division of the annual fund in 1983 and was named the first director-emeritus in 1988, having served 42 years.

Mrs. James Griffith (Virginia Vinson) Lawhon was the daughter of William A. Vinson, a founder of the legal firm Vinson & Elkins. Known as "Virgie," she was the chair of the women's division of the 1952 Maintenance Fund campaign. She was elected the Women's Committee president in 1953–55. For 13 years, she was recording secretary for the Society, in 1955–59 and 1962–70. She was also a vice president for 1959–62 and 1970–75. When she left the Board of Advisors in 1985, she had served 31 years.

Top: **Maurice Hirsch, Charles Jones, Max Levine and Gus Wortham, 1969.** Center: **Four Society presidents, from left: Charles Jones, John Cater, Maurice Hirsch and Fayez Sarofim, circa 1980.** Bottom: **Peter Marzio, Museum of Fine Arts, Houston director, and Symphony Executive Director Gideon Toeplitz with Stewart Orton, Houston Symphony Society chairman, 1990–91.** Right: **Dr. Charles F. Jones, Houston Symphony Society president, 1970–75, and chairman, 1977–80.**

W. Leland Anderson, a nephew to M. D. Anderson, was a 29-year board member, joining the board in 1955. He was vice president of Anderson-Clayton and Company and one of the first directors for the Texas Medical Center. In 1981, his daughter, Mrs. Russell Frankel (Julia Anderson), joined the Symphony's Board of Advisors; from 1993 to present she has been on the Board of Trustees. She and her husband co-chaired the 2008 Symphony ball, and she served on the Symphony's centennial steering committee.

Mrs. Leon Jaworski (Jeannette Adam) joined the board in 1956 and remained for the next 40 years. She was the Women's Committee president in 1959–61, the Society's recording secretary in 1977–80, and Annual Fund chair for the board and benefactors division in 1979. She also chaired the 1976 Star-Spangled Symphony Ball with Bing Crosby as the guest star and co-chaired the next ball two years later.

Mrs. Percy Edwin Turner (Isla Carroll) joined the board in 1956, the same year as her son-in-law, **Harris Masterson III**, each serving 22 and 23 years, respectively. His wife and Mrs. Turner's daughter by her first marriage to Frank Prior Sterling, Carroll Sterling Masterson was a 14-year board member, joining in 1966. Mrs. Stewart (Mariquita) Masterson, whose husband was first cousin to Harris Masterson, also served seven years, first serving on the Board of Advisors in 1983. Mrs. Turner's sister-in-law, Miss Florence Sterling, had served several years beginning in 1917.

Benjamin N. Woodson was recruited by Gus Wortham to be president of American General Insurance and moved to Houston in July 1953. His wife, Grace Cook Woodson, was a contemporary of Miss Hogg and in 1957 joined the board for 24 years. Ben Woodson supported the Symphony over 30 years by joining the board in 1961, with continuous service until 1998. In the 1970s, he served as treasurer. The first place prize for the Ima Hogg Competition, the Grace Woodson Memorial Award, was originally underwritten by Benjamin Woodson in her honor and is partially underwritten by endowment funds he contributed. Since his death, his daughter Mary Woodson Crowell and grandson **John Dennis III** have continued to underwrite this prize for the competition. Dennis has also served on the board in recent years.

Clive Runnells, Jr. joined the board in 1961, when he was president of Mid-Coast Cable Television and also a rancher. He served 41 years on the board and board of advisors.

Mrs. Alfred R. Neumann (Selma Smith) was a 35-year board member, whose husband was chancellor of the University of Houston Clear Lake. He also wrote the Houston Symphony's program notes for concerts for 18 years, from 1958 to 1975, and served on the board for six years. Selma was deeply committed to the annual fund campaign of the Houston Symphony and was the second president of the Houston Symphony League Bay Area in 1976. In 1977, she chaired the Houston Symphony League's first Houston Symphony radio marathon on KLEF FM. The Houston Symphony Society gave her a Gold Baton Award in 1995, the first awarded since 1972. An endowed prize for the Ima Hogg Competition was named in her memory.

Serving 37 years on the board of directors was **Mrs. I. L. (Bertha Gordon) Miller**, from 1963 to 1999. She was the daughter of Meyer Morris Gordon, sister to Harry and Aron Gordon, and mother of Dede Miller Weil and Arnold Miller. Dede Weil has been an active member of the board for 35 years. Miller's brother Harry B. Gordon, Sr. was on the board for 21 years, and brother Aron S. Gordon, head of Gordon Jewelers, was a director for eight years. Bertha Miller was also aunt to Frann Gordon Lichtenstein, who served briefly. Also part of the Gordon family on the board was Diane Gendel, a 19-year member who served as Houston Symphony League president, and whose father, Herman Shoss, played violin in the orchestra for eight seasons in the 1930s. She also co-chaired the 2006 Symphony ball.

Dr. Charles F. Jones joined Humble Oil in 1937 and was its president from 1964 until 1970 and then vice chairman until 1972, when he retired. Jones was elected to the board in 1969 as executive vice president, then president for 1970–75. He was one of the select group receiving a Gold Baton Award from the Society in 1972. In 1977, he became chairman of the Society for four years. He chaired the Board of Advisors in 1981–82. His wife, Edith, joined the board in 1973 for eight years.

Banker and Houston Symphony Society president **John T. Cater** came on the board in 1974. Before he was president from 1978 to 1980, he served on the nominating committee and chaired both strategic planning and finance committees. Subsequently he was chairman of the Society, chaired the Board of Advisors and served on the board of the Houston Symphony Endowment. Named a life trustee, he has 39 years of service.

 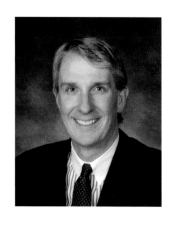  

For 34 years, **J. Hugh Roff, Jr.** was a member of the board, beginning in 1976. Roff was president of United Gas Pipe Line Company and later of Roff Resources LLC. In 1986–87, he was a vice president and chairman of the development committee for the Society. In 1988–89, he became president and then chairman of the Society in 1989–90.

Life trustee **Alexander "Mike" K. McLanahan** first joined the board in 1977. He was the 1993 Annual Fund chair and served as vice president of development in 1996–97 and 2005–08. McLanahan was chairman of the Houston Symphony Society from 1997 to 2001, and was named a life trustee in 2003. In 2006-07 he chaired the Symphony's Legacy Society. Now a retired investment manager, he was appointed by George H. W. Bush to the President's Committee on the Arts and the Humanities. His wife, Mary Ann McLanahan, has also eight years on the board.

John D. Platt joined the Society board in 1981 and was elected vice president and treasurer the next year. He was the 1982–83 finance chair and chair of the Houston Symphony Endowment for 1983–84. He was elected president for 1984–87 and became chairman in 1988. In 1997, he was named a life trustee.

Among others who served on the board for 30 or more years follow, with their first year of service: Theodore E. Swigart, 1933; Michel T. Halbouty, 1956; John F. Lynch, 1959; Immanuel Olshan, 1962; Mrs. Harold R. (Judy) DeMoss, Jr., 1972.

Other notable trustees with 20 or more years of service after joining the board during the first half-century include: Mrs. W. Scott (Ruth) Red, 1921; Mrs. Louis A. (Fannie) Freed, 1925; Dr. R. A. Tsanoff, 1929; Mrs. Andrew E. (Mary) Rutter, 1933; James L. Shepherd, Jr., 1936; J. W. Hershey, 1940; Isaac Arnold, Sr., 1944; Thomas Fletcher, Sr., 1945; Frank C. Smith, Sr., 1945; George A. Butler, 1945; J. W. Link, Jr., 1945; Mrs. Stuart (Katherine) Sherar, 1945; Simon Sakowitz, 1945; Harmon Whittington, 1945; Colonel W. B. Bates, 1946; Frank M. Law, 1946; James S. Abercombie, 1946; Warren S. Bellows, Sr., 1946; E. Leslie Hogan, 1949; Earl C. Hankamer, 1951; Robert W. Kneebone, 1953; James O. Winston, Jr., 1953; Dr. Hyman J. Schachtel, 1954; Mrs. William T. (Joan H.) Fleming, Jr., 1955; Mrs. Albert M. (Josie) Tomforde, 1955; Reuben W. Askanase, 1956; Mrs. S. Maurice (Susan Clayton) McAshan, Jr., 1956; Alfred C. Glassell, Jr., 1956; Dr. Richard J. Gonzalez, 1956; Leon Jaworski, 1956; Mrs. Wesley (Neva) West, 1956; Wesley W. West, 1960; Aaron J. Farfel, 1956; Mrs. Garrett R. (Phyllis) Tucker, Jr., 1957; Mrs. Thompson H. (Lucile) McCleary, 1957; Mrs. M. T. (Marion) Launius, Jr., 1959; Mrs. Greer (Jane) Marechal, 1959; Isaac S. Brochstein, 1961; Dr. Philip G. Hoffman, 1961; Allen H. Carruth, 1961; and Robin A. Elverson, 1961.

    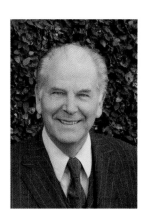

Houston Symphony Society presidents
Left: **First row: John T. Cater,** 1978–80 (chairman 1980–82); **E. C. Vandagrift, Jr.,** 1987–88; **Gene McDavid,** 1992–95; **Janice H. Barrow,** 1995–96; **Second row: Rodney Margolis,** 1999–2001; **Jeffrey B. Early,** 2001–03; **Michael Shannon,** 2003; **Ed Wulfe,** 2003–06 (chairman 2008–11).

Houston Symphony Society presidents and chairmen
Above: **First row: Jesse B. Tutor,** president 2006–09, and chairman, 2011 to present; **Robert B. Tudor III,** president, 2009–12; **Robert Peiser,** president, 2012 to present; **Frank Law,** shown here in 1960, had retired as chairman of First City National Bank in 1955. He was chairman of the Houston Symphony Society in 1948-49, and chairman of Houston Symphony Endowment, 1950–1959; **Warren S. Bellows, Sr.,** chairman in 1950–53. He was on the Society board for 20 years, and his son Warren, Jr., for 16. **Second row: Harmon Whittington,** chairman, 1953–56; **Joe F. Moore,** chairman, 1991–95; **Constantine S. Nicandros,** chairman, 1995–97; **Alexander McLanahan,** chairman,1997-2001; **Mike S. Stude,** chairman 2001–08.

In the latter half of the Symphony's history, these board members had 20 or more years of service: Mrs. Theodore W. (George) Cooper, 1964; Mrs. Edward W. (Ellen) Kelley, Jr., 1965; J. Hugh Liedtke, 1966; Mrs. C. Pharr (Betty) Duson, Jr., 1968; Robert T. Sakowitz, 1968; Maurice J. Aresty, 1969; Mrs. Charles R. (Rocky) Franzen, 1972; Rodney H. Margolis, 1973; Mrs. Edward O. (Janet) King, 1974; Mrs. Ike C. (Ruth) Kerridge, Jr., 1975; Charles W. Duncan, Jr., 1975; George B. Sweeney, Jr., 1976; Mrs. Rodney H. (Judy Erlich) Margolis, 1978; Dr. Grady L. Hallman, 1978; Dr. Margaret Waisman, 1978; Barry E. Kaufman, 1978; Mrs. Jerald D. (Katherine) Mize, 1978; L. Proctor "Terry" Thomas III, 1979; Stewart Orton, 1979; Charles D. Milby, 1981; Ermy Borlenghi Bonfield, 1981; Gordon B. Bonfield, 1983; Dr. Harvey L. Gordon, 1981; Ginny Elverson, 1982; Samuel D. Keeper, 1982; Robert M. Hermance, 1983; Jesse B. Tutor, 1983; Betty J. Tutor, 1993; Mrs. J. Stephen (Mary Lynn) Marks, 1984; Ulyesse LeGrange, 1985; Mrs. James A. (Helen) Shaffer, 1987; Gene McDavid, 1988; Anthony W. Hall, Jr., 1988; Charlotte A. Rothwell, 1988; Mrs. Thomas D. (Janice H.) Barrow, 1989; Arthur Newman, 1990; Stephen G. Tipps, 1991; Frederic Alan Weber, 1992; Mrs. Marvin (Joan Erlich) Kaplan, 1993; Terry A. Brown, 1993; and Edward C. Osterberg, Jr., 1995.

CHAPTER
XVI

THE VOLUNTEERS

In addition to board members who provided financial support in the early years, the board saw the need to authorize a committee to act as volunteer staff. The Houston Symphony Orchestra Association's auxiliary committee formed in 1931 with the purpose of selling subscriptions and tickets.

Card G. Elliott was the first chairman for two years. In 1933, the committee had an expanded mandate from the Association, and Miss Mary F. Fuller served as chairman in 1933–35. At the first meeting in 1933, "Dr. R.A. Tsanoff made a very forceful talk to the Committee stressing the importance of universal interest and subscription in the Symphony Orchestra."[1] The organization's secretary was Miss Mary Nugent Armstrong in 1933–36. Mrs. John Van De Mark was the next chairman for two years, followed by Mrs. J. Nye Ryman.

Others involved in this early group included Mrs. J. Moody Dawson, Mrs. E. L. Flowers, Mrs. H. A. Bybee, Miss Helen Saft, Mrs. Reba Hirsch, Hu T. Huffmaster, Harvin Moore, Mrs. Corinne D. Brooks, Mrs. Eugene Blake, Mrs. J. G. Flynn, Mrs. Eloise Helbig Chalmers, Dr. H. L. Bartlett, Miss Frances Patton, Miss Ruth Burr, Charles J. Robertson, Miss Louise Daniel and orchestra member Conway Shaw.

Among the activities of this group were soliciting donors to provide tickets to music teachers for their pupils and arranging public lectures by the conductor preceding each Symphony concert. The 1933 minutes of the committee also reflect the formation of a Little Symphony of 20 musicians from the orchestra, directed by Frank St. Leger, to give programs for schoolchildren. They considered details such as advertising and the selling of refreshments during the intermission at concerts. It was this group that made plans for the first children's concerts of the orchestra. The auxiliary committee was dissolved in 1937.

In its stead the Houston Symphony Society formed the Women's Committee, whose purpose was also to promote the sales of season tickets. Ima Hogg was appointed the first president of the Women's Committee, and for 75 years the Women's Committee (renamed the Houston Symphony League in 1978) has been a source of significant support for the Houston Symphony and of cultural and educational enrichment for our city.

For 50 years, the presidents of the Women's Committee/ Houston Symphony League served two-year terms, but that was changed to an annual appointment beginning in 1988. Ima Hogg

remained highly invested in the Women's Committee after her initial term and was involved in starting numerous new projects.

The volunteers continued with the annual campaign for renewing season ticket subscriptions until 2001, but management began handling new subscriber sales around 1953. From 1953 to the 1980s, the subscription renewal drive was known as the Red Wagon Drive—named after the box office wagon (usually painted red) of a circus. (Unsurprisingly, the drive was initiated by Ima Hogg.) As late as the 1990s, subscriptions volunteers found their supplies in a "red box" on wheels, located in a corner of the Jones Hall lobby.

The initial ticket sales efforts expanded to selling program ads in 1939, and the Women's Committee organized a Junior Patrons group (whose names were listed in the programs) to attend concerts in 1940. The program has been modified over the years but still exists today.

Fundraising

Another early activity begun in the 1940s included soliciting donations for the annual operating fund. In the early years, the Women's Committee was a major part of the drive, involving hundreds of women canvassing the city for individual donors. In the 1948–49 Maintenance Fund drive the Women's Committee raised more than half of the total funds. The Women's Committee also had a files chairman who kept donor and subscriber address lists, names of prospective subscribers and related annual fund

Previous spread: **Seated, Mary Louis Murphy with her zither and Women's Division chairman Ginny Schleuse at a 1975 Maintenance Fund meeting.** Above: **Student concert usher at a Houston Symphony Explorer concert, October 2012.** Top right: **The Women's Division of the 1961-62 Maintenance Fund drive met to report results.** Center right: **Ball chair Lilly Pryor with Sergiu Comissiona and Mickey Mouse at the Fantasia Ball in 1985.** Bottom right: **Houston Symphony League members bought a radio marathon auction item—lunch with Barbara Bush. From left, Linda Finger, Linda McReynolds, Barbara Bush and Roblyn Herndon, circa 1983.**

files. The committee was comprised of 400–500 workers, divided into teams with team captains and sections with section chairs. Some annual fund volunteers still recall the admonition of General Maurice Hirsch that they must pay personal visits to corporate donors, which they did, wearing hats and white gloves. While she was alive, Miss Hogg presented white orchids to the most successful committee members.

A fundraising ball was held in 1939 at the Houston Country Club, a Viennese ball chaired by Mrs. J. R. Parten and co-chaired by Mrs. Malcolm Lovett, which garnered $1,057.20 for the Houston Symphony. This was followed in the next two years by the Pan American Ball and the Yankee Doodle Ball, both chaired by Mrs. Ford Hubbard, Sr. The last of these was held just after the attack on Pearl Harbor, and balls were discontinued during the war. Balls were resurrected in 1976 by Mrs. Leon (Jeanette) Jaworski with the Star-Spangled Ball and guest star Bing Crosby. They were held biennially until 1986, when they became an annual major event of the League. Other balls from this period starred Joel Gray, Sammy Davis, Jr., and, in one unique year, Mickey Mouse. More than 30 gala balls have been staged since the late 1970s, often highlighted with a concert by the orchestra and sparked by a variety of creative themes ranging from The Old World Symphony Ball to Rock Me, Amadeus! Recent balls typically have garnered over $1 million.

Over the years, special money-raising events included such wide-ranging activities as a radio marathon, which was a weekend broadcast (on KLEF-FM) including an extensive catalog of premiums to be purchased; a collaboration with the Houston Antique Dealers Association at their annual show; assisting with registrations for a 10K fun run; a Saks Fifth Avenue-sponsored fashion show entitled the Maestro Collection, which kicked off the Houston social season each year; a Men's Event, usually with a sporting theme; and a series of distinctive dinner parties called Symphony Scores held in the spring at various homes and venues.

Some traditional fundraising events begun in past years still exist today: the glamorous Opening Night Party follows the Symphony's first concert of each season; a Symphony Store, begun in the lobby of Jones Hall at symphony concerts in 1992, annually raises substantial income from sales of music-related items and recordings; Magical Musical Morning, first held in 1997, is a delightful holiday party for children that features musical activities; an elegant gourmet Maestro's Wine Dinner (originally part of Symphony Scores, but since 2002 a separate event) supports the Ima Hogg Competition; and most recently in 2009, a Children's Fashion Show was created.

Education

As early as the 1930s, the Women's Committee arranged lectures as part of the marketing effort; by the 1950s, they offered regular speakers; and today's pre-concert lectures were originally organized by the League in the 1980s.

As with fundraising projects, some education endeavors of the League have flourished for a time and then been discontinued. Among these projects were Painting to Music (an idea of Miss Hogg's) and Special Transportation.

One of the oldest education activities of the Houston Symphony League is the student competition, which was begun in 1947 and is still very successful today.

The Women's Committee formalized a committee to oversee and provide ushers for school concerts in 1955, and it continues to do so today. The highly regarded Ima Hogg Young Artist Competition was begun in 1976.

In 1977, a docent program with Houston Symphony League volunteers was begun to enhance the concert experience of children attending school concerts. The docents-in-the-schools program was highly successful for many years and won awards in Texas, nationally and in Canada. One component of the docent program was the very popular Instrument Petting Zoo, which is still offered by Houston Symphony League volunteers today at family and summer concerts, in children's hospitals and at children's symphony social events.

League volunteer docents and others have also portrayed whimsical musical characters at children's symphony concerts and other events including "living" instruments, Perry the Penguin and Maestro Mouse.

A new education experience for adults was established in 1998—B# Brunch provided League members the opportunity to hear local musical luminaries or invited guest artists as presenters. Members of the Houston Symphony League subscribe to a series of lectures with leading music professionals of the city several times throughout the year. Also, for a time in the 1990s, League volunteers ran and made up a portion of the Houston Symphony Speakers Bureau, which offered gratis lectures about the activities of the Houston Symphony to community groups throughout the city.

A separate award was created to honor steadfast education volunteers in 2000. The Ardyce Tostengard Crystal Cello Award was named in memory of a dedicated education volunteer.

Service

Another area of Houston Symphony League enterprise is that of service. In the mid-1950s, the Women's Committee planned numerous parties for the orchestra, including a boat tour of the Houston Ship Channel to the San Jacinto battleground for several years running. From 1959 until 2004, the Houston Symphony

Top: **Left to right, Annette Colish and Julia Stark receiving Student Audition prizes from Winnie Safford Wallace in March 1948.** Center: **Charter members of the Bay Area Chapter of the Women's Committee, 1976: seated, from left, Selma Neumann and Lorain Merrill; standing, Pat Gibson, Alda Cannon, Fran Strong, Peggy Arisco, Julia Stark Wells, Margaret Barkley and Joan Wade.** Bottom: **The 2012–13 Houston Symphony League board.**

League also hosted an annual party for orchestra members and their families. Since 1979, the volunteers have offered orchestra coffees, and later full lunches, to the musicians during breaks at rehearsals several times a year.

For many years, the entertainment committee arranged dinners and receptions for guest artists and conductors, and a group of volunteers drove artists to and from the airport.

From time to time, the volunteers make a gift to the Symphony for specific purposes, such as buying cello chairs, the purchase of a harp for the orchestra, partial underwriting for a new Symphony recording, an education website and, in its 75th year, purchasing a new Steinway piano. When the new harp was purchased, the harpist position was endowed by Mr. and Mrs. Albert P. Jones. Nettie Jones was president of the Women's Committee from 1949 to 1951.

Affiliated Organizations

Regional committees were formed in 1952 and originally supported ticket sales in outlying towns. In 1975, auxiliary leagues were formed in the North and Bay areas. While the North Area League was discontinued in 2000, the Houston Symphony League Bay Area still is very active today. Both groups had a commitment to support the Houston Symphony with local events. The North Area held an annual English high tea to raise funds, and the Bay Area still holds a yearly fundraising home tour, A Day by the Bay. Both leagues worked to foster interest in their local schools for attendance at student concerts and formed docent chapters to present programs in their schools to enhance that experience, with the Bay Area group still running an award-winning docent program in the Clear Creek Independent School District. They also encouraged local students to participate in the Houston Symphony League student competition, and later the North Area staged their own Alice Flores-Smith Student Competition, named to honor the memory of a founding member. Each area league brought the orchestra to their local areas for both public and student concerts. Sounds Like Fun! concerts in the summer were presented in each area, and the North Area sponsored a pops concert each year in a local high school. The Bay Area held its first Atrium concert at the University of Houston Clear Lake in 1977. Today Bay Area members bus as a group to a series of Houston Symphony subscription concerts, and Bay Area volunteers assist Houston Symphony League volunteers in several of their projects.

For a few years in the late 1970s and early 1980s, EnCorps, an auxiliary group for young professionals, enjoyed success. Houston Symphony Partners, another young professionals group, followed in 1996, sponsoring such events as Mad As A March Hare, a silent auction. The Houston Symphony Dynamics, a team of teenagers from Houston-area high schools, began as an advisory group organized by Education Director Ginny Garrett in 1998 to advise and help promote the Houston Symphony's Teen Night Concert. In 2002, the group was renamed and became an official volunteer group of the Houston Symphony and remained active until 2005.

It is noteworthy that the Houston Symphony League has hosted several state and national conferences over the years. The state group met in Houston under two different names, as the Texas Women's Auxiliaries for Symphony Orchestras (TWASO) in 1967 and 1984 and as the Texas Association for Symphony Orchestras (TASO) in 1996 and 2008. Past presidents of TASO include two members of the Houston Symphony League: Ruth Kerridge and Helen Shaffer.

The national group, comprised of representatives from larger orchestras, was in Houston as the Association of Women's Committees in 1953, the Women's Association of Symphony Orchestras (WASO) in 1978, and the American Major Symphony Orchestra Volunteers (AMSOV) in 2011. Six members of the Houston Symphony League have served on the board of AMSOV since its founding: Mrs. Albert Jones , Miss Ima Hogg, Mrs. M. T. Launius, Jr., Mrs. Edward W. Kelley, Jr., Mrs. Thurmon Andress, and Mrs. James A. Shaffer. Nettie Jones, Ellen Kelley and Helen Shaffer served AMSOV as its president. In 1978, the League created its Volunteer of the Year Award, named to honor the memory of past president Ellen Kelley.

One more segment of volunteerism has been valuable to the Houston Symphony, particularly in the youth arena. The corporate underwriters for Saturday morning family concerts since the 1990s often provided employees to assist with pre- and post-concert children's activities, in addition to funding these events. These include Mervyn's Department Stores, Columbia Hospital Corporation of America, Time-Warner, Inc. and Weatherford International. And the Symphony has also benefited from other charitable organizations who have stipulated volunteering for the Houston Symphony as among their requirements of membership. Examples include First Junior Women's Club of Houston, which has provided teams of ushers for student concerts for many years, and the National Charity League, an organization of volunteering mothers and daughters who have assisted in various ways, particularly in the docent program.

The numerous and varied ways that a century of volunteers have served the Houston Symphony clearly demonstrate that their support has been critical to the success of the orchestra. From selling tickets, helping a child draw a bow across a violin, addressing envelopes, making deviled eggs for an orchestra luncheon or modeling a cello costume, to hosting a national convention, entertaining internationally famous guest artists or staging annual million dollar balls: volunteers have made it happen.

CHAPTER
XVII

EDUCATION AND COMMUNITY ENGAGEMENT

The primary educational activities of the Houston Symphony are performing concerts for children, including appropriate enhancement, creating opportunities for young musicians to compete and perform, and offering adult education experiences. Community Partnerships, a newer area, creates collaborations to reach new and non-traditional audiences.

From its very beginnings and continuing throughout its history, the Houston Symphony leadership has been deeply committed to education and, in particular, to the mission of providing a strong connection between the city's orchestra and its children. This dedication began with youth concerts and competitions in the early years and continues to the present day with Music Matters!, the title given to the Education and Community Engagement programs. This multi-faceted program offers symphonic education experiences for children and adults.

Supporting the Houston community has been integral to the Symphony's mission as well. Over the years, the musicians have performed in ensembles large and small for military personnel, hospitals, hurricane victims, rodeo fans, and many others. Unique programming like the annual Fiesta Sinfonica concert honoring Hispanic Heritage Month is well into its second decade with support from Chevron enabling the free, and very popular concert every September. On the eve of the Centennial, Symphony administrators created a new staff position, director of community partnerships, to formalize the process and broaden the reach of civic activities.

★ ★ ★

CHILDREN'S CONCERT

Thursday, December 9th, 3:00 P. M.

Program of Famous Dance Music Including
Ravel's "Bolero"

City Auditorium
25 CENTS — GENERAL ADMISSION — 25 CENTS

Adults accompanying school children are invited to attend. RESERVA-
TIONS MUST BE MADE THROUGH THE SCHOOLS.

for Music Matters! number some 70,000 patrons through approximately 30 concerts each year.

These concerts were usually conducted by staff conductors, among them Andor Toth, Al Urbach, A. Clyde Roller, Akira Endo, William Harwood, Toshiyuki Shimada, Gisèle Ben-Dor, Niklaus Wyss, Stephen Stein, Mariusz Smolij, Carlos Miguel Prieto, Rebecca Miller, Damon Gupton and Robert Franz; or by visiting conductors from other orchestras in Texas, such as Ezra Rachlin (Austin) and Victor Alessandro (San Antonio).

The concerts frequently included children's classical favorites such as *Peter and the Wolf, Tubby the Tuba* and selections from *The Nutcracker* ballet. Narration and visual additions helped make the music more accessible for young listeners. An early involvement of the Women's Committee in student concerts was the project of driving orthopedically handicapped children who could not ride the bus to concerts in private cars. For many years in the 1950s and 1960s, in a supportive collaboration with Houston Independent School District, the Women's Committee sponsored the *Painting to Music* project, inviting schoolchildren to create and submit artwork inspired by the music they heard at concerts.

In the early 1980s, a concern became prevalent that an education deficiency in math and science existed, and teaching emphasis shifted away from language arts and arts education. School field trips to concerts and museums had to offer content designed to correlate with math and science curricula in order to permit students to attend. The challenge was met by the Houston Symphony in several ingenious ways. First, a teacher guidebook was designed that included lesson plans that might present a numbers exercise or, for science, a simple acoustical experiment related to the concert performance. The narration at concerts reinforced

Student Concerts

The first concert known to be dedicated solely to students is noted in a *Galveston Daily News* article reporting that a concert for 2,500 schoolchildren was held at Houston's City Auditorium in April 1921.

In 1937, a regular series of student matinee concerts was coordinated with the Houston Independent School District, and by 1939, a children's committee of the Women's Committee was formed with Mrs. Dudley Sharp as chairman.

From the 1940s through most of the 1970s, schoolchildren from the greater Houston area were bussed to the concert hall several times a year for entertaining performances created for them. Ten student concerts were offered in the 1950s and as many as 18 by the 1970s.

Evidence of the importance of education to the Houston Symphony was the creation of the staff position of education coordinator in the 1970s. Education activities have flourished and been presented in numerous iterations over the decades, and today audiences

"The concerts frequently included children's classical favorites such as *Peter and the Wolf, Tubby the Tuba* and selections from *The Nutcracker* ballet."

these teachings. Secondly, to conform to the criteria of multiple exposure of the same learning event, a docent program began with volunteers taking a presentation to the school as a preview for the concert. The docents talked about the physical properties of orchestral instruments and allowed hands-on time called the Instrument Petting Zoo. Thirdly, the student concerts were divided into age groups with different emphases for early elementary grades through junior high school.

Until 1993, the majority of students paid a nominal fee to attend concerts. At that time, the daring move was made to obtain underwriting for student concerts, allowing thousands of children in Houston and nearby towns to attend concerts for free. The first major underwriter was the Houston Livestock Show and Rodeo, an organization that devotes huge resources to the benefit of children.

Previous spread: **Van Cliburn accepts the Texas Gulf Sulphur prize at his first Houston Symphony performance, 1947. To the right, conductor Ernst Hoffmann.**Top: **A student concert in the Music Hall, circa 1952.** Bottom: **Children love to make a big musical sound at the Instrument Petting Zoo.**

Junior Patrons

Although student concerts are the centerpiece of educational offerings, the earliest Houston Symphony children's project, and one that enjoys great longevity, was not part of these performances, but rather a method to raise funds and honor the children of symphony supporters by listing their names in the printed concert programs. This was the Junior Patrons project begun by the Women's Committee of the Houston Symphony Society in 1940. Over seven decades, these lists read like a roll call of prominent Houstonians. Examples from the first listing in the 1945–46 season include: Stewart Baker; Anne and Jane Lawhon; Ford Hubbard, Jr.; Clare Masterson; George C. Francisco, III; Isaac Arnold, Jr.; Nancy, Maconda and Isabel Brown; Allen and John McAshan; Sally Jane and Sells Neuhaus; Mimi Smith; A. A. Ledbetter, Jr.; Roy Cullen; Francita Stuart; Lyndall and Diana Wortham; William Pettus, Jr. and Jessica Hobby; and Harry and Cornelia Cullen. A listing in the 1968–69 programs included the name of future President George Walker Bush. The first chairmen of Junior Patrons were three young ladies: Josephine Abercrombie, daughter of Mr. and Mrs. J. S. Abercrombie; Betty Burrows, daughter of Mr. and Mrs. J. S. Burrows; and Joan Farish, daughter of Mr. and Mrs. W. S. Farish. Over the years, Junior Patrons have worn pins and enjoyed special advantages at family concerts such as reserved seating and visits backstage with concert guest artists, musicians, and conductors. The Junior Patrons program still exists today, and young members enjoy an annual special event, with musical activities and backstage access.

Competitions

For many of the Symphony's student concerts, a highlight of each was a solo appearance by a young musician. These artists were the winners of Houston Symphony student competitions. A statewide contest for junior and high school musicians was sponsored in 1946 by the Texas State Board of Education and Texas Gulf Sulphur Company to find a young soloist to appear in the Houston Symphony's radio broadcast series. The first winner was a 12-year-old pianist from Kilgore named Van Cliburn. Five more competitions in this series were held until 1952.

In the autumn of 1947, the Women's Committee began its own competition in which Houston area schoolchildren and teenagers were invited to compete for the opportunity to play as a student concert soloist with the orchestra. These young performers were challenged to perform a full concerto from the standard orchestral repertoire from memory. The Student Auditions committee was originally comprised of several women, including Miss Ima Hogg and Josie (Mrs. Albert M.) Tomforde, who served as the first judges. Others on the committee were Mrs. Albert Jones, Mrs. Aubrey Carter and Miss Nina Cullinan. Later, Austin Symphony conductor Ezra Rachlin came to Houston to judge, and eventually a panel of non-local professional musicians was utilized. Mrs. Tomforde, and later her daughter, Betty Tomforde Duson, chaired the competition for many years, and from 1978 until 1995 the competition even bore her name. Today it is known as the Houston Symphony League Concerto Competition. Winners over the years have frequently gone on to professional careers, and at least three (Marian Webb Wilson, cellist; Charles Tabony, violinist; and Hal Robinson, bass) became members of the Houston Symphony.

When Ima Hogg died in 1975, the Women's Committee, seeking to find a fitting way to honor her memory, created the Ima Hogg Young Artist Auditions. This competition for college level and young professional musicians has become internationally successful, offering cash prizes and guest artist opportunities with the Houston Symphony. The judging panel consists of music professionals from the ranks of nationally and internationally known conductors, critics, arts administrators and musicians. More than 100 applicants enter the preliminary round, and ten semi-finalists are invited to Houston for the piano accompaniment round. The field is narrowed to four finalists, who then play with the full orchestra in a live finals concert for the top prizes. The Ima Hogg Competition, as it is now known, has served as an impetus for the careers of countless professional musicians and world-renowned artists. Chairmen over the years have each contributed new enrichment and sophistication to the competition. Highlighting a "town and gown" aspect is the fact that the auditions were once held on two university campuses, the University of Houston and Rice University. Later Rice University became the permanent host site, and beginning in 1990 a poster design competition was conducted at the University of Houston School of Architecture. Today, submissions are sought from graphic artists throughout the nation.

Other innovations have been the radio broadcast of the event, the addition of the full orchestra for the finals round and the creation of an audience choice award. One hallmark of the competition's reputation is its outstanding level of Texas hospitality afforded the judges and competitors. In its 38 years of existence, the Ima Hogg Competition has involved more than 700 semi-finalists and more than 100 winners. To name only a few, they include such artistically acclaimed recording artists as harpist Yolanda Kondonassis, violinist Stephanie Chase, marimbist

Joseph Gramley and cellist Sophie Shao; professors of music such as David Wehr, Duquesne University; Gregory Sauer, Florida State University; and David Bilger, Curtis Institute of Music; and orchestra members such as Felicia Moye, concertmaster, Santa Fe Opera; Amy Porter, assistant principal flute, Atlanta Symphony; Katherine Needleman, principal oboe, Baltimore Symphony; Timothy Landauer, principal cellist, Pacific Symphony; Daniel McKelway, assistant principal clarinet, Cleveland Orchestra; Sarah Kwak, concertmaster, Oregon Symphony; and Scott Holshouser, principal keyboardist, and Frank Huang, concertmaster, both with the Houston Symphony.

Other Competitions

The Texas Composers' Contest was another competition begun in the 1940s as an idea of Ima Hogg's. The prize included cash along with a performance of the winning composition by the Houston Symphony. The competition was sponsored by the symphonies of Houston, Austin and Dallas, and in 1947 the orchestra presented the winning compositions at the first Texas Creative Arts Festival. In 1951, Ima Hogg noted that the Houston Symphony had sponsored the competition for more than five years, but would instead offer a commission that year to Texas composer David Guion. The result was his *Texas–Symphonic Suite*, which was performed in February 1952 and later recorded by the Houston Summer Symphony. The Texas Composers' Contest was briefly reactivated in 1960 by chairman Mrs. Craig F. Cullinan, Jr.

A brief two-year precursor to the Ima Hogg National Young Artist Competition was the Young Artists Competition, with generous prizes underwritten by Pennzoil United. The first was held in November 1968 and was chaired by Betty Tomforde (Mrs. C. Pharr) Duson and Josie (Mrs. Albert M.) Tomforde. The event was designed for highly qualified college and conservatory students of piano, violin and cello. Thirty-seven entrants comprised the field in the first year, and the prestigious judging panel was Gary Graffman, Vladimir Ashkenazy, Roy Harris, Sidney Harth, A. Clyde Roller and Houston Symphony Conductor-in-Chief André Previn.

In 1980, Gulf Oil Foundation endowed a new type of competition, the Gulf Oil Festival of Schools. Student musicians from the greater Houston area were auditioned by orchestra members, and those selected formed an entire student orchestra. This group then rehearsed and performed with the Houston Symphony seated side by side—student and professional. The set-up was quite challenging for the stage crew, with the stage needing to accommodate approximately 200 players. The project was discontinued after several years, but doubtless, these experiences created a lifelong memory for the young musicians,

Top: **The 1978 Ima Hogg Auditions: Andrea Nemecz, second prize; Ellen Kelley, Houston Symphony League president; Stephanie Chase, first prize; Jerry Priest, Audition Chairman; and Karen Lundgren, third prize.** Bottom: **Chairman Charlotte Rothwell presents the poster competition prize for the 1991 Ima Hogg Young Artist Competition to Michael Lee.** Left: **An early Junior Patrons button worn by children to concerts.**

who could evermore claim they had once "played with the Houston Symphony."

For ten years, from 1987 to 1997, the Houston Symphony League North Area (an auxiliary league of the Houston Symphony League) sponsored the Alice Flores-Smith Competition for high school musicians in its area. Named to honor a past president of the League, this competition was designed along similar criteria as the Concerto Competition. It was discontinued with the demise of the League in 1998.

Docent Program

Ann Koonsman, the first Houston Symphony education coordinator created the Houston Symphony Docent Program in 1978. Docent programs were new to symphony orchestras around the country at this time and, as noted previously, later were a vital component in giving schoolchildren multiple sequential learning experiences as mandated by tighter controls for field trips. The version Ms. Koonsman created offered volunteers a series that combined music education classes with training sessions for making in-school presentations. These presentations were designed to acquaint schoolchildren with the orchestral instruments they would be seeing and hearing at the concerts. For younger grades, docents performed a delightful puppet show with animal puppets portraying the four instrumental sections of the orchestra. Older students were given an informal lecture. The presentation for both groups ended with a hands-on experience with authentic instruments, whimsically named the Instrument Petting Zoo. The original docent class numbered some 25 volunteers, largely members of the Houston Symphony League.

In 1990, a Spanish language version of one puppet show (El Niño Musical) began being offered. Both the North Area and Bay Area symphony leagues developed their own programs, and for several years in the 1980s and 1990s, thousands of children were treated to a Houston Symphony Docent Program every year. The types of venues were also increased, with docents taking programs to local libraries and children's hospitals and performing for scout troops and art festivals. Another added feature was a set of four unique instrument costumes worn by docents and other volunteers: a life-sized clarinet, violin, timpani and tuba. The docents' Instrument Petting Zoo had a presence at all the Houston Symphony Sounds Like Fun! concerts in the summer and at the Family Concerts at Jones Hall.

The Houston Symphony Docent Program has won numerous awards at the state level and was given the Award of Excellence at the American Symphony Orchestra League Conference held in Toronto, Canada, in 1986.

Top: **Sounds Like Fun! concerts were led by Resident Conductor Mariusz Smolij in 2000–03.** Center: **Puppet show docents with the puppet character El Niño Musical on the far left.** Bottom: **A popular character from the docent puppet show, El Niño Musical (or the Musical Kid).**

160

Adult Education

It is a fairly common tradition that symphony orchestras throughout the country offer adult lecture series in connection with their concerts. In Houston, these have been offered in many ways over the years including radio and television broadcasts, talks to audiences immediately preceding a concert and separate lectures in various community venues such as libraries and senior citizen centers. Educational presentations have been offered for season ticket holders, volunteer support organizations, civic groups, continuing education classes at local colleges and universities and the general public.

The Women's Committee of the Houston Symphony took an interest in lectures and promotional talks for upcoming concerts in the early years. By the mid-1950s, a regular series of music appreciation speakers was offered; presenters included orchestra musicians and Symphony administrators. In this period, the Women's Committee was also very active in joining forces with local universities' music schools to promote attendance at Houston Symphony concerts and to encourage the inclusion of lecture content related to the musical compositions performed in Symphony programs. In yet another initiative, the Women's Committee volunteers worked with chamber ensembles of Houston Symphony musicians to bring orchestral music to small towns in the region.

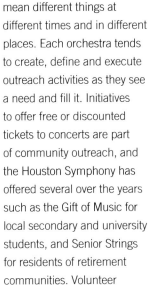

Beginning in the early 1960s, a highly respected music scholar and chairman of the music department of the University of Houston, Earl V. Moore, conducted a very successful eight-session lecture series for the Women's Committee. The lectures were well attended and led attendees through an in-depth look at the musical structure of the symphonic repertoire of the season. During the tenure of Music Director Sergiu Comissiona (1980–88), the Symphony began offering open rehearsals to the public. The effort was called Picnic With a Star because attendees were invited to bring a brown bag lunch to eat in the lobby after the rehearsal and hear a few words from local or visiting artists.

During the 1990s, yet another very popular series, Concert Connections, was offered on Saturday mornings preceding the open rehearsals. This was taught by noted musical historian and professor of music at the University of Houston Moores School of Music Howard Pollack, who lectured with entertaining piano

examples. In 1998, the highly successful B# Brunches were begun by the Houston Symphony League to offer members a benefit for their hard work on volunteer projects. Held in elegant homes four times a year with local musical luminaries or invited guest artists as presenters, these are still ongoing today.

The venture that has reached the greatest number of people and continues today is the series of pre-concert lectures called Prelude. These became standard practice in the mid-1980s with various local and visiting music authorities giving these lectures over the years.

Community Engagement

Symphony orchestra outreach is a broadly based term that can mean different things at different times and in different places. Each orchestra tends to create, define and execute outreach activities as they see a need and fill it. Initiatives to offer free or discounted tickets to concerts are part of community outreach, and the Houston Symphony has offered several over the years such as the Gift of Music for local secondary and university students, and Senior Strings for residents of retirement communities. Volunteer activities such as the Docent Program and, for a short time in the 1990s, a Speakers Bureau also constitute community engagement. Of course, in the broadest sense, any free public concert is a form of community outreach, and the Houston Symphony summer concerts at Miller Outdoor Theatre begun in the 1940s could be considered outreach.

For many years, outreach activities were offered informally by individual musicians. A player might establish a relationship with a school, a youth orchestra or some other entity, and provide musical tutoring or performances as a benefit. One example of the many instances of individual Houston Symphony musicians outreach is that of violist Kyla Bynum, cellist Marian Wilson, English hornist Larry Thompson, bassoonist Richard Hall and French hornist Jay Andrus, who gave coaching sessions in 1969 at Fleming Junior High School in collaboration with the school's music director, Luther Brown. Other examples include the many Houston Symphony musicians, such as timpanist David Wuliger, who coached members of the Houston Youth Symphony at rehearsals in the 1950s.

Above: **Jay Andrus helps a student horn player as part of the orchestra outreach program in 1969.**

In the 1990s, symphony orchestras across the country began to address the problem of shrinking and aging audiences. The idea spread that "breaking the barrier of the footlights" might be accomplished by demystifying individual classical musicians so they might become more relevant to non-traditional audience members. Some orchestras even included communication skills as well as instrument mastery as part of their audition process. It soon evolved that musicians might be trained to improve their ability in this area, and an early guru of the movement was a musician/entrepreneur/educator from the West Coast named Mitchell Korn. Along with several other orchestras in the country, the Houston Symphony engaged Korn in 1992 to work with a group of interested Houston Symphony musicians. The result was Musicians-in-Schools which was very successful.

Community partners have frequently figured successfully in symphony outreach, particularly through the education department. In the early 1970s, an arrangement with Channel 2, KPRC TV, presented orchestra musicians in talks and recitals on a local broadcast series. In the 1990s, KUHF radio broadcast a monthly program called "Music Matters on the Air," featuring personnel from the Symphony education staff. Continuing into the 1980s and 1990s, the Houston Symphony forged many creative partnerships with other arts and education organizations in the city. Some of these involved individual musicians and small ensembles and even chamber orchestra groups from within the full orchestra. Examples of these collaborative groups include Young Audiences of Houston, Very Special Arts (VSA) and the Texas Institute for Arts in Education. The education directors of the city's major arts organizations began meeting together in the late 1980s, sharing ideas and advice, and in 1998 the Houston Symphony hosted the Annual Meeting of the Education Directors of the American Symphony Orchestra League. A wide-ranging partnership with Houston's major arts organizations and HISD was mounted in 1990. In 1993, the Symphony partnered with the Houston Public Library, Young Audiences, and the Houston Zoo for a project featuring Babar the Elephant, based on the children's classic by Jean de Brunhoff and the music of Francis Poulenc. For a few years in the mid-1980s, the Symphony and the Museum of Fine Arts, Houston partnered in a presentation

series. The two organizations presented pianist and lecturer Jeffrey Siegel in his unique Keyboard Conversations. During another year, the Alley Theatre, Houston Ballet, Houston Grand Opera and the Houston Symphony collaborated to perform various iterations for each of their disciplines of *Romeo and Juliet* for area high school juniors, who studied the Shakespeare play as part of their English curriculum. The project was the subject of a 1991 special also produced by Channel 2, narrated by their popular newscaster Ron Stone. This film is now housed in the Smithsonian Institution.

For two years, 2000 and 2001, a unique project titled the Diversity Residency Program enjoyed success. This involved Rice University musicians serving a one-season internship performing as an orchestra member. These young players were mentored by Houston Symphony musicians and enjoyed special access to the conducting staff and administration as well.

On a full-scale orchestra level, many specially designed outreach concerts have been produced over the years. *Joy of Music* was presented annually during the holidays for special needs audiences and the *Houston Chronicle* Dollar Concerts begun in the 1960s both still exist today. The latter features the current winner of the Ima Hogg Competition. For several years, the Houston Symphony Teen Night Concert was given for area high schools that competed in selling tickets. The winning school was awarded a master class by a Houston Symphony staff conductor. Also popular for many years was the aforementioned Festival of Schools, a side-by-side concert with Houston Symphony players and student musicians. An annual Salute to Educators Concert was inaugurated in 1990, embracing and highlighting the education community and included awarding an annual Education Appreciation Award to an outstanding arts educator or administrator. Still presented early in the season each year is the appropriately themed Fiesta Sinfonica, which reaches out to Houston's Hispanic Latino community.

Probably the most successful full orchestra community outreach endeavor of the Houston Symphony is Sounds Like Fun! This series, which takes place in June and July every year, was the brainchild of a joint committee of staff, board and musicians meeting in 1986 seeking a way to find work for the orchestra during the summer when the schedule was not busy with concerts

Above: **Conductor-in-Residence Stephen Stein led education programming from 1992 to 1998.** Top right: **Associate Conductor Robert Franz entertained the family concert audience while conducting in a chicken suit.** Bottom right: **Franz and Junior Patrons.**

at Miller Outdoor Theatre (and later Cynthia Woods Mitchell Pavilion). The idea was to take the orchestra on tour to various non-traditional venues. The early years saw the orchestra going not only to churches, schools and community centers but also to a shopping mall, an equestrian center and the Houston Zoo.

Although the programs were geared for children and have featured clowns, visual enhancement, printed programs with musical games and puzzles, and audience participation, they are enjoyed by all ages. For several years through a partnership with the McDonald's Restaurants, the very popular children's clown, Ronald McDonald, was a part of Sounds Like Fun! concerts, guest conducting, leading audience sing-alongs, doing tricks and in general enhancing the fun atmosphere. The musicians are arrayed in colorful T-shirts and pre-concert activities such as student performing ensembles, strolling costumed characters and the ever-popular docent Instrument Petting Zoo are all part of the fun. Sounds Like Fun! has enjoyed successful underwriting over the years.

The other major development of Houston Symphony community outreach, which came about in 1999, was Community Connections. Musicians-in-Schools laid the groundwork for this ambitious program that would take musicians into venues of their choice with a free program of their own design such as recitals or coaching sessions. These performances could be as soloists or in small ensembles. Modeled after a similar activity by the Chicago and St. Louis orchestras, where some dozen musicians were involved, the Houston Symphony musicians responded with such enthusiasm (almost 100%) that

Community Connections became the largest such symphony orchestra community outreach program in the nation. As with Sounds Like Fun!, Community Connections continues to attract major underwriting and is still very successful today.

Other recent and new community outreach projects include Fidelity FutureStage, Symphony Scouts and residencies to further Houston Independent School District band and orchestra programs for secondary schools on an in-depth level. Fidelity FutureStage was a program sponsored by Fidelity Investments in four cities. Fidelity provided instruments for high school music students and sponsored musical competitions in each city to give high school students the chance to perform with each orchestra in concert, as well as the chance to receive music instruction from professional musicians in their school. Symphony Scouts is a four-series program for four- to six-year-olds, providing an intimate environment for them to learn the instrument families.

As education and community engagement enter the next century, the goal remains the same: to introduce the world of orchestral music to school children, encourage music makers to pursue their passion, nurture concert goers to hear music in new ways, empower educators to use music as a tool in classrooms, bring families together and engage all parts of the community.

Symbolically and yet, significantly defining the role of education and community engagement, is the title now employed by the department overseeing these efforts: Music Matters!

CHAPTER

XVIII

POPS AND SPECIAL SERIES CONCERTS

Conductor Ernst Hoffmann made an early attempt to present concerts along the lines of the Boston Pops concerts that the Boston Symphony had begun in 1885, which included light classics and the popular music of the day. Hoffmann led the first trial Popular Concert of the Houston Symphony on January 24, 1937. The next season, the Symphony had a concert series of pop programs, with such guests as pianist Albino Torres and the Rice University Band. Unfortunately, the concerts didn't sell particularly well and were abandoned.

Aside from the outdoor summer concerts modeled on the Boston Pops and started in 1940 at Miller Outdoor Theatre, pops concerts were not sold as a package until the 1942–43 season—they continued until December 1945, with from four to six concerts per season. During this period, there were headliners such as Percy Grainger, Oscar Levant and Alec Templeton. The schedule of 1942–43 concerts notes that two extra "Pop" concerts were given in November and December 1942, for the entertainment of servicemen.

Three years after the war, Henke & Pillot grocery stores picked up the ball and sponsored a series of free pops concerts by the Symphony in 1948–53. In 1954, another paid subscription season of seven pops concerts was instituted by Ferenc Fricsay and lasted until 1956.

Foley's department store sponsored a Spring Series of Pops in 1969, leading to Sounds of the 70's concerts in 1970–71. Featured on this series were artists Henry Mancini, Kenny Rogers and The First Edition, Ray Charles, Doc Severinsen, Jack Benny and Victor Borge.

From 1983 to the present, a regular subscription pops season has been offered. In 1984, the six-concert pops programs were conducted by assistant conductor Toshiyuki Shimada, Sergiu Comissiona and various visiting conductors. In 1985, Exxon became a major sponsor of pops concerts, and in 1986 the Houston Symphony hired its first principal pops conductor, Newton Wayland. Wayland shaped the pops programs until 1993. From 1993 to 1998 Conductor-in-Residence Stephen Stein was the primary conductor for pops programming. Michael Krajewski is the present principal pops conductor, hired in 2000.

Holiday Concerts

Another opportunity for pops programming arose with the New Year's Eve concert that became a tradition for the Houston Symphony. André Kostelanetz conducted the orchestra in City Auditorium in 1951, with guest artist and soprano Dorothy Kirsten. Kostelanetz continued as the Symphony's conductor of choice for this event until the early 1960s, using the Music Hall for at least a decade until

Jones Hall was built. Among the other guest artists when he was on the podium: André Previn, Phyllis Curtin and Beverly Sills.

Arthur Fiedler took over the New Year's Eve concerts by 1964, continuing the tradition until 1972. Various guest conductors, and occasionally the music director, led the concerts thereafter. After the concerts, the stage was cleared for dinner and dancing, and patrons toasted the New Year. The last one held in Jones Hall was in 1995.

Christmas concerts gained popularity in the 1950s. In a precursor to today's family concerts, the annual Children's Christmas Party featured television personality Bob Keeshan, or Captain Kangaroo, and was begun in 1958 as an introduction to music for pre-school children. Houston was the first city to present him with the orchestra—he returned for at least six years.

The Christmas concerts that had become formalized annual events beginning in 1968 were known as the Sounds of Christmas in the 1975 Foley's-sponsored presentation. Beginning in 1984, the Christmas pops concert was offered in the subscription brochure and is still offered today.

Handel's *Messiah*

The Houston Symphony first performed Handel's *Messiah* on December 3, 1940, with combined church choirs (450 strong) of Houston. The next year, the event was repeated in December.[1]

It was performed for the first time on a subscription series in December 1952. Andor Toth conducted with a mixed chorus from Austin, Davis, Lamar and San Jacinto High Schools, who performed

"Today's *Houston Chronicle* Dollar Concert is an annual event featuring the first prize winner of the Ima Hogg Competition."

the "Hallelujah Chorus" from *Messiah*. In 1958, the "Hallelujah Chorus" was on a March program and in 1959 was featured in December.

In April 1966, Sir John Barbirolli conducted the piece with the Houston Symphony Chorale and the University of Houston Concert Choir at the Music Hall. In 1968, the Houston Symphony Chorale and the orchestra presented *Messiah* as part of a larger Christmas concert.

During the 1970s, it was presented sporadically, using the University of Houston choruses or the Houston Symphony Chorus. For several years, it was presented at the First Baptist Church, Park Place Baptist Church or Westbury Baptist Church.

Associate conductor Mario Benzecry conducted the piece in 1973, using the University of Houston Choruses at the Music Hall. The following year saw the beginning of a string of Houston Symphony Chorus presentations with the Houston Symphony.

From at least 1990 to the present, *The Messiah* has become an annual event presented in Jones Hall with the Houston Symphony Chorus.

Houston Chronicle Dollar Concert

The first Dollar Concert sponsored by the *Houston Chronicle* was a pops concert in 1960, with guest conductor Arthur Fiedler and an audience of 8,000.[2] The idea was "conceived by Mr. John T. Jones, Jr., a vice-president of the Houston Symphony Society and publisher of the *Houston Chronicle*, who visualized the wide audience that could be reached by this low admission price."[3] Tickets for one dollar were available in the lobby of the *Houston Chronicle* building or the Houston Symphony office at the Music Hall (until Jones Hall opened in 1966). Tickets were also often sold at other locations around the city. Among the other conductors of these concerts in this era were Vladimir Golschmann, Sir Malcolm Sargent, Sir John Barbirolli, André Kostelanetz, Walter Hendl, André Previn, Helen Quach and Morton Gould. In the 1960s, there were three to five Dollar Concerts each year. Today's *Houston Chronicle* Dollar Concert is an annual event featuring the first prize winner of the Ima Hogg Competition.

Previous spread: **Principal Pops Conductor Michael Krajewski**. Above: **Michael Krajewski greets the audience at the 2012 Very Merry Pops concert.** Left: **Caroline Wiess, chairman of the 1944 Pops Committee, with soprano Beatrice Hagan.**

CHAPTER
XVIV

TOURING

Touring, while financially costly, is beneficial for a symphony orchestra for many reasons. The musicians strengthen their ties by traveling and living together, they hone their performances by frequent repetition of the specific limited repertoire programmed for tours, they learn to adjust to the acoustics of a different performance space night after night, and perhaps most importantly, the musicians take great pride in proving their quality and reputation as an orchestra beyond the scope of their own home city.

While the downside aspects of touring—the constant travel, and strange hotels and food each day with little time for rest—do exist, they are somewhat offset by the freedom from the daily responsibilities of life at home and the excitement of seeing new places. Wonderful stories of experiences on tours linger for years to become part of an orchestra's lore.

Ernst Hoffmann led the first Texas tour of six cities in the 1938–39 season and a short three-city Texas tour in the spring of 1940. During World War II, the orchestra maintained a busy schedule touring military bases throughout Texas and Louisiana from November 1942 to April 1945. The first international venue for the orchestra occurred during this period—the Good Will Tour of the Houston Symphony Orchestra to Monterrey, Mexico, on November 12 and 13, 1943. Tours of Texas cities continued until 1947, the last under the baton of conductor Ernst Hoffmann.

In 1950 and 1954, Efrem Kurtz led the orchestra on a Midwest tour and, after 1951 and 1953, on tours of the Southeast. Regional touring continued until March 1956. The 1955 tour took the orchestra to West Texas and New Mexico with conductor Milton Katims. The 1956 tour of the Southeast U.S. with Katims and Maurice Bonney was the last until Sir John Barbirolli led the first East Coast tour in 1964. This ambitious tour celebrated the golden anniversary season and included 19 cities. Red Pastorek recalled the conditions of the 1960s Midwest tours: "in the middle of the winter, on the buses, travelling 36 hours a day… there were a couple of times we had the bathroom-down-the-hall kind of a place—old railroad station, downtown hotel, it was a small town, just absolutely pitiful. David Wuliger, who was our timpanist at the time, used to come with a special bag with him to these hotels. Open it up and there was a rope ladder in it. He would tie the ladder to the radiator and stick it by the window so in case this place burned down, he was the first one out!"[1]

Barbirolli's leadership of spring tours continued each year until 1967. During the 1967 West Coast tour, the orchestra and Barbirolli flew on a DC-7, a four-engine plane that management had booked as inexpensively as possible. The pilots reported that in letting down the wheels to land in Oregon, a hydraulic line broke—no flaps, no steering and no brakes. Days later, in San Francisco, the hydraulics went out again. The orchestra committee met with management to say that the orchestra was not getting back on the airplane, so they needed another airplane.[2]

Conductor-in-Chief André Previn toured the Eastern and Midwest United States in 1968 and 1969. The 1970 East Coast tour was led by conductor Hans Schweiger. Trips to the East Coast were on the schedule between 1973 and 1976, with Lawrence Foster conducting. Then, in May 1979, the orchestra and conductor Erich Bergel traveled to play at Cuauhtémoc and Acapulco, Mexico, with soloist Yo-Yo Ma. Musicians in the cello section amused themselves with a poker game on the plane to Mexico City.[3]

In 1982, the orchestra participated in Festival Casals in San Juan, Puerto Rico, with Sergiu Comissiona. The year 1983 brought a 70th anniversary East Coast tour, followed in succeeding years by East Coast, national and regional tours.

Christoph Eschenbach conducted a special concert in January 1989, the Inauguration Salute to the First Lady (Barbara Bush) at Kennedy Center in Washington, D.C. He led annual tours in the years following. Singapore was the destination for a June 1990 tour. After 1991 appearances at the Kennedy Center and Carnegie Hall, the orchestra was featured at the Pacific Music Festival in Japan.

During the 1992 European tour, Eschenbach was asked to present a private concert of chamber music in Cologne, Germany, with principal and titled players from the Houston Symphony. The

Previous spread: **Cellist Chris French's touring trunk bears the marks of past tours.** Above: **A running poker game on tour was made easier with a custom-made table to fit in the bus aisle, 1965.** Top right, clockwise: **Good Will Tour of the Houston Symphony Orchestra, Laredo, Texas, 1943. Houston Symphony members in Singapore, June 1990. Houston patrons of the 1997 European tour toast the orchestra. Left to right: Barry Burkholder, Tom Barrow, Janet Burkholder and Janice Barrow.**

GOOD WILL TOUR OF THE HOUSTON SYMPHONY ORCHESTRA

ERNST HOFFMANN -- Conductor

TO MONTERREY, MEXICO VIA BOWEN TRAILWAYS BUSES.

Laredo, Texas, November 12, 1943

group, known as the Houston Symphony Chamber Players, served as faculty to Japan's Pacific Music Festival and toured Japan in 1993, 1994 and 1995, then toured Europe in 1994 and 1997. In the summers of 1996 and 1997, they appeared at Chicago's Ravinia Festival.

After an East Coast tour in 1994, the orchestra returned to the Pacific Music Festival in 1995. The Shell 1997 European tour began in London and continued to France, Amsterdam, Germany and Austria. Shell sponsored the 1998 U.S. tour with Christoph Eschenbach. Eschenbach's last tour with the orchestra was the European Festival 2000, with appearances in Germany and Switzerland.

No touring of the orchestra occurred after 2000 until the orchestra presented

itself at Carnegie Hall in January 2006. The orchestra's first concert at Carnegie Hall was in 1965 with Barbirolli, making 2006 the 14th performance there. The orchestra was invited back by Carnegie Hall for a January 2010 concert, when the orchestra presented its multimedia production, *The Planets–An HD Odyssey*. They presented the program in the following days in Florida. This piece was featured in the Houston Symphony's sold-out seven-city tour of the United Kingdom in October 2010.

The orchestra and Maestro Graf were invited to participate in Carnegie Hall's 2012 Spring for Music series in May. A month later, the group was the first orchestra from the United States invited to perform at the Festival of the World's Symphony Orchestras in Moscow, Russia.

"Christoph Eschenbach conducted a special concert in January 1989, the Inauguration Salute to the First Lady (Barbara Bush) at Kennedy Center in Washington, D.C."

Far left: **Tom Barrow, son of Leonidas and Laura Thomson Barrow, early subscribers to the Houston Symphony.** Left: **Andrés Orozco-Estrada with a buckle presented by Mayor Annise Parker.** Center: **Robert Franz leads the 100th birthday concert at Miller Outdoor Theatre.** Bottom, from left: **Bernice Beckerman. Donald Ray Jackson, stage manager. Chris French, one of the Bad Boys of Cello.**

APPENDIX

173

CHIEF CONDUCTORS AND MUSIC DIRECTORS

1913–16	Julien Paul Blitz
1916–18	Paul Bergé
1931–32	Uriel Nespoli
1932–35	Frank St. Leger
1936–47	Ernst Hoffmann
1948–54	Efrem Kurtz
1954	Ferenc Fricsay
1955–61	Leopold Stokowski
1961–67	Sir John Barbirolli
1967–69	André Previn
1971–78	Lawrence Foster
1980–88	Sergiu Comissiona
1988–99	Christoph Eschenbach
2001–13	Hans Graf
2013–	Andrés Orozco–Estrada

ASSISTANT AND PRINCIPAL GUEST CONDUCTORS

1915	Maurice L. Derdeyn, *Assistant Director*
1921	William Reher
1935–36	Alfred Hertz, Vittorio Verse, Modeste Alloo, *Guest Conductors*
1937	Austin Ledwith, *Assistant Conductor*
1941–43	Joseph A. Henkel, *Assistant Conductor*
1943–48	Joseph A. Henkel, *Associate Conductor*
1953–54	Andor Toth, *Assistant Conductor*
1955–58	Maurice Bonney, *Associate Conductor*
1958–62	Ezra Rachlin, *Guest Conductor*
1965–70	A. Clyde Roller, *Associate Conductor*
1969–70	Antonio de Almeida, *Principal Guest Conductor*
1970–73	A. Clyde Roller, *Resident Conductor*
1973–74	Mario Benzecry, *Associate Conductor*
1975	Akira Endo, *Associate Conductor*
1978–80	C. William Harwood, *Exxon/Arts Endowment Assistant Conductor*
1978–79	Michael Palmer, *Guest Conductor*
1979–81	Erich Bergel, *Principal Guest Conductor*
1980–81	C. William Harwood, *Associate Conductor*
1981–83	Sir Alexander Gibson, *Principal Guest Conductor*
1981–85	Toshiyuki Shimada, *Assistant Conductor*
1985–87	Toshiyuki Shimada, *Conducting Associate*
1986–93	Newton Wayland, *Principal Pops Conductor*
1987–88	Richard Fletcher, *Assistant Conductor*
1987–91	Niklaus Wyss, *Associate Conductor*
1988–89	Gisèle Ben–Dor, *Assistant Conductor*
1989–91	Gisèle Ben–Dor, *Resident Conductor*
1992–98	Stephen Stein, *Conductor–in–Residence*
1999–2000	Christopher Confessore, *Interim Education and Outreach Conductor*
2000–03	Mariusz Smolij, *Resident Conductor*
2000–	Michael Krajewski, *Principal Pops Conductor*
2003–06	Carlos Miguel Prieto, *Associate Conductor*
2004–05	Damon Gupton, *American Conducting Fellow*
2005–07	Rebecca Miller, *American Conducting Fellow*
2007–08	Brett Mitchell, *American Conducting Fellow*
2008–11	Brett Mitchell, *Assistant Conductor/ American Conducting Fellow*
2008–	Robert Franz, *Associate Conductor*

HOUSTON SYMPHONY CONCERTMASTERS

1913–15, 1916–17	Benjamin J. Steinfeldt
1915–16	Louis Arnouts
1918	E. D. Saunders
1931–37	Josephine Boudreaux
1937–43	Joseph Gallo
1943–46	Olga King Henkel
1946–72	Raphael Fliegel
1972–79	Ronald Patterson
1978–79	Alan Traverse, *Co-Concertmaster*
1981–87	Rubén González
1987–2005	Uri Pianka
2006–08	Angela Fuller
2010–	Frank Huang

ORCHESTRA MEMBERS

With calendar dates of service

Composition of this list was drawn primarily from program listings and, as such, may be incomplete.

*Contracted substitutes
**Extra players

Abel, Charles, *Violin*, 1931
Acosta, D., *Bass*, 1937–38
Adams, C. A., *Horn*, 1916
Adams, E., *Trumpet*, 1944–46
Adams–Young, Lora, *Violin*, 1980–81
Adkins, Alexandra, *Violin*, 2000–
Adkins, Durward, *Viola*, 1948–49
Ailman, Carroll, *Viola*, 1948–49
Ailman, Suzanne, *Cello*, 1948–49
Aldin, A., *Bass*, 1940–41
Allen, S., *Violin*, 1942–44
Alley, R., *Horn*, 1944–46
Altenbach, Richard, *Violin*, 1985–89
Althage, Ed, *Trumpet*, 1916–17, 1931–33
Altobelli, Peter, *Horn*, 1950–52
Alvarado, Benito, *Violin*, 1936–38, 1940–44, *Bass Clarinet*, 1944–65, Librarian, 1941–43
Amick, H. B., *Trombone*, 1932–46
Anastasi, Martin, *Viola*, 1936–41, *Contrabassoon*, 1938–1941, Librarian, 1936–41
Anaya, Francisco, *Bassoon*, 1913, *Trombone*, 1913–15
Anderson, Oskar, *Flute*, 1940–42, 1945–48

Andrix, George, *Viola*, 1957–58
Andrus, Jay, *Horn*, 1963–95
Apgar, Horace, *Bass*, 1949–50
Arbiter, Eric, *Bassoon*, 1972–
Armstrong, R. W., *Viola*, 1931–32
Arnouts, Louis, *Violin*, 1913–16, Librarian, 1913–15
Asher, G., *Trombone*, 1944–45
Atherholt, Benjamin, *Bassoon* and *Contrabassoon*, 2012*
Atherholt, Robert, *Oboe*, 1984–2012
Aue, Margaret, *Cello*, 1955–57
Austin, James, *Trumpet*, 1959–77
Avelar, Albert, *Percussion*, 1936–37
Babb, Elizabeth, *Cello*, 1974–76, Assistant Librarian, 1974–76
Backlund, Linda, *Viola*, 1967–69
Bacon, Thomas, *Horn*, 1977–88
Baillett, Bradley, *Flute* and *Piccolo*, 2007–08
Baird, Mary, *Violin*, 1949–51
Baldassari, Alfred, *Viola*, 1949–50
Ball, Geraldine, *Percussion*, 1946–52
Balliett, Bradley, *Bassoon*, 2007–08*
Balogh, Lajos, *Cello*, 1957–62
Balsley, Floyd L., *Oboe*, 1937–41
Banke, Lois, *Piano*, 1956–61*
Banuelos, Antonio, *Bass*, 1936–40
Banuelos, Jose, *Cello*, 1936–37, 1940–41
Barach, Daniel, *Viola*, 1954–55
Barbour, Arthur J. H., *Organ*, 1913–14
Barguy, Mr., *Horn*, 1931
Barnard, William, *Organ*, 1958–60*, 1960–68
Barnett, Clifton, *Trumpet*, 1931–32
Barney, Betty, *Violin*, 1948–50
Barnhill, Allen, *Trombone*, 1977–
Barone, Clement, *Flute* and *Piccolo*, 1948–59
Barozzi, Socrate, *Violin*, 1963–67
Bartlett, Dr. H. Leigh, *Violin*, 1931
Bartold, Gabriel, *Trumpet*, 1948–49
Barton, Charles, *Timpani*, 1931–32
Bates, Earl, *Clarinet*, 1947–48
Battista, Ned, *Trumpet*, 1965–83
Bauch, Arthur, *Viola*, 1949–51
Bay, Thomas, *Cello*, 1967–93
Baykash, Edward, *Violin*, 1957–69
Baz, Manuel Rivera, *Piano*, 1913
Beach, Myrtle W., *Violin*, 1951–52
Beach, Vance, *Cello*, 1949–52
Bean, David, *Trombone* and *Bass Trombone*, 1960**, 1961–66
Beard, Richard, *Horn*, 1943–44, 1947–48
Beck, Chris M., *Bass*, 1931–34, 1935–36
Beck, Eileen, *Harp*, 1933–34
Beck, Mrs. A. H., *Violin*, 1932–33
Becker, Zillah, *Violin*, 1931–32
Beckerman, Bernice, *Viola*, 1977–97
Behrendt, Robert, *Viola*, 1949–50
Behrle, L., *Violin*, 1944–45
Bekker, Yuriy, *Violin*, 2006*
Bellino, Frank, *Viola*, 1952–53
Benedetti, Italio, *Clarinet*, 1932–35, *Bass Clarinet*, 1937
Benner, Raymond, *Bass*, 1950–52
Bennett, Clyde, *Bassoon*, 1941–48
Bennett, George, *Violin*, 1953–81
Bennie, V., *Viola*, 1945–46
Bernhart, A., *Bass*, 1946–47
Beversdorf, Thomas, *Trombone*, 1946–48
Bhosys, Waldemar, *Oboe*, 1938–40
Birdwell, Edward, *Horn*, 1956–58**, 1961–62
Bizet, Yvonne, *Violin*, 1956–57
Black, William, *Bass*, 1956–87, 1988–99
Blackburn, Roger, *Trumpet*, 1973–74
Blech, L., *Horn*, 1944–46
Blinoff, N., *Viola*, 1942–43
Bloch, H., *Bass*, 1941–42
Block, Mrs. Sam V., *Violin*, 1931–32
Bobbe, Jerry, *Cello*, 1970–71
Boffa, Alexander, *Bass*, 1949–55, 1957–65
Boffa, Marcella Conforto, *Violin*, 1949–77
Bonacorso, Joseph, *Violin*, 1954–55
Bonney, Maurice, *Viola*, 1955–58

Boone, Bert D., *Trombone*, 1913–16, 1917–18
Borden, Nadine, *Cello*, 1946–48
Bossart, David, *Bassoon*, 1961–62
Boudreaux, Josephine, *Violin*, 1916–18, 1931–37
Bourne, Harry R., *Bass*, 1931–41, 1947–48, *Tuba*, 1932
Bourne, Marjorie A., *Harp*, 1937–40, 1941–44
Boxley, Katie, *Violin*, 1932–35
Boyle, David, *Cello*, 1976–78
Bradley, W. Scott, *Organ*, 1917–18
Bragers, Joseph, *Violin*, 1931–33
Bragg, Margaret, *Violin*, 1974–2013
Braun, Harry, *Violin*, 1948–49
Breaker, Lois, *Harp*, 1944–45
Breivogel, Jean, *Cello*, 1946–48
Bretschger, Fred, *Bass*, 1990–92
Bridges, Alfred, *Viola*, 1957–58
Briggs, Mary Agnes Johnson, *Timpani*, 1943–46, *Percussion*, 1949–51, 1956–61**
Briggs, Milton, *Horn*, 1949–60
Briscoe, D. L., *Violin*, 1940–41
Bristow, D. L., *Violin*, 1941–42
Brockstein, Irvin, *Percussion*, 1948–49
Brooks, Wayne, *Viola*, 1977–
Brourman, Jacques, *Violin*, 1954–56
Brown, M. J., *Violin*, 1940–42
Brown, Melissa Moore, *Cello*, 1957–58
Brown, N., *Harp*, 1941–43
Brown, Peter, *Cello*, 1957–58
Brown, Richard, *Percussion*, 1972–80
Brown, Robert, *Violin*, 1966–68
Brown, S., *Timpani*, 1942–43
Brubaker, David, *Violin*, 2001–03, 2013*
Brubaker, Marina, *Violin*, 1989–
Bruetting, Carl, *Horn*, 1947–48
Bruinsma, Frank, *Cello*, 1971–72
Bruno, J., *Horn*, 1943–44
Bruno, J. A., *Violin*, 1913–14
Brusilow, Nathan, *Clarinet*, 1948–54
Bryan, Mr., *Bassoon*, 1931
Buchanan, Caroline, *Viola*, 1962–64
Bucy, Paula, *Cello*, 1955–57
Budrow, Winston, *Bass*, 1974–77
Bures, Jan, *Horn*, 1967–75
Burger, Robert, *Bassoon*, 1948–53
Burke, Paul V., *Cello*, 1931–44
Burton, James, *Bassoon*, 1962–64
Butin, Wade, *Horn*, 2009–10*, 2010–11**, 2012–*
Butler, Jeffrey, *Cello*, 1986–
Buytendorp, E., *Bass*, 1945
Buytendorp, H. J., *Bass*, 1938–40, 1942–43, 1944–45
Bynum, Kyla, *Viola*, 1956–59, 1967–92
Caballero, William, *Horn*, 1985–89
Callahan, Margaret Bailey, *Violin*, 1944–48
Campbell, Douglas, *Horn*, 1983–84
Cancelosi, Robert, *Cello*, 1962–63
Caplan, Arnold, *Violin*, 1931–32
Carkeek, Lois, *Violin*, 1955–57
Carlton, Edith Lord, *Viola*, 1931–40, 1942–44
Carpenter, Iva, *Violin*, 1915–18, 1931–37
Carr, Norman, *Violin*, 1949–50
Carrel, N., *Clarinet*, 1937–41
Carroll, Edward, *Trumpet*, 1975–76
Carroll, Jack, *Trumpet*, 1931–34, 1935–36
Cassel, Ernest, *Violin*, 1948–65
Caughey, D. Walter, *Cello*, 1934–35
Caughey, W. Walter, *Viola*, 1934–35
Chabra, J., *Oboe* and *English Horn*, 1944–45
Chalmers, Shirley, *Clarinet*, 1943–45
Chandler, William, *Violin*, 1990–96
Chapin, Earl, *Horn*, 1950–52
Chapman, Martha, *Violin*, 1980–
Chapman, William, *Trombone*, 1959-60**
Charlton, Athelstan R., *Cello*, 1914–18, 1931–36, Librarian, 1917–18
Chase, Ben, *Viola*, 1948–49
Chaudhuri, Genevieve, *Cello*, 1957–61
Chausow, David, *Violin*, 1970–87

Chelpanov, Oleg, *Violin*, 2013–*
Cho, Hyunjin, *Cello*, 1968–85
Chuberk, Doris, *Violin*, 1953–56
Chung, Mi-Hee, *Violin*, 1981–
Ciccarelli, Anthony, *Clarinet*, 1949–54
Cichowicz, Vincent, *Trumpet*, 1944–45
Cima, C., *Horn*, 1916–18
Cinquemani, J., *Trumpet*, 1942–43
Clayton, Caroline, *Viola*, 1964–68
Clayton, Merle, *Cello*, 1960–62, 1963–68
Clinesmith, Benjamin, *Cello*, 1965–67
Clow, Irma Louise, *Harp*, 1936–38
Coffman, Lynn, *Violin*, 1960–66
Cohan, Carol, *Viola*, 1957–60
Cohen, Gilbert, *Trombone and Bass Trombone*, 1949–51
Colburn, Lois, *Cello*, 1943–45
Cole, Donald, *Cello*, 1948–50
Cole, Maisie, *Violin*, 1966–68
Collins, Ellis P., *Viola*, 1913–14, 1916–18
Collins, Margot, *Violin*, 1955–64
Collins, Richard, *Violin*, 1953–65, 1969–70
Colvig, David, *Flute*, 1948–85
Comanda, Enzo, *Violin*, 1964–66
Compean, Carlos, *Trumpet*, 1956–61**
Compean, Jose, *Viola*, 1945–48
Connell, Eugene, *Viola*, 1951–52
Connell, Winston, *Viola*, 1931, 1950–51
Connolly, Fred, *Violin*, 1933–37, 1938–39
Coomara, Rohini, *Cello*, 1969–70
Cooper, W. L., *Flute*, 1916–17
Copher, M., *Violin*, 1942–43
Corder, David, *Trumpet*, 1961–65
Corruccini, Rebecca, *Violin*, 2007–08
Corse, Joe, *English Horn*, 1935–36
Cowan, Harry, *Violin*, 1968–71
Craypo, Rian, *Bassoon*, 2007–
Creccotti, Peter, *Trumpet*, 1956–57
Croft, Mrs. L. R., *Violin*, 1935–36
Crouse, Wayne, *Viola*, 1951–83
Crouzet, Eugene, *Violin*, 1913–14
Csengery, Ronald, *Violin*, 1966–68
Cullens, H., *Viola*, 1939–40
Currier, N. Woodbury, *Bass*, 1938–42
Daigle, Martha, *Violin*, 1945–46
Dailey, A. H., *Violin*, 1914–17, 1931
Davies, Marion, *Cello*, 1948–63
Davis, Al A., *Trombone*, 1934–45, 1954
Davis, D., *Violin*, 1942, 1944–46
Davis, Dorothy, *Violin*, 1949–50, 1957–65
Davis, Paul S., *Horn*, 1933–35, 1936–41
Davis, Robert, *Trombone and Bass Trombone*, 1951–59
Davis, Shirley W., *Violin*, 1956–58
De Chaudron, Albert, *Violin*, 1915
De Fulvio, V., *Bass*, 1946–47
De Milita, Vincent, *Flute*, 1917–18, 1934–35
de Rudder, A., *Cello*, 1931
De Rudder, Henri, *Viola*, 1934–38
De Rudder, Mike, *Cello*, 1931–40
De Santis, Modesto, *Oboe and English Horn*, 1948–53
Dean, D., *Percussion*, 1942–43
Deck, Warren, *Tuba*, 1977–80
deGranda, Alvaro, *Violin*, 1960–61
DeGroote, Helen, *Violin*, 1958–59
DeGroote, Lucien, *Cello*, 1957–60
DeJon, Roe, *Viola*, 1935–36
Del Signore, Brian, *Percussion and Timpani*, 1988–
Denoff, Avrom J., *Violin*, 1954–55
Denton, James R., *Cello*, 1988–
Derden, Doris Musgrave, *Violin*, 1957–94
Derdeyn, Maurice L., *Violin and Viola*, 1913–17
DerHovsepian, Joan, *Viola*, 1999–
DeRudder, Louis, *Cello*, 1931–32, 1934–38, 1942–43, 1947–49, 1950–78
DeSantis, Mary, *Violin*, 1951–53
Desiato, James, *Oboe*, 1948–49
Deutsch, Robert, *Cello*, 1977–2007

Deviney, Christopher J., *Percussion*, 1998–2003
DeWitt, John, *Trumpet*, 1982–
DeWitt, Roger, *Oboe*, 1940–42
Di Vito, Michael, *Violin*, 1949–50
Diaz, Elena, *Violin*, 1959–91
Dickie, James, *Bassoon*, 1954–58
Diehl, Anton, *Violin*, 1913–18
Diehl, Eugene O., *Violin*, 1913–18
Diehl, Gabrielle "Soeurette," *Violin*, 1931–32
Diehl, William, *Horn*, 1913–14
Diliberto, Frank, *Bass*, 1965–66
Dines, Judy, *Flute*, 1992–
Dinitz, Adam, *English and Horn Oboe*, 2007–
Dixon, Newell, *Bass*, 1965–78, 1979–96
Dodge, Miss, *Harp*, 1931
Doolan, L., *Bass*, 1940–41
Dorfman, Herman, *Horn*, 1948–57
Dorough, Aralee, *Flute*, 1985–
Dorsett, C., *Violin*, 1944–47
Doyle, Catherine, *Violin*, 1931–36, Librarian, 1931–36
Draper, Barbara, *Cello*, 1951–52
Dregalla, Dorothy, *Harp*, 1945
Drescher, Cliff, *Flute and Piccolo*, 1931–40, 1943–48
Dror, Danny, *Violin*, 1965–69
Dudley, Michael, *Cello*, 1987–89*
Dulgerska, Assia, *Violin*, 2007–
Dunlap, Nettie Mae, *Violin*, 1932–33
Dunlay, W. H., *Viola*, 1913–14
Dvorak, Kevin, *Cello*, 1978–
Dybwad, Harold, *Oboe*, 1916–17
Dye, N., *Violin*, 1937–38
Dyer, Max, *Cello*, 1983–84
Dyson, G., *Trombone*, 1934–35
Eakin, Charles, *Bass*, 1950–52
Easton, Anitra, *Violin*, 1933–34
Easton, Thomas Gail, *Clarinet*, 1960–61**
Eberi, Carl, *Viola*, 1946–47
Edelen, Frederick, *Cello*, 1994–2004
Edley, Philip, *Bass*, 1949–73
Egilsson, Arni, *Bass*, 1965–69
Ehrenwerth, Gizella, *Violin*, 1949–50
Ehrhardt, Ernest, *Cello*, 1966–68
Elkin, Leo, *Violin*, 1956–61
Ellefsen, Walter, *Viola*, 1948–49
Elliott, Gretchen, *Cello*, 1968–69
Elliott, Thomas, *Viola*, 1968–76, 1986–2004
Elliott, Willard, *Bassoon and Contrabassoon*, 1946–49
Ellison, Paul, *Bass*, 1966–87
Elster, R., *Timpani*, 1942–43
Ermolenko, George, *Violin*, 1981–82
Erwin, E., *Trombone*, 1942–44
Erwin, W., *Viola*, 1943–45
Escalante, M. Rivera, *Violin*, 1913
Escott, Merlin, *Bass*, 1947–48
Estabrook, Ray, *Violin*, 1913–14, 1915–17
Etchison, Mr., *Oboe*, 1931
Evans, George N., *Flute*, 1913–18
Faget, Louis, *Cello*, 1936–37
Fagira, Leon, *Horn*, 1931–32
Fako, Nancy Jordan, *Horn*, 1963–64
Falconieri, Frank, *Bass*, 1949–51
Falk, D., *Violin*, 1940–41
Fantz, Lemonine, *Trombone*, 1956–59*
Farkas, Stefan, *Oboe and English Horn*, 2004–06
Farley, D., *Trombone*, 1935–36
Farmer, L., *Cello*, 1945–46
Fasshauer, Carl, *Cello*, 1949–51, 1962–67
Fawcett, Herbert, *Bassoon*, 1959–61
Fawcett, Patricia, *Flute and Piccolo*, 1959–61
Feldt, Eleanore, *Cello*, 1934–36, 1937–43
Fellows, F., *Violin*, 1937–43
Fellows, Naomi, *Violin*, 1940–48
Fenstermacher, Leroy, *Viola*, 1958–59
Ferguson, Robert, *Clarinet*, 1942–43, Bass Clarinet, 1946–48
Fields, Clyde, *Clarinet*, 1913–16
Fields, Dall, *Bassoon*, 1916–17
Figuiera, Leon, *Horn*, 1932–34

Filerman, Peter, *Viola*, 1966–75, 1976–81, Assistant Librarian, 1967–68, Librarian, 1968–74
Fineberg, Fraya, *Percussion*, 1967–97
Fink, Mrs. Sam, *Violin*, 1931–32, 1934–35
Finlay, Lloyd C., *Violin*, 1915–17
Fippinger, Gerald, *Horn*, 1953–61
Firak, John, *Viola*, 1950–53
Firzt, Joseph, *Violin*, 1951–52
Fischer, Jonathan, *Oboe*, 2012–
Fliegel, Raphael N., *Violin*, 1936–37, 1939–44, 1945–95
Forbes, V., *Violin*, 1943–44
Fradkin, Jules, *Viola*, 1961–66
Franchini, Anthony Joseph, *Violin*, 1945–46
Fransee, Gabriel D., *Violin*, 1931–32 and *Viola*, 1933–37
Fransee, W. F., *Viola*, 1931–37
Fraser, Barbara, *Violin*, 1956–61
Frederick, Michael, *Bassoon*, 1993–94
Freeman, Phillip, *Trombone and Bass Trombone*, 2007–
Freilich, Felix, *Violin*, 1954–55
French, Christopher, *Cello*, 1986–
Frey, Willy, *Violin*, 1951–54
Friszt, Joseph, *Violin*, 1952–53
Frusina, Mihaela, *Violin*, 1998–
Frye, Elizabeth, *Violin*, 1957–58
Fulgham, Henry, *Percussion*, 1956–72
Fuller, Angela, *Violin*, 2006–08
Furbay, Helen, *Violin*, 1951–57, 1961–72
Gaedecke, Charles W., *Trumpet*, 1915–16
Galindo, Julien M. "Julio", *Cello*, 1913–14
Gallo, Joseph, *Violin*, 1937–43, 1953–69
Galperin, Sergei, *Violin*, 1995–99, 2002–
Gans, I., *Viola*, 1941–42
Garcia, Gail, *Viola*, 1980–81
Garfield, Rebecca Powell, *Flute*, 2012–**, 2012–*, *Piccolo*, 2013–*
Garian, Paul, *Violin*, 1946–48
Garland, Timothy, *Violin*, 2000–05
Garrett, Carol, *Viola*, 1967–69
Garrett, David, *Cello*, 1989–2001
Gatwood, Colin, *Oboe*, 1991–
Gebhardt, Viola, *Violin*, 1931–32
Gelus, Edward, *Violin*, 1936–37
Geschmay, Peggy, *Violin*, 1965–68
Gest, Samuel, *Cello*, 1953–54
Geyer, Charles, *Trumpet*, 1978–81
Ghitalla, Armando, *Trumpet*, 1949–51
Giat, Sampson, *Oboe and English Horn*, 1955–57
Gibbs, Leonard, *Viola*, 1963–66
Gibson, Hugh, *Viola*, 1963–94
Gilbert, P., *Timpani*, 1938–41
Gilkey, V., *Violin*, 1942–43
Girko, Steve, *Clarinet*, 1974–75
Glassman, Frank, *Trombone*, 1944–48
Glier, Herman, *Bass*, 1931
Gold, Arthur, *Bass*, 1941–42
Goldberg, Harry, *Violin*, 1931–32
Goldblum, Edward M., *Oboe*, 1936–37
Golden, Joseph, *Horn*, 1948–51
Goldschmidt, Bernhard, *Violin*, 1956–58
Goldstein, Linda, *Viola*, 1981–
Goldstein, Louis C., *Violin*, 1931–36
Gonzalez, Henry, *Bass*, 1963–65
Gonzalez, Rodica, *Violin*, 1990–
Gonzalez, Ruben, *Violin*, 1980–87
Goodearl, Nancy, *Horn*, 1981–
Goodman, I., *Bass*, 1942–43
Gorguraki, Victor, *Violin*, 1954–68
Gorisch, Eunice, *Violin*, 1948–53, *Viola*, 1953–54
Gorisch, Stephen, *Cello*, 1948–49, 1954–76
Goshkowitz, Harry, *Violin*, 1950–51
Gottwald, John, *Bass*, 1931–42, 1943–49
Gould, A., *Bass*, 1942–43
Gould, Charles, *Bassoon*, 1972–75
Gower, W., *Horn*, 1945–46
Grace, J. G., *Violin*, 1931–32

Graham, Robin, *Horn*, 1976–77
Gray, F., *Trumpet*, 1942–43
Gray, J., *Trombone*, 1943–44
Green, Albert, *Viola*, 1950–57
Green, Donald, *Trumpet*, 1974–75
Green, Oliver, *Clarinet and Bass Clarinet*, 1951–56
Greenberg, Louis, *Oboe*, 1931–32, 1935–37
Gribanovsky, Dmitry, *Bass*, 1943–47
Griffin, Elsie, *Violin*, 1936–37
Griffin, Randall, *Clarinet*, 1990–91
Griffith, Mark, *Percussion*, 2004–
Grimwood, Lavanna, *Bass*, 1977–78
Grodner, Murray, *Bass*, 1948–51
Grossman, Ben, *Bass*, 1913–16, 1917–18, 1931–37
Grotsky, Paul, *Violin*, 1948–49
Grunbaum, M., *Violin*, 1939–42
Grymonpre, Richard, *Viola*, 1972–76
Guberman, Nathan I., *Violin*, 1931–37
Guderian, Mack, *Trumpet*, 1976–86
Guinn, Roy Neil, *Trombone and Bass Trombone*, 1959–61
Gundry, Roland, *Violin*, 1949–50
Gutierrez, Fred, *Violin*, 1931–41, 1945–48
Gutierrez, Jesus, *Bass*, 1913–18, 1931–40
Gutierrez, José, *Clarinet*, 1931–36
Gutierrez, José (Sr.), *Horn*, 1915, 1918
Gutierrez, Patricio, *Cello*, 1913–18, 1931–32, 1935–38; *Piano*, 1915; *Celesta and Organ*, 1936; *Horn*, 1932
Guttman, R., *Piano*, 1913–14
Haardt, O. H., Jr., *Violin*, 1932–35
Haenni, Verena, *Viola*, 1959
Hail, Ernest R., *Clarinet*, 1913–18
Haitto, Heimo, *Violin*, 1965–66
Halbouty, James J., *Violin*, 1937–38
Halen, David, *Violin*, 1984–92
Halen, Eric, *Violin*, 1986–
Hall, Don, *Violin*, 1957–58
Hall, H., *Violin*, 1937–38
Hall, Richard, *Bassoon*, 1964–93
Hall, William, *Trumpet*, 1956–60*
Haltmar, A., *Tuba*, 1915–18
Hammersley, Vera, *Bass*, 1944–45
Hanley, William, *Violin*, 1958–59
Hanselman, John, *Trombone*, 1959–60*
Hansen, Erling, *Flute and Piccolo*, 1963–67, Librarian, 1964–68
Harper, Kenneth, *Bass*, 1991–92*
Harris, Daniel, *Violin*, 1959–60
Harris, F., *Violin*, 1943–44
Harrison, Ernest, *Oboe*, 1946–48
Hart, Albert C., *Percussion*, 1915–16
Hart, Dorothy, *Violin*, 1947–48
Heck, August, *Horn*, 1936–37
Hedegus, L., *Viola*, 1939–40
Heim, Alyn, *Percussion*, 1952–53
Heine, W., *Trumpet*, 1943–44
Hendrix, Howard, *Clarinet*, 1957–60*
Heneger, Gregg, *Bassoon and Contrabassoon*, 1975–93
Henkel, E., *Violin*, 1937–38
Henkel, Joseph, *Violin*, 1937–48
Henkel, Olga King, *Violin*, 1938–49
Henniss, Bruce, *Horn*, 1995*, 1996–2007
Herdeman, Emily, *Violin*, 2011–12*
Herdliska, Phyllis, *Viola*, 1971–
Hernandez, Frank, *Viola*, 1936–46, *Violin* 1946–48, Librarian, 1943–44
Herrera, Eleanor Traverse, *Cello*, 2006–07*
Hershey, S. W., *Violin*, 1934–36
Hertog, Y., *Violin*, 1943–45
Hess, W. T., *Cello*, 1913–18
Hester, Barbara, *Oboe*, 1955–94
Hester, Byron, *Flute*, 1953–90
Hiller, Roger, *Clarinet*, 1956–59
Hinds, Artie Lee, *Violin*, 1948–49
Hinds, Mary Ann, *Percussion*, 1954–56
Hine, Joy, *Viola*, 1960–61
Hirsch, Albert, *Violin*, 1949–50
Hirsch, Rosetta, *Violin*, 1913–17
Hirsch, Stacy, *Violin*, 1983–89
Hlavaty, Henry F., *Violin*, 1931–40, 1946–49, 1950–53, *Viola*, 1940–42, 1945–46

Hlinka, Jan, *Viola*, 1941–42
Hodge, Leslie, *Piano*, 1935–36
Hoebig, Desmond, *Cello*, 1992–96, 2001–04
Hoeppner, Fred, *Cello*, 1948–49
Hoffman, Alice, *Viola*, 1946–48
Hoffmann, Robert C., *Violin*, 1956–57
Holdman, Ronald, *Timpani*, 1986–
Holland, Jack, *Horn*, 1957–58
Holloway, J. H., *Trumpet*, 1934–35
Holshouser, Scott, *Keyboard*, 1986–
Horner, Jerry, *Viola*, 1956–57, 1959–63
Hornstein, Max, *Violin*, 1937–38, 1940–42, 1943–46, *Viola*, 1942–43, 1946–48
Horrocks, James, *Horn*, 1966–67*, 1971–98
House, Leonard A., *Cello*, 1931–32
Howard, Miss, *Harp*, 1931
Howell, Ruth, *Violin*, 1931
Howey, Donald, *Bass*, 1999–
Howland, Nellie, *Harp*, 1931–36, *Percussion*, 1936
Hoxey, M., *Oboe*, 1917–18
Huang, Frank, *Violin*, 2011–13
Hughes, George, *Trombone*, 1913–18
Hughes, Gina, *Flute*, 2012–*
Hughes, Glenn, *Trombone*, 1959–60*
Hughes, Mark, *Trumpet*, 2006–
Humphries, J. M., *Timpani* and *Percussion*, 1931, 1933–35
Hurwitz, Mrs. Harry, *Violin*, 1934–35, 1936–37
Hussman, Arthur H., *Flute*, 1913–16, 1931–32
Hutson, Emily, *Viola*, 1931–34
Huttner, Maximilian, *Violin*, 1951–53
Hyde, Virginia, *Violin*, 1953–57
Ilku, Julius, *Bass*, 1954–55
Illenyi, Ferenc, *Violin*, 1991–
Illes, George, *Violin*, 1931–33
Illions, Seymour, *Viola*, 1953–56
Incognito, Paul J., *Violin*, 1917
Inouye, Mark, *Trumpet*, 2004*, 2005–06
Isaacson, I., *Bass*, 1943–44
Jakey, Lauren, *Violin*, 1959–60
Jakez, Carlos, *Oboe*, 1913–15
Jakubowicz, Alfred, *Violin*, 1950–52
Janeba, Kathleen, *Harp*, 1958–60**
Jassel, Gregor, *Violin*, 1931–32,1934–35, 1936–40, 1941–42, 1943–50
Jelagin, Juri, *Violin*, 1948–65
Jelagin Harrin, Vera, *Violin*, 1948–90
Jenkins, Marian, *Violin*, 1913–15
Jett, David, *Trombone*, 1948–49
Jewett, Allison Garza, *Flute* and *Piccolo*, 2006–07*, 2007–
Jiang, Quan, *Violin*, 2004–11*
Jiang, Wei, *Viola*, 1999–
Joh, Kiju, *Violin*, 2007–
Johnson, Helen, *Violin*, 1932–33
Johnson, Kurt, *Violin*, 2001*, 2002–
Johnson, Lisa, *Violin*, 1982–84
Johnson, Robert, *Horn*, 2012–*
Johnson, Thruston, *Violin*, 1955–56
Johnston, James, *Bass*, 1934–35
Jones, B., *Harp*, 1938–41
Jones, Frank C., Jr., *Violin*, 1935–38
Jones, L. C., *Violin*, 1940–42
Jones, Mrs. R. B., *Violin*, 1933–34
Jones, Robert, *Viola*, 1962–63
Jones, Robert, *Organ*, 1969–76**
Joseph, Charles, *Violin*, 1950–51
Ju, Haeri, *Cello*, 2007–
Jungling, A., *Cello*, 1931–33
Kadz, Robert, *Cello*, 1963–65
Kahila, Frances Albertin, *Bassoon*, 1936–44
Kahila, Kauko, *Trombone*, 1941–44
Kainz, A., *Horn*, 1942–43
Kalesnykaite, Rasa, *Violin*, 2006–07*
Kamins, Benjamin, *Bassoon*, 1981–2004
Kaplan, Sidney, *Violin*, 1931, 1934–35
Karcher, Joseph R., *Violin*, 1935–49, 1960–66
Karon, Jan, *Violin*, 1968–84
Kashy, Jean-Louis, *Flute* and *Piccolo*, 1961–63
Kauffman, Amy, *Violin*, 1999–2000
Kaufman, Zelik, *Violin*, 1948–49
Kaza, Roger, *Horn*, 1995*, 1996–2010

Kearns, Frank W., *Viola*, 1931–35
Kec, Vaclav, *Viola*, 1944–45
Keightley, Patricia John, *Harp*, 1955–56*
Keller, Grace, *Viola*, 1917–18, 1931–37
Kelly, Kevin, *Violin*, 1977–
Kelly, Kristen, *Violin*, 1992-94, 1995-97, 1999-2001
Kelser, John, *English Horn*, 1931–36, *Oboe*, 1932, 1934
Kendall, Odin M., *Viola*, 1913–18
Kepner, Paul Rubenstein, *Flute*, 1936–48
Kerker, Joachim, *Violin*, 1949–51
Kerns, Frank W., *Viola*, 1932–33
Kessler, E., *Horn*, 1941–42
Key, C., *Horn*, 1946–47
Kierstead, Karin, *Violin*, 1971–77
Kimmes, Jane, *Violin*, 1989–94*
King, Bonnie, *Cello*, 1970–76
King, Mr., *Oboe*, 1931
Kirk, David, *Tuba*, 1982–
Kirkham, Dr. H. L. D., *Violin*, 1931–37
Kirmse, Leona, *Violin*, 1931–33
Kishkis, Alfred, *Bass*, 1951–52
Kitai, Anthony, *Cello*, 2000–01*, 2001–
Klapper, Jeremy, *Violin*, 1989–94
Klingbeil, Bruce, *Cello*, 1961–62
Klingelhoffer, William, *Horn*, 1978–80
Klinkon, Ervin, *Cello*, 1958–61
Knapp, Marjorie, *Violin*, 1949–52
Knaus, J., *Trombone*, 1942–43
Knox, T., *Trombone*, 1942–43
Knutsen, K., *Cello*, 1946–47
Koch, David, *Bass*, 1969–70
Kolda, Marjorie Rutz, *Horn*, 1942–44
Kopp, M., *Cello*, 1944–45
Kornacher, Thomas, *Violin*, 1963–64
Koster, Elizabeth, *Viola*, 1959–61
Kovac, J., *Bass*, 1944–46
Krasnoff, Norton, *Trumpet*, 1951–55
Krasow, Bernard, *Viola*, 1946–49
Kraus, Felix, *Oboe*, 1949–50
Krohn, Roderick, *Violin*, 1950–51
Kubitschek, F., *Horn*, 1945–46
Kuhnel, Ernest E., *Trombone*, 1913–14, 1915–18, 1931–34
Kunin, Inessa, *Violin*, 1982–94
Kushleika, Vithold, *Viola*, 1936–41
Kushner, W., *Clarinet*, 1942–43
Lainhart, John C., *Violin*, 1934–35
Laitenen, Leonard, *Viola*, 1946–48
Lakits, E. J., *Oboe*, 1932–35
Lambert, Lawrence, *Trumpet*, 1937–42, 1946–54, 1956–57
LaMonaca, Caesar, Jr., *Horn*, 1953–75
LaMonaca, Mary Critelli, *Violin*, 1966–76
Landsman, Julie, *Horn*, 1982–85
Langone, Inga Mark, *Violin*, 1962–63
Lantz, Harry, *Cello*, 1948–51
Lao, Si-Yang, *Violin*, 1998–
Larson, Eric, *Bass*, 1999–
Latiolais, Margery, *Bass*, 1952–56
Laughton, Kirk, *Horn*, 1980–81
Lazzaro, Vincent, *Trombone*, 1951–55
LeBaron, B., *Cello*, 1938–41
Ledwith, Austin, *Bassoon*, 1936–40
Lee, Hitai, *Violin*, 1985–
Lee, Mary Elizabeth, *Piano* and *Celesta*, 1970–76
Lee, Myung Soon, *Cello*, 1976–
Lee, Owen, *Bass*, 1994–96
Lee, Soon-Ik, *Violin*, 1978–80
Leek, Anne, *Oboe*, 1993–
Leeker, A., *Violin*, 1943–44
Leff, Benjamin, *Violin*, 1934–36
LeGrand,Thomas, *Clarinet*, 1986–
Leguia, Luis G., *Cello*, 1958–59
Lera, T., *Violin*, 1937–38
Lerner, Jeffrey, *Clarinet*, 1952–56, 1957–59*, 1959–67
Leverett, S., *Violin*, 1942–43
Levinson, David, *Cello*, 1941–42
Levitt, Harry, *Violin*, 1932–35
Lewin, Daniel, *Violin*, 1987–88
Lewis, H., *Violin*, 1943–44
Lewis, Morton, *Bass Clarinet*, 1957–59
Liese, Ralph, *Trombone*, 1948–72
Lippel, Henri, *Cello*, 1942–43
Lippman, S., *Violin*, 1918

Liu, Xiaodi, *Oboe*, 2011–12*
Lockwood, Hilton, *Viola*, 1949–56
Lombardi, Louis, *Violin*, 1948–49
Longnecker, Gloria, *Percussion*, 1956–57*
Lube, Albert, *Trombone*, 1940–41, 1945–51, 1955–77
Lube, Joe, *Trumpet*, 1934–37, *Xylophone*, 1934
Ludwig, Sarah, *Violin*, 2011–12*
Lugaro, Arturo, *Bass*, 1913–15
Lukatsky, Joseph, *Oboe*, 1937–38
Lunden, Alice, *Bass*, 1948–49
Lyon, Peggy, *Flute*, 1959–60*
Lyon, R., *Violin*, 1946–47
Lytle, Hub, *Bassoon*, 1931–32
MacBlain, Charles, *Violin*, 1917–18
Macchiaroli, Roger, *Bass*, 1961–63
MacDonald, A. L., *Cello*, 1939–41
MacDonald, G. C., *Cello*, 1939–41
Macelaru, Cristian, *Violin*, 2005–06*
Macias, Juan, *Cello*, 1938–39
MacLane, J., *Cello*, 1944–45
MacLennan, Mrs. R. G., *Cello*, 1931–38
Magill, Samuel, *Cello*, 1980–86
Maguire, Jean, *Cello*, 1949–51
Mahr, Barbara, *Cello*, 1959–62
Mainzer, Joan, *Harp*, 1951–53
Malone, David, *Bass*, 1978–
Mamlock, Theodore, *Violin*, 1970–71
Mann, A., *Violin*, 1941–42
Manno, Leonard, *Bass*, 1936–45, 1947–49, 1958–77
Mansfield, Newton, *Violin*, 1948–49
Marcus, Morris, *Violin*, 1948–49
Marcuse, Walter, *Trumpet*, 1941–42
Mark, Inga, *Violin*, 1956–57
Marsh, E., *Flute*, 1943–44
Marsh, Robert E., *Horn*, 1952–53
Marshall, D., *Viola*, 1945–46
Marshall, David, *Violin*, 1977–82
Marten, James H., *Bassoon*, 1915–18, *Librarian*, 1915–17
Martin, Gwendolyn, *Violin*, 1958–60
Martin, Leslie, *Cello*, 1933–45, 1946–48
Martin, Tony, *Percussion*, 1947–48
Martini, Mr., *Bass Clarinet*, 1931
Martinson, Roy, *Cello*, 1950–56
Masters, Jacqueline, *Violin*, 1963–65
Mathews, John, *Bass*, 1949–50
Mathwig, Leroy, *Violin*, 1965–66
Matthews, Billye J., *Flute*, 1956–58*
Matthews, M., *Harp*, 1945–46
Maxman, George, *Violin*, 1983–87
Mayfield, Lynette, *Flute*, 1973–92
Maynard, Betty, *Harp*, 1946–48
Mays, R., *Trombone*, 1945–46
Mazzari, Fred, *Cello*, 1969–78
McAndrew, Josephine Citron, *Violin*, 1971–90
McCollum, C., *Violin*, 1942–43
McCormick, Jeanette, *Horn*, 1942–44
McCracken, Emma Jo, *Violin*, 1949–50
McCracken, Patricia, *Harp*, 1956–58, 1958–59*
McCrorey, Donald, *Violin*, 1964–71
McCroskey, John, *Trombone*, 1972–99
McCulley, Edamay, *Violin*, 1948–49
McDaniel, Prudence, *Cello*, 1989–90
McIlwain, Glen, *Flute*, 1948–49
McIntyre, C., *Violin*, 1942–43
McIntyre, Mary Shelley, *Violin*, 1943–53, 1954–78
McIntyre, Richard R., *Cello*, 1933–35, 1946–47
McIntyre, Verna, *Violin*, 1942–48, 1954–57, 1962–75
McKinney, Bruel, *Oboe*, 1943–45
McLaughlin, H., *Percussion*, 1943–44
McMillan, Steven, *Violin*, 1980–81
McMurray, Michael, *Bass*, 1980–, *Assistant Librarian*, 1981–
McNelly, Nancy, *Cello*, 1961–62
Mei, Ni, *Violin*, 2005–06*
Mendelsohn, Leon, *Horn*, 1948–49
Mercado, Rodney, *Violin*, 1948–49
Meyers, Cynthia, *Flute* and *Piccolo*, 1997–2006
Michaux, E., *Horn*, 1916
Mikulski, Charles, *Violin*, 1967–68

Miller, Dennis, *Tuba*, 1980–81
Miller, Doris, *Viola*, 1945–48
Miller, F. H., *Violin*, 1913–14, 1917–18
Miller, Frances, *Violin*, 1936–37
Miller, Gilbert, *Clarinet*, 1948–49
Miller, H., *Viola*, 1943–46
Miller, L. L., *Bassoon*, 1931, *Bass Clarinet*, 1937–43
Miller, Otto, *Cello*, 1914–15, 1916–18
Miller, W., *Bass*, 1945–46
Mills, Fred, *Trumpet*, 1958–61
Miner, D. Frank, *Bass*, 1932–33, 1934–37
Miner, Janice, *Oboe* and *English Horn*, 1963–65
Ming, Qi, *Violin*, 1995–
Mintz, J. H., *Violin*, 1932–33
Mirrow, Seymour, *Violin*, 1956–58, 1959–62
Mobley, F., *Violin*, 1915–17
Molfino, Colleen, *Harp*, 1960–61*
Molfino, Gaetano, *Viola*, 1948–53, 1954–55
Molloy, Thomas, *Viola*, 1964–67, 1968–, *Assistant Librarian*, 1971–, –75
Monarch, Patricia, *Bassoon*, 1944–47
Moncada, Violeta, *Viola*, 1956–92
Montague, W. S., *Cello*, 1932–37
Montlack, Sol, *Viola*, 1941–42
Moore, David Allen, *Bass*, 1996–99
Moore, Mr., *Violin*, 1931
Moore, Ray E., *Bass*, 1942–56, *Librarian*, 1943–67, *Assistant Librarian*, 1964–66, *Curator*, 1967–72
Moran, Deborah, *Violin*, 1983–2010
Morgan, Charles R., *Bassoon*, 1931–32
Mori, Elmer, *Bass*, 1954–55
Morris, Farrell, *Percussion*, 1960–61*
Morrison, Bruce N., *Oboe* and *English Horn*, 1960–62
Morrow, B., *Trumpet*, 1940–41
Moscovitz, Shaler, *Viola*, 1964–70
Moses, Miss, *Violin*, 1931
Mosler, Leo, *Percussion*, 1948–51
Mosny, Elizabeth, *Violin*, 1961–82
Motto, L., *Cello*, 1937–46
Moyes, Dorothy, *Cello*, 1947–87
Moyes, John, *Horn*, 1946–66
Mucci, Victor, *Violin*, 1948–49
Mueller, F., *Oboe*, 1916–17
Mueller, Frederick, *Bassoon*, 1956–57*
Mueller, R., *Violin*, 1944–45
Muenzer, Albert, *Violin*, 1966–77
Muniz, I., *Violin*, 1936–37
Murphy, R., *Violin*, 1943–44
Musiol, Adolph, *Viola*, 1959–60
Muzyk, Jacek, *Horn*, 2011–12
Nassy, James, *Violin*, 1953–54
Neal, Christopher, *Violin*, 2001–
Neal, Vera Fransee, *Violin*, 1931–33, 1936–48
Neidlinger, Buell, *Bass*, 1962–64
Nelligan, George, *Cello*, 1932–35
Nelson, George E., *Viola*, 1932–33
Nelson, Walter P., *Horn*, 1931–42
Newell, Louise Payler, *Viola*, 1958–63
Newell, Thomas E., Jr., *Horn*, 1957–63
Nigrine, Henry, *Viola*, 1953–55
Nikiforoff, Vladimir A., *Timpani*, 1931–35, *Percussion*, 1936–42, 1943–46
Nolan, Roberta, *Violin*, 1965–66
Norris, Mary, *Violin*, 1933–35
Northrup, J. W., Jr., *Violin*, 1931–33
Norton, Doris C., *Violin*, 1956–57
Novak, Lyuba, *Cello*, 1956–57
Novotny, Joseph, *Tuba*, 1948–49
Noyes, Martha, *Cello*, 1958–59
Nunemaker, Richard, *Clarinet, Bass Clarinet* and *Saxophone*, 1967–
Oatman, Ole, *Bass*, 1936–37
O'Bannon, Everett, *Violin*, 1957–58
Obregon, Elena, *Viola*, 1961–63
O'Brien, Donald, *Clarinet*, 1962–63
Ochsenschlager, Barbra, *Bass*, 1946–48
O'Connor, Leslie, *Percussion*, 1916
O'Donnell, J. H., *Trombone*, 1931–32

Ognibene, Vincent, *Violin*, 1960–61
O'Hare, Kerry, *Viola*, 1992–98
Oliveira, John, *Violin*, 1969–90
Olsen, Vera, *Bass*, 1945–47
Oman, Paul, *Trumpet*, 1959–60
Orazi, Ennio, *Cello*, 1954–55
Orloff, Basil, *Violin*, 1966–69
Orzechowski, H., *Bass*, 1942–43
Osborne, Tommy, *Trumpet*, 1931–32
Ossewaarde, Jack H., *Organ*, 1957–58*
Owen, Jennifer, *Violin*, 1999–
Pacetti, Beatrice, *Violin*, 1931–32
Paderewski, Joseph, *Cello*, 1951–56
Pae, Carol, *Viola*, 1956–57
Page, Paula, *Harp*, 1984–2013
Paglia, Mario, *Violin*, 1967–81
Palasota, Pete, *Oboe*, 1941–43
Paquay, E., *Horn*, 1932–33, 1934–36
Parcher, Mr., *Trumpet*, 1931
Parker, Gaines, *Viola*, 1940–42, 1947–51, *Violin*, 1946–47
Parker, Stephenson, *Cello*, 1949–50
Parker, T., *Viola*, 1943–44
Parquay, A., *Horn*, 1931–32
Pascal, George, *Viola*, 1989–
Pasenhofer, Arlo, *Violin*, 1938–41
Pastorek, Christine Louis, *Violin*, 1969–
Pastorek, Robert, *Bass*, 1964–
Patrick, William R., *Violin*, 1913–18, 1931–34, 1935–43
Patterson, Ronald, *Violin*, 1972–80
Paul, S. J., *Trumpet*, 1913–18
Pazemis, Ann, *Oboe*, 1943–44
Peccoraro, Anthony, *Flute*, 1917–18
Pecha, Emory, *English Horn* and *Oboe*, 1941–42
Peck, Clifford C., *Violin*, 1914–17
Peck, David, *Clarinet*, 1975–86, 1991–2013
Pelizzari, J., *Clarinet*, 1946–47
Perry, Louis, *Violin*, 1931–32
Perry, Robert, *Violin*, 1958–82
Perry, Roy E., *Tuba*, 1931, 1932–48
Person, Sheldon, *Viola*, 2011–
Peterson, V., *Oboe*, 1945–46
Pfister, Ralph, *Violin*, 1950–52
Pharris, David, *Clarinet*, 2013–*
Pianka, Uri, *Violin*, 1987–2005
Pickar, Richard, *Clarinet*, 1959–60
Pickthorne, E., *English Horn*, 1932
Picthorn, J. D., *English Horn*, 1931–32
Pierson, Karen, *Bassoon*, 1994–2008
Piller, D. H., *Bassoon*, 1917–18
Pimbert, Octave, *Violin*, 1931
Pitman, Wanda Lou, *Trumpet*, 1943–46
Piton, C., *Horn*, 1917
Pitts, Timothy, *Bass*, 1993–2009
Platt, R., *Trombone*, 1942–43
Pledge, Genevieve, *Violin*, 1931–35, 1936–45
Plesner, Joy, *Viola*, 1961–2004
Plummer, Carolyn, *Violin*, 1974–86
Poepping, Noel, *Bassoon* and *Contrabassoon*, 1935–36
Polak, C., *Viola*, 1944–45
Pollitt, Walter, *Piano*, 1916–17
Popkin, Mark, *Bassoon*, 1950–51
Porfiris, Rita, *Viola*, 1995–2010
Posman, L., *Bassoon*, 1940–41
Potiomkin, Alexander, *Clarinet* and *Bass Clarinet*, 2011–12**, 2012–
Poulos, Helen, *Violin*, 1959–63
Powell, Mrs. Nettie Mae, *Violin*, 1931
Powers, W., *Horn*, 1944–45
Pozner, J., *Violin*, 1944–45
Pricer, L. J., *Viola*, 1932–33
Prisk, Anthony, *Trumpet*, 2002–
Pu, William, *Violin*, 1990*, 1991–2002
Pullman, M., *Flute*, 1944–45
Pursch, C. L., *Viola*, 1916–18, 1931
Qi, Ming, *Violin*, 1993–96
Querfurth, Rudolph, *Viola*, 1949–50
Radley, Joan, *Cello*, 1962–64
Raffaelli, Gino, *Violin*, 1954–57
Ragnon, Raymond, *Cello*, 1916–17
Ralske, Eric, *Horn*, 1987*, 1988–94
Ralyea, H., *Viola*, 1937–38
Randel, V., *Violin*, 1939–40
Randolph, William H., Jr., *Clarinet*, 1956–62

Rantucci, Claudia, *Violin*, 1964–66
Rasoplo, E., *Violin*, 1934–35
Ray, Willard, *Cello*, 1956–58
Raykhtsaum, Aza, *Violin*, 1980–84
Ready, William, *Violin*, 1933–34
Rees, Dana, *Cello*, 1967–69
Reid, Kittrell, *Trumpet*, 1935–42, 1943–44, 1945–53, 1954–66
Reines, Nat, *Bassoon*, 1953–54
Remington, Alan, *Bassoon*, 1954–57
Remington, Janet, *Harp*, 1948–51
Renzulli, Arthur, *Bass*, 1952–54
Ribitsch, Frank, *Piccolo* and *Flute*, 1942–44
Ricci, Joseph, *Horn*, 1916–17
Rice, Richard, *Viola*, 1950–52
Rice, Robert H., *Clarinet*, 1931, *Bass Clarinet*, 1931–33
Richardson, James R., *Clarinet*, 1914–17
Richter, Eckhardt, *Cello*, 1954–55
Rigby, Helen, *Oboe*, 1936–38
Ring, Alden, *Cello*, 1962–69
Rinkoff, S., *Violin*, 1931–32
Risley, C. G., *Trumpet*, 1931–40
Rittner, Charles, *Bass*, 1913–14, 1915–18
Rizzo, Joseph, *Oboe*, 1942–43
Robbins, H. H., *Trumpet*, 1932–34, 1935–36
Robbins, John, *Trombone*, 1959–60*
Robbins, Mrs. Evelyn E., *Violin*, 1931–35
Roberts, Betty, *Viola*, 1931–35
Roberts, Louis, *Cello*, 1980–81
Robins, Miss, *Violin*, 1931
Robinson, Dorothe, *Violin*, 1956–93
Robinson, Harold, *Bass*, 1977–85
Robinson, J. Jeff, *Bassoon* and *Contrabassoon*, 1993–
Robinson, Keith, *Bass*, 1948–75
Robinson, Sharon, *Cello*, 1972–73
Roehl, Elmer, *Bassoon*, 1935–36
Roman, Franz, *Oboe*, 1913–15, *Clarinet*, 1931, 1933–34, 1935–37
Romick, H., *Violin*, 1934–35
Romick, J., *Viola*, 1937–38
Roos, Phillip, *Violin*, 1913–17, 1933–36
Rose, Beatrice Schroeder, *Harp*, 1953–84
Rose, William, *Tuba*, 1949–77
Rosenblatt, Louis, *Oboe* and *English Horn*, 1954–55
Rosenzweig, Hyman, *Violin*, 1931–34
Roth, W., *Viola*, 1944–46
Rouleau, J., *Violin*, 1945–46
Routt, Julia Jack, *Violin*, 1931–37
Rower, Walter, *Cello*, 1951–54
Rubenstein, Jaques, *Violin*, 1936–37
Rubin, Betty, *Violin*, 1963–65
Runyan, Hal, *Cello*, 1943–49, Assistant Librarian, 1946–47
Rupert, Leslie D., *Horn*, 1938–42
Russ, W. K., *Trombone*, 1931–32
Russell, Miss, *Violin*, 1931
Russell, Mrs. W. L., *Violin*, 1931–40
Russell, Stella, *Violin*, 1940–48
Russo, Anthony, *Clarinet* 1917–18, 1931–33, 1935–37, 1939–48, *Bassoon*, 1917
Ruttenberg, Louis, *Oboe*, 1968–91
Ruttenberg, Margaret, *Violin*, 1972–95
Rutz, H., *Violin*, 1933–34
Ruzek, Donald, *Bassoon*, 1951–52
Ryba, Mr., *Cello*, 1931
Ryman, Mr., *Violin*, 1931
Saam, Frank, *Violin*, 1950–51
Sacchi, Leo, *Horn*, 1964–82
Sachs, Michael, *Trumpet*, 1986–88
Saft, Arthur, *Violin*, 1913–14
Saibel, Maxwell, *Horn*, 1938–43
Saltzman, Sidney, *Bass Clarinet* and *Clarinet*, 1948–51
Sanchez, E., *Flute*, 1916–17, 1937–38
Sanders, Eugene, *Violin*, 1913–14
Sandrock, D., *Cello*, 1944–46
Sanner, B., *Viola*, 1944–45
Sarsky, B., *Violin*, 1941–42
Sauer, C. Edward, *Violin*, 1914–15, 1931–48
Saunders, E. D., *Violin*, 1913–18
Saunders, Joseph, *Cello*, 1969–70

Sawyer, John F. "Del", *Trumpet*, 1957–59
Sazer, Victor, *Cello*, 1948–50
Scavelli, Ramon, *Viola*, 1955–58
Schadeberg, Theodore, *Violin*, 1933–35
Schaeffer, Naomi, *Viola*, 1946–48
Schaffer, Richard, *Trumpet*, 1967–2001
Scheer, Wilma, *Violin*, 1932–33
Schellhase, Elizabeth, *Horn*, 2008–09*
Schenk, R., *Viola*, 1943, *Violin*, 1944
Schlamme, Marie, *Violin*, 1939–48
Schlegel, L., *Viola*, 1938–39
Schmidt, Harry, *Violin*, 1932–34
Schmit, E. E., *Piccolo* and *Flute*, 1931–43
Schmitt, James, *Horn*, 1953–57
Schoen, Curt, *Bassoon*, 1931, 1932–36
Schoettle, Elmer, *Piano*, 1960–63*
Schramm, Mrs. Harold, *Violin*, 1917–18
Schubert, Christian, *Clarinet*, 1996–
Schults, Clarice, *Violin*, 1934–35
Schultz, Herbert, *Clarinet*, 1948–49
Schulze, Ralph, *Bassoon* and *Contrabassoon*, 1949–72
Schuster, D., *Oboe*, 1916
Scott, Alan, *Cello*, 1956–59
Seale, T., *Trombone*, 1938–42
Seaver, Cedric, *Viola*, 1932–35
Seibert, Charles, *Percussion*, 1916–17
Seidler, W., *Violin*, 1938–43
Selders, Dr. Raymond E., *Flute*, 1931–33
Seletsky, Harold, *Clarinet*, 1955–56
Settanni, Eugene, *Violin*, 1968–80
Seykora, Frederick, *Cello*, 1959–60
Shachner, H., *Bass*, 1941–42
Shadeberg, T., *Violin*, 1933
Shaffer, Elaine, *Flute*, 1948–53
Shand, Sherman, *Viola*, 1969–72
Shapiro, Fay Barkley, *Viola*, 1981–
Shapiro, Mark, *Bass*, 1983–
Sharp, T., *Trumpet*, 1941–43
Shaw, Burke, *Bass*, 2000–
Shaw, Conway R., *Violin*, 1913–14, 1931–33
Shaw, Ted, *Clarinet*, 1931–32
Sher, Allen, *Cello*, 1951–54
Shideler, C., *Cello*, 1945–46
Shideler, H., *Violin*, 1944–45
Shiragami, Sae, *Violin*, 1996–99
Shook-Cleghorn, Barbara, *Violin*, 1966–96
Shoop, Betty, *Viola*, 1948–49
Shoss, Herman, *Violin*, 1931–39
Sigel, Joanne, *Violin*, 1949–50
Sigerson, S., *Horn*, 1932
Sijersen, Sijer, *Horn*, 1932–37
Silber, E., *Viola*, 1940–41
Silivos, Sophia, *Violin*, 1994–
Silverman, Arthur, *Viola*, 1954–56
Silversteen, Rosemary, *Violin*, 1971–73
Silverstein, Joseph H., *Violin*, 1949–53
Simon, James, *Percussion*, 1951–86
Simon, Nancy Heaton, *Violin*, 1953–62
Simon, Sebastian, *Cello*, 1941–42
Simonsen, Johan, *Violin*, 1950–74
Skavenna, Alexander, *Viola*, 1934–35
Sklar, Martin, *Bass*, 1962–65
Skoldberg, Phyllis, *Violin*, 1957–59
Skovron, Stanley, *Viola*, 1948–50
Slater, M. W., *Piano*, 1913–15
Slaughter, Robert, *Viola*, 1955–56
Sloan, K. Bert, *Celesta*, 1948–51*, 1956–64*
Slocomb, Carol Robertson, *Flute* and *Piccolo*, 1968–96
Slocomb, Donald G., *Clarinet* and *E-Flat Clarinet*, 1959–60*, 1963–96
Smedvig, Rolf, *Trumpet*, 1977–78
Smiley, S., *Violin*, 1942–43
Smith, Albert, *Violin*, 1945–48
Smith, Betty, *Violin*, 1946–48
Smith, Brinton Averil, *Cello*, 2005–
Smith, Emil F., *Horn*, 1913–15, 1917–18
Smith, Harold, *Bass*, 1954–59

Smith, Lee R., *Violin*, 1913–18, Librarian, 1917
Smith, Mrs. L. R., *Harp*, 1916
Smith, Paul, *Violin*, 1931
Snider, Phillip, *Tuba*, 1981–82
Snyder, A. W., *Percussion*, 1933–35, *Celesta*, 1934
Snyder, Lloyd, *Horn*, 1946–48
Sobel, L., *Violin*, 1934–35
Sollner, Fred, *Bass*, 1947–48
Southerland, Henry, *Viola*, 1939–44
Sozinova, Olga, *Violin*, 1991–94
Spiga, Carlo, *Violin*, 1965–66
Stafford, Mrs. W.A., *Viola*, 1936–37
Stalarow, H. S., *Violin*, 1932–35
Stanley, Joan Harter, *Violin*, 1961–80
Stanton, Philip, *Horn*, 1975–83, 1984–2012
Steel, M., *Cello*, 1941–44
Steensrud, Eric, *Viola*, 1961–66
Steer, B., *Violin*, 1945–46
Steer, D., *Viola*, 1945–46
Stehn, Leonard, *Cello*, 1962–63
Steinfeldt, Benjamin J., *Violin*, 1913–15, 1916–17
Stephenson, Betty, *Violin*, 1968–87, 1988–95
Stephenson, James, *Violin*, 1968–95
Stetler, Charles, *Violin*, 1934–36, 1937–38
Stevens, Ralph, *Cello*, 1931
Stewart, Jane, *Violin*, 1981–82
Stokes, Elmore Ewing, *Percussion*, 1913–17, 1932–56
Stokes, J. S., *Horn*, 1916
Stone, Robert, *Bass*, 1948–49
Stonefelt, Al, *Trumpet*, 1966–67
Storch, Laila, *Oboe*, 1948–55
Strauss, Matthew, *Percussion*, 2004–
Strba, Daniel, *Viola*, 1992–
Stroh, Edward, *Violin*, 1948–49
Stroikoff, Vladimir, *Cello*, 1932–34
Strong, Donald, *Horn*, 1956–59*
Stuart, Robert, *Clarinet*, 1937–42
Stuchberry, G., *Trumpet*, 1942–43, 1945
Sullivan, John, *Trumpet*, 1934–41, 1945–46, 1947–50
Summers, Richard, *Oboe* and *English Horn*, 1953–54
Sutherland, Maxine, *Bassoon*, 1957–59
Svahn, Gustav, *Horn*, 1913–16, 1917–18
Swain, James, *Cello*, 1963–66
Swanson, Howard, *Violin*, 1952–56
Tabony, Charles, *Violin*, 1977–2012
Tally, Charlotte, *Violin*, 1931–35, 1936–38
Talmage, Bernard, *Flute*, 1932–34
Tankersley, James, *Horn*, 1957–77
Tanner, H., *Bass*, 1945–46, 1953–54
Taylor, Helen, *Oboe* and *English Horn*, 1965–67
Taylor, Thomas, *Horn*, 1950–53
Teare, Amy, *Violin*, 1981–
Tedeschi, F., *Trombone*, 1917–18
Tetzlaff, Daniel, *Trumpet*, 1946–48
Tetzlaff, Jane, *Cello*, 1945–48
Thal, Max, *Viola*, 1946–48
Thayer, Henry George, *Violin*, 1914–18, 1932–36
Thayer, Julie, *Horn*, 2009–12
Thomas, E., *Violin*, 1944–45
Thomas, Brian, *Horn*, 1995–
Thompson, C. V., *Flute*, 1931–33, 1934–37
Thompson, Larry, *Oboe* and *English Horn*, 1967–2003
Thorne, John, *Flute*, 1992–2013
Thorp, V., *Violin*, 1942–44
To, Yan, *Violin*, 1989–99
Tobey, Joseph, *Cello*, 1952–53
Tobin, Bernice, *Cello*, 1943–45
Tomforde, Mrs. Albert, *Violin*, 1934–35
Topolsky, Marvin, *Bass*, 1955–56
Torres, Albino, *Viola* and *Piano*, 1935–36, *Piano*, 1947–49, *Celesta*, 1947–48
Toth, Andor, *Violin*, 1949–55
Toth, Deborah, *Cello*, 1981–86
Tracht, Myron Edward, *Bassoon*, 1948–50

Tracy, Grace Sarvis, *Oboe* and *English Horn*, 1957–60
Trainovitch, John, *Violin*, 1946–48
Trautwein, Isabel, *Violin*, 1996–98
Traverse, Alan, *Violin*, 1978–99
Trepel, Shirley, *Cello*, 1963–90
Trongone, Edward, *Oboe*, 1946–48, 1957–61*
Tucci, Paul R., *Bassoon*, 1958–81
Tuck, Darrell, *Timpani*, 1941–42
Tucker, K. R., *Bassoon*, 1932–35
Tushin, Aaron, *Viola*, 1938–42
Twaddell, Elizabeth, *Bass*, 1956–60
Urbach, Alfred, *Cello*, 1946–57
Valkenier, Bernard, *Horn*, 1937–41
Valkovich, Susan, *Violin*, 1981–2004
Vamos, Roland, *Violin*, 1950–51
van Horn, J., *Viola*, 1945–46
Van Tongeren, Helen, *Violin*, 1948–49
Vaughan, M., *Cello*, 1941–42
Velasco, Francisco, *Cello*, 1913–14
Venitelli, Salvatore, *Viola*, 1958–59
VerMeulen, William, *Horn*, 1990–
Villani, Alfred, *English Horn* and *Oboe*, 1936–41, 1942–48, *Oboe* 1957–61**
Voiers, Erma, *Violin*, 1934–47
Wadler, Irving W., *Violin*, 1933–35, 1939–78, *Viola*, 1935-39
Waggoner, William, *Trombone*, 1956–59*
Wagner, Elise, *Bassoon*, 2008–
Wagner, Mrs., *Violin*, 1932
Walker, Virginia, *Percussion*, 1960–90**
Walp, Robert, *Trumpet*, 1983–
Warner, H., *Viola*, 1944–45
Washburn, Franklin E., *Violin*, 1933–37, 1938–42, 1946–48
Washburn, S., *Cello*, 1943–44
Waterman, K., *Horn*, 1944–45
Waters, David, *Trombone* and *Bass Trombone*, 1966–2007
Waters, Lee, *Percussion*, 1935–37, 1945–46
Wauchope, Kendrick, *Bass*, 1970–93
Weaver, Raymond, *Oboe*, 1950–84
Webb, E., *Cello*, 1945–46
Weberpal, Hellen, *Cello*, 2012–13*
Wechsler, Harvey, *Violin*, 1975–76, 1980–89, 1990–2000
Wegner, N., *Trumpet*, 1943–44
Weingart, Edmund, *Violin*, 1949–50
Weiss, Arlene, *Bass Clarinet*, 1956–57
Weiss, Herman J., *Timpani*, 1913–18, *Timpani* and *Percussion*, 1931–38
Welch, William P., *Viola*, 1949–88
West, W. E., *Trombone*, 1916–17
Westerbrook, Ray, *Violin*, 1913–14
Westermeier, T., *Bassoon*, 1932–33, 1934–35
Westervelt, Robert, *Horn*, 1948–49
Wexler, Miriam, *Violin*, 1957–59
Wexler, Shirley, *Viola*, 1959–67
White, Bradley, *Trombone*, 2000*, 2001–
White, Patricia, *Bassoon*, 1947–49
White, Ralph, *Trumpet*, 1934–36
Wieland, Eugene, *Horn*, 1949–50
Wiggins, A., *Organ*, 1937–40
Wilkenfeld, Jake, *Trumpet*, 1931–32, 1934–35
Wilkinson, W. W., *Horn*, 1931
Wilkomirski, Michael, *Violin*, 1958–59, 1965–72, *Viola*, 1959–61
Williams, Chester Vere, *Trumpet*, 1913–18
Williams, George, *Trombone*, 1931
Williams, Rachel, *Viola*, 1942–44
Williams, Shirley, *Violin*, 1955–56
Williams, Wendy, *Flute*, 1991–92*
Williamson, George, *Trombone*, 1931–35, 1936–39
Willrich, John C., *Violin*, 1913–18, 1931–32
Wilson, Barbara, *Bass*, 1955–62
Wilson, E., *Bass*, 1943–44
Wilson, Marian Webb, *Cello*, 1959–2000
Wilson, William, *Viola*, 1951–53
Wilt, James, *Trumpet*, 1989–2004
Winborn, Edward, *Trumpet*, 1960–61*
Winder, Max, *Violin*, 1949–62
Woldt, John William, *Horn*, 1946–47

Wolfe, Harvey S., *Cello*, 1956–59
Wolsfeld, Myrtle, *Violin*, 1948–51
Womack, George, *Percussion*, 1980–2004
Wong, Xiao, *Cello*, 2000–
Woodridge, A. L., *Violin*, 1933–34
Woods, M., *Viola*, 1943–45
Wright, Donald B., *Viola*, 1954–57
Wright, Harold, *Clarinet*, 1951–52
Wu, Christine, *Violin*, 2001–05
Wulfe, Jack, *Cello*, 1953–56
Wuliger, David, *Timpani*, 1946–86
Wylie, Robert, *Horn*, 1956–60*
Xu, Siwen, *Violin*, 1994–2004
Yan, Tong, *Violin*, 2012–
Yarger, Mr., *Violin*, 1931
Yasdanfar, Ali, *Bass*, 1996–99
Yeh, Shen, *Violin*, 1995–2001
Yeskin, Doris, *Violin*, 1949–50
York, Norman, *Bass*, 1951–52
Yu, Yuan-Qing, *Violin*, 1994–95
Zajicek, Rudolph, *Violin*, 1951–54
Zaratzian, Harry, *Violin*, 1943, *Viola*, 1943–44
Zeger, Ruth, *Violin*, 1981–
Zeper, Louis, *Violin*, 1948–49
Zhang, Tina, *Violin*, 2012–13
Zimbler, Helen, *Bass*, 1960–61
Zirbel, Ted, *Flute*, 1931–32
Zuckermann, Norbert, *Violin*, 1962–63
Zuo, Jun, *Violin*, 1995–2005
Zuppas, Nick, *Violin*, 1951–54

HOUSTON SYMPHONY CHORUS

CHORUS DIRECTORS

1946–67	Alfred C. Urbach
1967–68	A. Clyde Roller
1968–69	Wayne Bedford
1969–77	Donald Strong
1977–86	Virginia Babikian
1986	Edward Polochick
1986–	Dr. Charles Hausmann

CHORUS ASSISTANT DIRECTORS

1948–53	Arthur A. Hall
1950–57	Ruth Mary Ruston
1961–68	Wayne Bedford
1968–69	Don Strong
1968–70	Eleanor Grant
1968–70	Azaleigh McGinnis
1968–77	Thomas Avinger
1969–70	Lonnette Prather
1970–73	Virginia Babikian
1973–74	Azaleigh McGinnis
1974–77	Virginia Babikian
1977–78	Raymond Witt
1978–79	John Burnett
1979–86	David Wehr
1980–82	Thomas Avinger
1986	Charles Hausmann
1988–90	Holly Kooken
1990–97	Betsy Weber
1997–2002	Eduardo Garcia–Novelli
2002–04	Roger S. Keele
2004–06	A. Jan Taylor
2006–08	Richard Robbins
2008–09	Justin Smith
2009–12	Paolo Gomes
2012–13	Kevin Klotz

CHORUS MANAGERS

1975–81	Sandy Graf
1981–86	Lee Stevens
1986–87	Claudia Leis
1987–88	Sherry Terry
1988–98	Marilyn Dyess
1999–2002	Cheryl McIver Whinney
2002–11	Susan Scarrow
2011–	Sarah Berggren

HOUSTON SYMPHONY CHORUS MEMBERS

Current members with service over 20 years, in order of longevity

Peropoulos, Peter
Grady, John
Nussmann, David G.
Cheadle, William
Gahr, Mary
Bush, Barbara
Browning, Robert
Sessions, Tony
Rogan, Carolyn
Gatlin, Clarice
Izzo, Chuck
Field, Richard
Vazquez, Tony
Bailey Adams, Melissa
El-Saleh, Rachel
Cutler, Roger
Alban, Bob
Bond, John
James, Stephen
Kinsey, Berma
Lewis, Joyce
Bratic, Nancy
Magnuson, Pamela
Alms, Ramona
Voigt, Mary
Sommer, Paige
Howard, Catherine
Howe, George
Williams, Lee
Bumpus, Pat

BUSINESS MANAGERS

1913–14	William Kendall
1913–18	Ernest Hail
1931–34	Bernard Epstein
1938	Theodore F. Gannon
1939–41	Harry R. Bourne
1942–43	Margaret McCament
1944	Homer Springfield
1945	Margaret McCament
1947–48	Francis R. Deering

MANAGERS AND EXECUTIVE DIRECTORS

1948–74	Tom M. Johnson
1975–76	James L. Wright
1976–81	Michael Woolcock
1981–87	Gideon Toeplitz
1989–2000	David M. Wax
2001–05	Ann Kennedy
2005–09	Matthew VanBesien
2010–	Mark C. Hanson

GENERAL MANAGERS

1984–90	Tom Fay
1991–2001	James N. Berdahl
2002–03	Jeff Woodruff
2003–05	Matthew VanBesien
2005–	Steven Brosvik

STAFF MEMBERS

With ten or more years of service (last title is shown)

Barney, E. Lynn, *Librarian*, 1985–92

Berdahl, James, *General Manager*, 1991–2001

Bratlie, Merle, *Director of Artistic Services*, 1989–

Brassow, Sally, *Controller*, 1998–

Cantrell, Peggy, *Accounting Assistant*, 1982–91

Clark, Lee Allen, *Director of Business Affairs*, 1982–91

Clements, Michael, *Customer Services Manager*, 1982–93

Crenshaw, Noel, *Stage Technician*, 1963–98

Currlin, Alice Bruce, *Public Relations Director*, 1955–70

Daily, Roger, *Director, Music Matters!*, 2001–

Davenport, Josephine, *Computer Services Assistant*, 1985–96

Demel, Madeline, *League Activities Coordinator*, 1970–81

Desmarais, Aurelie, *Senior Director of Artistic Planning*, 1996–

Dinitz, Amanda, *Director of Executive Operations*, 2003–

Fabry, Zoltan, *Stage Technician*, 1993–

Fails, Heather, *Manager, Ticketing Database*, 2003–

Fasshauer, Carl, *Assistant to the General Manager*, 1955–73

Garrett, Ginny, *Director of Education and Community Relations*, 1980–81, 1983–2001

Giles, Nancy, *Director, Annual Fund*, 1995–2000, 2003–07

Gulla, Philip, *Director, Technology*, 2003–

Jackson, Don, *Stage Manager*, 1967–2005

Jackson, Donald Ray, *Stage Manager*, 1988–

Johnson, Tom, *General Manager*, 1948–73

Juvan–Savoy, Connie, *Publications Manager*, 1987–97

Kendrick, Simone, *Secretary to the Executive Director*, 1980–94

Kent, Art, *Senior Director of Public Affairs*, 1997–2008

LaRocque, Jan, *Manager of the Patron Database*, 1984–

Liese, Ralph, *Orchestra Personnel Manager*, 1969–79

Lopez, Melissa, *Director of Marketing, Single Ticket & Group Sales*, 1996–

Maloch, Suzanne, *Director of Human Resources*, 1994–2006

McLaughlin, Daphne, *Accounting Assistant*, 1981–90

McMurray, Michael, *Assistant Librarian*, 1982–

Medvitz, James T., *Librarian*, 1974–84

Middleton, Kay, *Receptionist*, 1982–

Moore, Ray E., *Librarian*, 1943–72

Pawson, Michael D., *Chief Financial Officer*, 2003–13

Raines, Virginia, *Executive Secretary*, 1963–76

Rall, Anita, *Auditor*, 1939–72

Ross, Maria, *Payroll Manager*, 1998–

Salge, A. J., *Network Systems Engineer*, 2004–

Seay, Thalia, *Maintenance Fund Secretary*, 1956–58, 1963–71

Simmons, Mildred, *Annual Fund Coordinator*, 1972–81

Stinson, Betty, *Executive Assistant*, 1981–90

Takaro, Tom, *Librarian,* 1998–

Taylor, Glenn, *Chief Marketing Officer,* 2004–

Urbach, Alfred, *Personnel Manager,* 1948–49, 1955–64

Walker, Marlene, *Advertising Manager/ Publisher,* 1986–97

Wax, David M., *Executive Director,* 1987–2000

Wenig, Steve, *Director of Community Partnerships,* 2004–

Westerfelt, Chris, *Manager, Accounts Payable and Special Projects,* 1995–

Wilson, Carol, *Manager, Music Matters!,* 1995–2012

HOUSTON SYMPHONY ORCHESTRA ASSOCIATION 1913–14

OFFICERS

Mrs. Edwin B. Parker
President
Miss Ima Hogg
First Vice-President
Frantz Brogniez
Second Vice-President
H. F. MacGregor
Treasurer
Mrs. Z. F. Lillard
Recording Secretary
Mrs. William Abbey
Corresponding Secretary

BOARD OF DIRECTORS

Mrs. William Abbey
Mr. J. B. Bowles
Mr. D. B. Cherry
Mr. J. S. Cullinan
Mrs. R. C. Duff
Miss Blanche Foley
Mr. Ike Harris
Mrs. Jules Hirsch
Mr. Jesse H. Jones
Mrs. Will Jones
Mr. Will Kendall
Mr. Abe Levy
Dr. Edgar Odell Lovett
Mr. H. F. MacGregor
Mrs. Joseph Mullen
Mrs. E. A. Peden
Miss Laura Rice
Miss Ella Smith
Mrs. James Schuyler Stewart
Mrs. J. Lewis Thompson
Mrs. Turner Williamson
Mr. Henry Stude
Mrs. Gentry Waldo

ADVISORY COMMITTEE

Dr. Henry Barnstein
Mrs. J. O. Carr
P. W. Horn
Dr. William S. Jacobs
Mrs. Harris Masterson
Mrs. W. B. Sharp
Mrs. C. C. Wenzel

HOUSTON SYMPHONY SOCIETY

PRESIDENTS

1913–17	Mrs. Edwin B. Parker
1917–21	Miss Ima Hogg
1921–31	Mrs. H. M. Garwood
1931–34	Joseph A. Mullen, M.D.
1934–36	Joseph S. Smith
1936–42	Walter H. Walne
1942–46	Hugh Roy Cullen
1946	Joseph S. Smith
1946–56	Miss Ima Hogg
1956–70	General Maurice Hirsch
1970–75	Dr. Charles F. Jones
1975–78	Fayez Sarofim
1978–80	John T. Cater
1980–82	Richard G. Merrill
1982–84	Ellen Elizardi Kelley
1984–87	John D. Platt
1987–88	E. C. Vandagrift, Jr.
1988–89	J. Hugh Roff, Jr.
1989–92	Robert M. Hermance
1992–94	Gene McDavid
1994–96	Janice H. Barrow
1996–99	Barry Burkholder
1999–2001	Rodney H. Margolis
2001–03	Jeffrey B. Early
2003	Michael E. Shannon
2003–06	Ed Wulfe
2006–09	Jesse B. Tutor
2009–12	Robert B. Tudor III
2012–	Robert A. Peiser

CHAIRMEN

1946–48	Gus S.Wortham
1948–50	F. M. Law
1950–53	Warren S. Bellows, Sr.
1953–56	Harmon Whittington
1977–80	Dr. Charles F. Jones
1979–80	Fayez Sarofim, Vice–Chairman
1980–82	John T. Cater
1982–84	Richard G. Merrill
1984–88	Ellen Elizardi Kelley
1988–89	John D. Platt
1989–90	J. Hugh Roff, Jr.
1990–91	Stewart Orton
1991–95	Joe F. Moore
1995–97	Constantine S. Nicandros
1997–2001	Alexander K. McLanahan
2001–08	Mike S. Stude
2008–11	Ed Wulfe
2011–	Jesse B. Tutor

HOUSTON SYMPHONY SOCIETY

BOARD OF DIRECTORS AND ADVISORY BOARD MEMBERS, 1913-2013

(including ex-officio members)
*Life Trustee

Mrs. William Abbey
Mrs. Clark Abbott
J. S. Abercombie
Mrs. J. S. Abercrombie
Samuel Abraham
Edgar D. Ackerman
Mrs. Alwin Adam
Joanne Adams
Kenneth S. Adams, Jr.
L. S. Adams
Stephen M. Aechternacht
Dr. William W. Akers
Mrs. Paul A. Akscyn
Carolyn W. Alexander
Stanford Alexander
Wayne S. Alexander
Albert B. Alkek
Joe L. Allbritton
Doris Fondren Allday
Bonnie Allen
Herbert Allen
Mrs. J. D. "Bucky" Allshouse
Mary Ambrose
Eugene V. Amoroso
Frank Amsler
Col. James Anderson
D. Kent Anderson
Dillon Anderson
Mrs. W. Leland Anderson
Mrs. William A. Anderson, Jr.
Paul M. Anderson
W. Leland Anderson
Lilly Kucera Andress
Frank Andrews
The Honorable Jesse Andrews
Mrs. Rawle Andrews
Congressman William R. Archer
Maurice J. Aresty
Thomas G. Armstrong
Isaac Arnold, Sr.
Isaac Arnold, Jr.
Antoinette T. Arnold
William N. Arnold
Roman Arnoldy
Reuben W. Askanase
J. Evans Attwell
John F. Austin, Jr.
Mrs. John F. Austin, Jr.
John S. Bace
Philip A. Bahr
Clayton Baird
Capt. James A. Baker
Mrs. James A. Baker
James A. Baker, Jr.
Mrs. James A. Baker, Jr.
James A. Baker
W. Browne Baker
B. Ben Baldanza
Robert C. Baldwin
Mrs. Rubalee Hankamer Ball
Gene C. Bankston
Mrs. Perry O. Barber, Jr.
Thomas C. Barber, II
Samuel A. Barclay III
Thomas G. Barksdale
T. D. Barlow
T. J. Barlow
Mrs. John T. Barnefield
Dr. Marguerite Ross Barnett
Allen Barnhill
Dr. Henry Barnston
Janice H. Barrow*
Allan Bartlett
Mrs. T. D. Barziza
Danielle Batchelor
Col. W. B. Bates
Mrs. Ben Battelstein
Phillip Battelstein
Charles Baughn
Dean Baxter
Thomas Bay
R. O. Beach, Sr.
Charles C. Beall, Jr.
Mrs. Thomas H. Bearden
Michael Bearer
Gary V. Beauchamp
Tim Beauchemin
David J. Beck
Mrs. John A. Beck, Jr.
Tom Becker
Richard A. Behlmann
Edward H. Belanger
Warren S. Bellows, Sr.
Mrs. Warren S. Bellows, Sr.
Warren S. Bellows, Jr.
Karl R. Bendetsen
Col. Paul G. Benedum
Harry E. Bennett
Leslie Bennett
Mrs. J. W. Bentley
Mrs. Lloyd M. Bentsen, Jr.
Conrad Bering, Jr.
Milton S. Berman
Arthur S. Berner
Philip J. Berquist
James M. Berry
Joel H. Berry
Mrs. Noel J. Bertelli
S. R. Bertron
Mrs. T. J. Bettes
Dr. Devinder Bhatia
Dr. Thomas M. Biggs
Dr. Charles E. Bishop
Darlene Bisso
Ira J. Black
Mrs. J. G. Blaffer
Mrs. John H. Blaffer
Mrs. Robert Lee Blaffer
Francis M. Blair
Mrs. Robert F. Bland
Neil Bland
Jack S. Blanton
Mrs. Eddy Blanton
William N. Blanton
Leon W. Blazey, Jr.
Dr. Edward Blitz
Peter G. Block
Ed Bodde
Lisa R. Bogert
Anthony Bohnert
James B. Boles
George Boltwood
Ermy Borlenghi Bonfield
Gordon B. Bonfield
B. F. Bonner
Marilou Bonner
Ann Bookout
Ms. Marie Taylor Bosarge
Ted Bosquez
J. A. Bousquet
Mrs. William G. Bowen
William J. Bowen
Michael Boxberger
Meherwan P. Boyce
Carole Boyd
Howard T. Boyd
Judge Edward S. Boyles
Mrs. Richard Brackett
Michael B. Bracy
Rev. Patrick O. Braden, C.S.B.
Robert S. Braden
Mrs. Luke C. Bradley
Walter Bratic
George Bregman
Alfredo Brener
Alex Brennan-Martin
Robert J. Brennecke
J. Mark Brewer
Mrs. David M. Bridges
B. I. Bridgwater
Dr. Robert L. Briggs
Alison Leland Brisco
Mrs. Birdsall Briscoe
Geary Broadnax
Benjamin Brochstein
Isaac S. Brochstein
Samuel J. Brochstein
Catherine Campbell Brock
Ruth White Brodsky
Martin Brody
Frantz H. Brogniez
Linda J. Broocks
Ian Brookbanks
Mrs. Ethel Brosius
E. Conway Broun
Edgar W. Brown
George R. Brown
Herman Brown
Mrs. Herman Brown
Leonard O. Brown
Mrs. Edgar W. Brown, Jr.
Mrs. G. Norman Brown
Mrs. Hart Brown
Mrs. John D. Brown
Norma Jean Brown
Ronald Brown
Terry Ann Brown
Robert Brubaker
General A. D. Bruce
Mrs. George Bruce
Mrs. George S. Bruce, Jr.
Susanna G. Brundrett
Bill Brunger
Mrs. John S. Brunson
Earleen Bryan
L. R. Bryan, Jr.
Miss Carolyn Bryan
Mrs. Guy M. Bryan
Bob J. Bryant
Mrs. William C. Buchanan
Alan R. Buckwalter III
Mrs. Robert Buell

Dr. Roger J. Bulger
John O. Bullington
Thomas A. Bullock
Nancy Bumgarner
Mrs. Edward W. Burbank, Jr.
Ralph B. Burch
Reagan Burch
Barry Burkholder
Cynthia Burns
John D. Burns
R. Jeff Burns
Mrs. Julian S. Burrows
Prentiss C. Burt
John D. Burton
Justice Brett Busby
Mrs. M. Clyde Butcher
William F. Butin
Carol A. Butler
George A. Butler
Mrs. George A. Butler
Mrs. John R. Butler
P. H. Butler
P. P. Butler
Charles L. Bybee
Mrs. Charles L. Bybee
Cheryl Byington
Mrs. W. David Cade
Dixon H. Cain
H. W. Cain
James C. Calaway
Richard H. Caldwell
T. J. Caldwell
Mrs. Ben A. Calhoun
Charles Callery
James T. Callier
Arthur A. Cameron
Dougal Cameron
Mrs. R. Trent Campbell, Jr.
D. B. Cannafax
Mrs. William Calvin Cannon
Armando Cantu
Mrs. Carol A. Carlson
George Carmack
David M. Carmichael
Martha Carnes
Mrs. J. O. Carr
Phillip J. Carroll
Allen H. Carruth
Mrs. Allen H. Carruth
Bruce Carter
John B. Carter
John F. Carter II
Miss Agnese Carter
Mrs. Aubrey Leon Carter
Victor N. Carter
Mrs. Victor N. Carter
Lynn Caruso
M. Lyle Cashion
Art Caspar
Leonel J. Castillo
Max Castillo
John T. Cater*
Ann Cavanaugh
H. Scott Caven, Jr.
Jack Chadderdon
Robert C. Chambers
Mrs. Robert Lee Chance
Donna Josey Chapman
Mrs. John E. Chapoton
John Chase
D. B. Cherry
Mrs. D. B. Cherry
Adair B. Chew
Col. W. A. Childress
Mrs. John H. Chiles
Vincent Chiodo
Robert M. Chiste
Lawrence A. Ciscon
Jane M. Cizik
Robert Cizik
Bernard F. Clark, Jr.
Jane Clark
Janet F. Clark
Michael H. Clark
Mrs. Robert L. Clarke
Orson C. Clay
Benjamin Clayton
William Lockhart Clayton
Lora R. Clemmons
Emily Fairfax Coates
Audrey Cochran
Brandon Cochran
Dr. Chester G. Cochran
Ernest H. Cockrell

Mrs. Ernest H. Cockrell, Jr.
Sue Coffey
George Cohen
Ryan Colburn
John A. Cole
Ken W. Cole
Mrs. Leslie Coleman
Joseph A. Collard
Everett D. Collier
Gus Comiskey, Jr.
Dr. John P. Comstock
Peter R. Coneway
Randall R. Conklin
The Honorable John B. Connally
Mrs. André F. Connan
Brendan Connaughton
Mrs. E. Harold Conner
Tracey Conwell
John H. Cooper
Mrs. Theodore W. Cooper
George Copley, Sr.
James F. Cordes
Donald E. Cornett
George Cottingham
Mrs. Fred T. Couper, Jr.
Dr. Charles B. Covert
Janis H. Cox
Mills Cox
Mrs. Robert L. Cox
Paul K. Crafts
Jay C. Crager, Jr.
E. Lillo Crain
Glen R. Cramer
Miss A. Cranford
H. Scott Craven, Jr.
Mrs. Rorick Cravens
Cheryl D. Creuzot
R. Nelson Crews
Carolyn Crites
John W. Croft
Dr. Carey Croneis
Thomas N. Crowell
Eileen T. Crowley
Robert J. Cruikshank
Agnes G. Crump
Professor Joseph Crump
Hugh Roy Cullen
Mrs. Hugh Roy Cullen
Roy Henry Cullen
Craig F. Cullinan, Jr.
Mrs. Craig F. Cullinan, Jr.
Joseph Stephen Cullinan
Nina J. Cullinan
Naurice Cummings
C. Baker Cunningham
Harold R. Cunningham
J. Brown Cutbirth
The Honorable Lewis Cutrer
Dr. Scott Cutler
Thomas D'Alesandro IV
Barbara S. Daniel
Christopher J. Daniel
Miss Louise Chalmette Daniel
Mrs. Mary Evans Daniel
Mrs. James D. Dannenbaum
Richard R. D'Antoni
Renée R. Danziger
Horace Darton
Jeff Dastmalchian
Leslie Barry Davidson
Brian E. Davies
Britt D. Davis
Frank B. Davis
Sherry Filé Davis
Tom Martin Davis
Mrs. James R. Dawley III
Moody Dawson
Mrs. J. Moody Dawson
Mark P. Day
Bertrand de La Noue
John M. de Menil
Alexander de Toth
Mrs. D. De Vries
Mrs. R. R. Dean
Mrs. Alexander Dearborn
Cindy Deere
Francis R. Deering
James B. DeGeorge
Linnet F. Deily
Robert Del Grande
Mrs. Clotaire D. Delery, Jr.
Marc P. Delesalle
Lorraine Dell
Louis F. DeLone

Mrs. Harold R. DeMoss, Jr.
Viviana Denechaud
Mrs. John P. Dennis, Jr.
John P. Dennis, III
John P. DesBarres
Mrs. Henry Desenberg
Mrs. J. Desey Desenberg
Mrs. Alex Deutser
Brenda DeVore
Gene Dewhurst
Tammy Dewhurst
Dr. James P. DeWolfe
Baron Enrico di Portanova
Francisco V. Diaz
Mrs. H. H. Dickson
Jan Meyer Diesel
Noah Dietrich
R. G. Dillard, Jr.
Mrs. Chris Dixie
Jack N. Doherty
Michael Doherty
Susanna Dokupil
A. J. Dow
Patrick M. Dreckman
Mrs. John S. Drew
Mickey A. Driver
Daniel Dror
Mrs. Daniel Dror
Glenn Dubin
Lee M. Dubow
Ray Lofton Dudley
Mrs. Ray Lofton Dudley
Mrs. R. C. Duff
Mrs. Elva Kalb Dumas
Charles W. Duncan, Jr.
John H. Duncan
Mrs. John H. Duncan
Archie W. Dunham
Clinton D. Dunn
Susan A. Dunten
W. McComb Dunwoody
Mrs. C. Pharr Duson, Jr.
Ms. Gayle Dvorak
Roy L. Dye, Jr.
J. C. Dygert
Jeff Dyke
Osborne J. "Jeff" Dykes, III
Jeffrey B. Early
Gary D. Easterly
Dr. H. J. Ehlers
The Honorable Granville W. Elder
John W. Elder
Judge J. A. Elkins, Sr.
James A. Elkins, Jr.
Lucas T. Elliot
Card G. Elliott
Mrs. C. G. Elliott
Thomas Elliott
Sydney T. Ellis
Robin A. Elverson
Virginia Elverson
W. C. English, Jr.
Gene H. Englund
Bernard Epstein
Maurice Epstein
R. D. Ernst
Clark Kent Ervin
Mellie Esperson
Patrick Esquerre
John Esquivel
Mrs. Junius F. Estill, Jr.
Gayle P. Eury
J. W. Evans
R. Joan Fadden
Mrs. Henry B. Fall
Aubrey M. Farb
Harold Farb
Aaron J. Farfel
Stephen P. Farish
Mrs. Stephen P. Farish
Stephen P. Farish III
Mrs. William Stamps Farish, Sr.
Mrs. William Stamps Farish, Jr.
William S. Farish III
Mrs. William S. Farish III
David E. Farnsworth
R. A. Farnsworth, Sr.
Robert Farrell
William G. Farrington
Mrs. William G. Farrington
George R. Farris
Mrs. Davis Faulkner
Kelli Cohen Fein
D. D. Feldman

Arlen G. Ferguson
Harry Ferguson
José-Pablo Fernandez
Robert L. Field
Sam Field
Robert L. Field
Marvy A. Finger
Mary B. Finger
Ronald J. Finger
Mrs. Ronald J. Finger
Wayne Fisher
Tom Fitzpatrick
Thomas Flaxman
Lamar Fleming, Jr.
Mrs. William T. Fleming, Jr.
Glenn F. Fletcher, Jr.
Thomas Fletcher, Sr.
Thomas Fletcher, Jr.
Chris Flood
Mrs. Edward L. Flowers, Jr.
Richard W. Flowers
Mrs. James G. Flynn
Miss Blanche Foley
Mrs. Louis Fontenot
Charles E. Foster
Craig A. Fox
Thomas A. Fox
Joe H. Foy
Felix Fraga
Don Fancher
William H. Francis, Jr.
Mrs. William H. Francis, Jr.
C. J. Francisco
Julia Anderson Frankel
S. David Frankfort
Byron Franklin
Mrs. Charles R. Franzen
The Honorable Kenneth Franzheim II
Mrs. Wilson Morris Fraser
Wilson P. Fraser
Mrs. Wilson P. Fraser
Carl B. Frazer
Mrs. Louis A. Freed
N. W. Freeman
Layne Bryan French
Richard W. French, Jr.
Herbert Frensley
J. Kent Friedman
Deborah J. Fritsche
Mrs. A. H. Fulbright
Miss Mary F. Fuller
Princess Tazilio von Furstenberg
Mary Fusillo
W. H. Gabig
Dr. Michael Gagliardi
Dr. V. G. Gallina
Barry Galloway
Barry J. Galt
Frank T. Garcia
Martha Garcia
Paul M. Garmany
Mrs. James A. Garrity
Dr. George G. Garver
Mrs. H. M. Garwood
Gabriel M. Gelb
Allen Gelwick
Diane Gendel
Mrs. I. G. Gerson
Carl P. Giardini
Robert Gibbs
Scott Gieselman
Mrs. Edith Sweeney Giles
Linda Challis Gill
Miss Ina Gillespie
Mrs. Fred Gillette
Malcolm Gillis
B. B. Gilmer
Daffin Gilmer
Mauro Gimenez
Jeffery J. Gimpel
Alfred C. Glassell, Jr.
Stephen W. Glenn
Wayne E. Glenn
Jan Glenz
Julius Glickman
D. Stephen Goddard, Jr.
Mrs. William Gray Godfrey
Herbert Godwin
Mrs. Otto E. Goedecke
Wayne K. Goettsche
Jack E. Golden
W. J. Goldston
Enrique González
Dr. Richard J. Gonzalez

Baxter D. Goodrich
John Paul Goodwin
Aron S. Gordon
Dr. Harvey L. Gordon
Harry B. Gordon, Sr.
Mrs. Thomas J. Gordon
Dr. David Gottlieb
Hans Graf
Ms. Lauretta S. Graf
H. Devon Graham, Jr.
Mrs. John F. Grant
Rob Grant
Carla Graubard
Eric Graves
Saundria Chase Gray
Daniel C. Green
John E. Green, Jr.
Mrs. Clifford Green
J. B. Greenfield
Robert G. Greer
Martin Gregersen
Charles R. Gregg
Lloyd Gregory
Mrs. R. P. Gregory
R. P. Gregory
William A. Grieves
Dorothy H. McDonnell Grieves
Gerald D. Griffin
John A. Griffin
Lee Griffin
William Griffin III
James P. S. Griffith
Donald L. Griswold
Randolph Lee Groninger
Jenard Gross
Richard H. Gross
Mrs. Herman Grotte
Peter Gruenberger
Larry J. Gunn
Mrs. Ralph Ellis Gunn
Janet Gurwich
T. C. Guseman
William D. Gutermuth
Frank Gutherie
Frank C. Guthrie
Stanley Haas
Dr. Norman Hackerman
Maureen Hackett
Mrs. Edgar D. Haden
H. Frederick Haemisegger
Mrs. H. Frederick Haemisegger
J. Michael Hafner
James A. Hageman
Lee Hager
Ernest Hail
Michel T. Halbouty
Eric Halen
Anthony W. Hall, Jr.
Gordon B. Hall, Jr.
Dr. Grady L. Hallman
Peter G. Ham
Charles W. Hamilton
Lawrence Hamilton
George Hamman
Mrs. John Hamman, Jr.
Dr. Michael P. Hammond
Earl C. Hankamer
Mrs. David Hannah, Jr.
George Hansen
John P. Hansen
Susan Arnoldy Hansen
Mark C. Hanson
Harry C. Hanszen
Mrs. Harry C. (Katherine) Hanszen
Mrs. Harry C. (Alice) Hanszen
James W. Hargrove
Temple Hargrove
Lute Harmon
Mrs. Clayton M. Harrell
Robert S. Harrell
William E. Harrell
Dr. William H. Harris
Ike Harris
L. L. Harris
Robert W. Harrison, Jr.
Mrs. Karl F. Hasselmann
Dr. Eric J. Haufrect
Kathleen D. Hayes
John Hazard
Mrs. G. Allen Heidbreder
Erwin Heinen
Mrs. John H. Heinzerling
Fritz Heitmann
A. Helberg

Mrs. F. A. Helbig
Cathy Helms
J. C. Helms
Heidi Ann Helton
Wolf Hengst
Robert M. Hermance
Mrs. John W. Herndon, Jr.
Robert R. Herring
Yvonne Herring
R. Dean Herrington
J. W. Hershey
Mrs. J. W. Hershey
Frank C. Herzog
Mrs. J. L. Hester
George Heyer
Mrs. R. E. Hibbert
Suzanne Hicks
Miss Blanche Higginbotham
Brodrick W. Hill
D. Sloan Hill
George A. Hill, Jr.
Mrs. George A. Hill, Jr.
Jackson Hinds
Gerald D. Hines
Mrs. Barbara F. Hines
Dr. W. H. Hinton
Doug Hinzie
Mrs. Albert Hirsh
Mrs. Jules Hirsch
Mrs. Maurice Hirsch
General Maurice S. Hirsch
Henry F. Hlavaty
The Honorable William P. Hobby, Jr.
Mrs. William P. Hobby
William P. Hobby
Carroll Ray Hochner
Robert E. Hodge
Mrs. Stanley A. Hoffberger
Richard Hoffert
Dr. Philip G. Hoffman
The Honorable Roy Hofheinz
Mary Frances Hofheinz
Mayor Fred Hofheinz
E. Leslie Hogan
Mike Hogg
Miss Ima Hogg
Mrs. W. H. Hogue
The Honorable Oscar F. Holcombe
Christine Holland
Dr. Gary L. Hollingsworth
Robert E. Hollingsworth
Morris Honore
Harold S. Hook
Scott A. Hooper
William D. Hoops
Professor P. W. Horn
Allen R. Houk
D. Lynn Houston
Dr. William V. Houston
Newton K. Hoverstock
Allan E. Howard
Mrs. George F. Howard
Mrs. Lynn Howell
Paul N. Howell
Ford Hubbard
Ford Hubbard, Jr.
Mrs. Ford Hubbard, Jr.
Mrs. Marvin Huckaby
David V. Hudson, Jr.
Diana M. Hudson
Mrs. Edward Joseph Hudson, Sr.
Roy Michael Huffington
R. Michael Huffington
Mark Hughes
Mrs. J. L. Huitt
Donald F. Hunt
Mrs. J. Collier Hurley
William Marvin Hurley
Mrs. Harry Hurt
Barbara Hurwitz
Patti B. Hurwitz
Mrs. Wille Hutcheson
Mrs. Alexander F. Imlay
Mrs. J. G. Imlay
Mark B. Inabnit
Culton Ingram
Jerry Inzerillo
John A. Irvine
George M. Irving
Robert Charles Ivey
Manfred F. Jachmich
Grover G. Jackson
Rev. William States Jacobs
Arthur E. Jago

Brian James
Paula Jarrett
Leon Jaworski
Mrs. Leon Jaworski
Susan Pinson Jeffers
The Honorable Dwight Jefferson
Ronald H. Joe
Susan Joerger
A. Clarke Johnson
C. G. Johnson
Craig D. Johnson, M.D.
Dr. Craig O. Johnson
Earl L. Johnson
J. M. Johnson
Miss Alathena Johnson
Mrs. John M. Johnson
Richard J. V. Johnson
Robert M. Johnson
Thomas M. Johnson
Willard N. Johnson
Mrs. Murrell M. Johnston
Ralph A. Johnston
Mrs. Ralph A. Johnston
Russell L. Jolley
Robert Jolly
Mrs. Albert P. Jones
Allen N. Jones
Dr. Charles F. Jones
Mrs. Charles F. Jones
Dr. Samuel P. Jones
Frank G. Jones
Gainer B. Jones
Gainer B. Jones, Jr.
Jesse Holman Jones
Mrs. Jesse H. Jones
John T. Jones, Jr.
Mrs. John T. Jones, Jr.
Kenneth F. Jones
Mrs. Will Jones
Don D. Jordan
Russell C. Joseph
Mrs. Harry T. Jukes
Dr. Blair Justice
Dr. Rita Justice
R. B. Kahle
F. P. Kalb
Catherine Kaldis
Francis S. Kalman
Steven P. Kanaly
Joan Kaplan
Bradley C. Karp
Stephen J. Karper
Barry E. Kaufman
Paul Kayser
Roger Kaza
Jared M. Kearney, Jr.
Richard Keating
Mrs. Howard B. Keck
Thomas J. Keefe
Samuel D. Keeper
Dr. Danny R. Kelley
Edward W. Kelley
Ellen Elizardi Kelley
Hugh Rice Kelley
L. C. Kemp, Jr.
William E. Kendall
Simone P. Kendrick
Ann Kennedy
Robert E. Kepke
Mrs. I. C. Kerridge, Jr.
James L. Ketelsen
Edward Kiam
Mrs. L. R. Kier
Justin Kimball
Mrs. Edward O. King
Ms. Chris King
Robert Vernon King
Mrs. H. A. Kipp
Dr. I. Ray Kirk
William A. Kirkland
Milton Kirshbaum
Mary Louis Kister
Keith Klaver
Leonard P. Kline
Robert W. Kneebone
Mrs. V. Scott Kneese
David D. Knoll
Mrs. Phillip Koelsch
Barney F. Kogen
Donald Kovalevich
Bobbie Kristinik
Ryan Krogmeier
Mrs. J. H. Kurth, Jr.
Mrs. J. Allen Kyle

R. Bruce LaBoon
Abe I. Lack
Julio S. Lagarta
E. M. Lallinger
Seth Lamb
Charles L. Lamme
Caesar LaMonica
Deanna Lamoreux
Neil B. Lande
Dr. H. M. Landrum
Mrs. Frederick L. Landry
R. S. Langham
Steve Langham
David H. Langstaff
George Lanier
Robert C. Lanier
Susan Lapin
Roslyn R. Larkey
Arthur Laro
Priscilla Freeman Larson
Thomas C. Latter
Levi Laub
M. T. Launius, Jr.
Mrs. M. T. Launius, Jr.
F. M. Law
Theodore N. Law
Mrs. Theodore N. Law
Sam Lawder
Mrs. James Griffith Lawhon
Rev. William A. Lawson
Kenneth Lay
Clyde W. Lea
J. Sayles Leach
Mrs. Paul V. Ledbetter
Ethel Kaye Lee
Peg Lee
Anne Leek
Ulyesse J. LeGrange
Dr. Daniel E. Lehane
Dr. Alfred E. Leiser
Alison Leland
E. G. Leonardon
Jenifer Loenpacher
A. Ronald Lerner
Al R. Lever
Mrs. Joseph L. Levin
H. Fred Levine
Max Levine
Mrs. Max Levine
Rochelle Levit, Ph.D.
Abe Levy
Miss Harriet Levy
George H. Lewis, Jr.
Lucy H. Lewis
William Bradley Lewis
Dr. Robert I. Lewy
Ken Liberton
Frann Gordon Lichtenstein
Dr. Harris A. Lichenstein
J. Hugh Liedtke
Mrs. G. Burton Liese
Ralph Liese
Ms. Lida Light
Mrs. Z. F. Lillard
Kevin J. Lilly
Professor Emil Lindenberg
William L. Lindholm
Jacques Lindon
The Honorable Jon Lindsay
J. W. Link
J. W. Link, Jr.
Ms. Patsy Link
Mrs. Thomas C. Liston
H. Arthur Littell
Mrs. Erik Littlejohn
Alan N. Livingston
Larry Livingston
Mrs. Louis G. Lobit
Dr. Alan H. Lockwood
E. W. Long, Jr.
Meredith J. Long
Janiece M. Longoria
Mrs. Franciso Lorenzo
Benton F. Love
Jeannette Loverdi
Dr. Edgar Odell Lovett
Mrs. H. M. Lovett
James R. Lowe
Thomas S. Lucksinger
H. M. Lull
Oral L. Luper
Walter L. Luthy
Mrs. J. M. Lykes, Jr.
April J. Lykos

A. J. Lynch
John F. Lynch
Mrs. James E. Lyon
Mrs. Walter R. Lytz
G. A. Mabry
H. F. MacGregor
Mrs. H. F. MacGregor
Cora Sue Mach*
Steven P. Mach
Joseph M. Macrum
Beth Madison
General M. M. Magee
John F. Maher
Mrs. Clarence M. Malone, Jr.
Sultana Mangalji
Carolyn Mann
Dr. Michael Mann
Dr. Paul M. Mann
Tommy Mann
Edward Marcus
Lawrence E. Marcus
Mrs. Greer Marechal
Frank Maresh
Rodney H. Margolis*
Judy E. Margolis
Robert J. Marino
Brad Marks
Irving William Marks
J. Stephen Marks
Jay Marks
Mary Lynn Marks
Mrs. Howard M. Marmell
Douglas Marshall
Whitfield Marshall
Mike Marvins
Ike Massey
David Massin
Mrs. H. Masterson
Harris Masterson III
Mrs. Harris Masterson III
Mariquita Masterson
James Masucci
Ronald D. Matthews
Thomas K. Matthews II
Thomas K. Matthews III
Dr. Malcolm L. Mazow
Jackie Wolens Mazow
W. Baker McAdams
Fraser A. McAlpine
Mrs. S. Maurice McAshan, Jr.
Robert McAughan
Brian P. McCabe
Elisabeth McCabe
Billy McCartney
Barbara McCelvey
David P. McClain
David McClanahan
Mrs. Thompson H. McCleary
Franklin N. McClelland
Mrs. L. F. McCollum
The Honorable Jim McConn
J. R. McConnell
Lori B. McCool
Judge T. Lamar McCorkle, Jr.
Sanford E. McCormick
Mrs. J. D. McCraney
John J. McCutchen II
Mrs. John J. McCutchen
Mrs. Bert T. McDaniel
Gene McDavid*
George E. McDavid
R. Thomas McDermott
Rebecca A. McDonald
John T. McDonnell
Dr. John W. McFarland
Mrs. Ira McFarland
Mrs. Charles P. McGaha
Judi McGee
Stuart R. McGill
N. C. McGowan
E. Clyde McGraw
Mrs. Frank J. McGurl
G. Bruce McInnes
Mary Ann McKeithan
Dolly Madison McKenna
Alexander K. McLanahan*
Mary Ann McLanahan
Diane McLaughlin
J. W. McLean
Charles E. McMahen
Dennis J. McMahon
Cathy McNamara
A. G. McNeese, Jr.
Nancy G. McNeil

Linda McReynolds
Dr. Wilbur L. Meier, Jr.
J. W. Meinhardt
Peter Menikoff
C. William Merchant
James M. Mercurio
Richard G. Merrill
Allen A. Meyer
George B. Meyer
Mrs. George B. Meyer
Leopold L. Meyer
Randall Meyer
Kevin O. Meyers
Kirk B. Michael
Dr. Osama I. Mikhail
Charles D. Milby
Marilyn Miles
E. L. Miller
Mrs. Isadore L. Miller
Richard E. Miller
Russell J. Miller
Mrs. S. I. Miller
Dr. Susan M. Miller
Mrs. William James Miller
JoAnne Mills
James A. Milne
Richard L. Minns
Cynthia Woods Mitchell
Dr. Earl Douglas Mitchell
E. Lee Mitchell
George P. Mitchell
John P. Mitchell
Michael Mithoff
Ginni Mithoff
Jerald David Mize
Katherine Taylor Mize
Mrs. Jack H. Modesett, Jr.
Robert V. Moise
Phyllis Molnar
Charles H. Montford
Alvin S. Moody, Jr.
Shearn Moody, Jr.
Dr. Earl V. Moore
Joe F. Moore
Michael Dean Moore
Preston Moore
Thomas Moore
William E. Moore
John J. Moran
Mrs. John J. Moran
W. T. Moran
Dr. W. E. Moreland
S. Reed Morian
Paul R. Morico
Mrs. Robert E. Moroney
Jan F. Morrell
Michael B. Morris
Pamela Anne Morris
Pat Morris
S. I. Morris
Jo Morrison
Nancy Morrison
Walter J. Morrison
T. C. Morrow
Wright Morrow
Mrs. Wright Morrow
Mrs. John L. Mortimer
Robert Adam Mosbacher, Sr.
Edward J. Mosher
Mrs. Edward J. Mosher
Mrs. Harry J. Mosser
Donald Moyer
Dave Mueller
Joseph A. Mullen, M.D.
Mrs. Joseph A. Mullen
Joseph V. Mullen
Dr. Barry Munitz
W. C. Munn
Dennis Murphree
Mrs. Daniel L. Murphry
Mrs. Gerald Ross Murphy
Rev. John F. Murphy
Frank H. Murray
Fred F. Murray
Joe Murrill
Patricia Muske
Mrs. I. S. Myer
E. William Nash
Underwood Nazro
Mrs. Underwood Nazro
Mrs. J. W. Neal
Sally M. Neblett
Paul J. Neff
Mrs. Haywood Nelms

Fred A. Nelson
Fred M. Nelson
Richard C. Nelson
Thomas S. Neslage
Mrs. Hugo Neuhaus
Mrs. Hugo V. Neuhaus, Jr.
W. Oscar Neuhaus
Dr. Alfred R. Neumann
Mrs. Alfred R. Neumann
Arthur Newman
Constantine S. Nicandros
Tassie Nicandros
Jim H. Nichols, Jr.
Holly Nielsen
John O. Niemann, Jr.
Mrs. James C. Niver
Judge James L. Noel, Jr.
Judge John P. Noel
Roy Nolen
William M. Noonan
Mrs. Richard Norsworthy
Earle North
Scott S. Nyquist
Steven C. Oaks
Dr. E. E. Oberholtzer
Doris J. O'Connor
Ralph S. O'Connor
Lisa Launius O'Leary
Mrs. Olaf La Cour Olsen
Immanuel Olshan
Dana Ondrias
Bryan E. O'Neill
Edward Oppenheimer
Sergio Ortiz
Hanni Stern Orton
John S. Orton
Katharine Orton
Stewart Orton*
Dee S. Osborne
Richard O'Shields
Mrs. Jack H. Ossewaarde
Dr. Susan Osterberg
Edward C. Osterberg, Jr.
Kenneth Dale Owen
Mrs. Kenneth Dale Owen
Terrell W. Oxford
Mrs. W. A. Paddock
William C. Padon III
Paula Page
Dr. Rod Paige
Willilam Pannill
Dr. Michael N. Papadopoulos
Mrs. Edwin B. Parker
Mrs. Jonathan E. Parker
R. Allison Parker
Michael Parmet
R. Alan Parrish
Zack S. Parrish, Jr.
Tiba Parsa
Mrs. J. R. Parten
Carl Pasechtag
Christie A. Patrick
Larry J. Patrick
Larry Payne
Laurence J. Payne
Mrs. Edgar Pearson
Shirley McGregor Pearson
Judge John W. Peavy, Jr.
Mrs. George E. B. Peddy
Mrs. E. A. Peden
Robert A. Peiser
Marshall Pengra
Herbert W. Penning, Jr.
Charles A. Perlitz, Jr.
Charles E. Perry
George A. Peterkin
Mrs. George A. Peterkin
Brenda J. Peters
Mrs. Lovett C. Peters
Fran Fawcett Peterson
Sarah A. Peterson
Geoffroy Petit
Travis H. Petty
Eckhard Pfeiffer
Harry J. Phillips, Jr.
J. L. Phillips
Theo W. Pinson III
Ronald A. Piperi
Chester M. Pitts III
Dr. Kenneth S. Pitzer
John D. Platt
Mrs. Albert Plummer
Jack Plunkett
Mrs. J. A. Pondrum

David G. Pope
Mrs. John Post
Hugh Potter
Michael Poulas
Don G. Powell
Greg Powers
Ronald L. Powers
James S. Prentice
Mrs. Herman Pressler
Ken Price
Mrs. Denton C. Priest
David Proctor
F. C. Proctor
John M. Proffitt
Ms. Jody Proler
Daniel F. Prosser
David Pruner
Stephen D. Pryor
Mrs. William Pryor
Gloria G. Pryzant
Dana Puddy
Joseph P. Quoyeser
Mrs. Henry H. Rachford, Jr.
Mrs. Cooper K. Ragan
Veazy Rainwater
Mrs. Lula Bryan Rambaud
William M. Ramos
J. Dale Ramsey
Ron Rand
Mrs. Bud A. Randolph
Richard Ransome
Lila Rauch
Ricky Anthony Raven
Hugh M. Ray
Billy R. Reagan
John Reagan
F. John Reck
Mrs. Samuel Clark Red
Walter Scott Red
Mrs. W. Scott Red
Charles F. Reed, Jr.
Geroge F. Reed
Lawrence S. Reed
Mrs. Lawrence S. Reed
Roman F. Reed
Leslie Reichek
Mrs. Charles Reimer
Dr. Neil Reisman
Carl E. Reistle, Jr.
Jeffrey B. Reitman
Dr. Margo K. Restrepo
Sally K. Reynolds
Miss Laura Rice
Joel Richards, III
Gunter H. Richter
Russell Riggins
H. John Riley, Jr.
Mrs. Mildred Sage Roach
James Robb
Dr. Richard Robbins
Mrs. Herbert Roberts
Bruce Robertson
Mrs. Charles J. Robertson, Sr.
Dr. Hampton Robinson
Emrye Robinson
John M. Robinson
Nelson Robinson
P. H. Robinson
James W. Rockwell
Mrs. James W. Rockwell
Mrs. Gerald H. Roeling
J. Hugh Roff, Jr.*
Frank V. Rogers
Regina J. Rogers
Shelby R. Rogers
Dr. Alejandro L. Rosas
Edwin Rose, Jr.
Helen B. Rosenbaum
JoAnn Rosenberg
Dr. Allen R. Ross
Walter M. Ross
Charlotte A. Rothwell
Miss Mary Elizabeth Rouse
Roland M. Routhier
William J. Rovere, Jr.
Kathi Rovere
Clive Runnells, Jr.
George Rupp
H. L. Rush, Jr.
Mrs. Willard L. Russell
Anthony Russo
Joe E. Russo
Mrs. Andrew E. Rutter
John Rydman

Mrs. Henry R. Safford
Miss Helen Saft
Miss Mildred Sage
Bernard Sakowitz
Robert Tobias Sakowitz
Simon Sakowitz
Tobias Sakowitz
Robert B. Sale, Jr.
Most Reverend Enrique San
    Pedro, S. J.
Manolo Sanchez
Michael B. Sandeen
Daniel S. Sanders
David Saperstein
Walter W. Sapp
Fayez Sarofim
Louisa Stude Sarofim
Charles A. Saunders
Mrs. Edna W. Saunders
Omar A. Sawaf
George Sawtelle
Dr. Granville M. Sawyer
Philip Sayles
Dr. P. H. Scardino
Dr. Hyman J. Schachtel
Mathew Schatzman
W. G. Scheibe
Dr. Alexander Schilt
Gerald J. Schissler
Mrs. Richard Schissler, Jr.
Lee D. Schlanger
Mrs. L. William Schleuse
James A. Schlindwein
Pierre Schlumberger
Kenneth L. Schnitzer
Anne Schnoebelen
Max Schuette
John Schuhmacher
E. R. Schumacher
Dr. Mark Schusterman
Paul N. Schwartz
W. Marc Schwartz
Fred S. Schwend
Dr. H. Irving Schweppe, Jr.
John B. Scofield
John McGregor Scott
Richard W. Scott
Eddy Scurlock
Robert A. Seale, Jr.
Bill Sears
Percy Selden
Mrs. W. Harold Sellers
Cleveland Sewall
Mrs. Cleveland Sewall
Helen Shaffer
Mrs. W. T. Shanks
Michael E. Shannon*
Marc Shapiro
Dr. Timothy Sharma
J. William Sharman, Jr.
Mrs. Dudley C. Sharp
Mrs. Frank W. Sharp
Mrs. Walter Benona Sharp, Sr.
W. Bedford Sharp
W. Bedford Sharp, Jr.
Mrs. W. Bedford Sharp, Jr.
Lee M. Sharrar
Burke Shaw
Miss Mabel Shearer
Robby Shelton
Donna Shen
Steve Shepard
Don Shepherd
James L. Shepherd, Jr.
Stuart Sherar
Mrs. Stuart Sherar
Mrs. Richard Maylan Sheridan
Valerie J. Sherlock
Mrs. Dallas B. Sherman
W. A. Sherman
Stanley W. Shipnes
Irvin M. Shlenker
Michael G. Shoup
Thomas W. Sigler
L. E. Simmons
Tom Simmons
Harry W. Simms
Jerome B. Simon
B. Douglas Simpkins, Jr.
Dr. Ronald E. Sims
Steven J. Singer
Charles R. Sitter
Mrs. J. W. Slaughter
Robert Sloan

Buck Small
S. J. Small II
A. Frank Smith
A. Frank Smith, Jr.
Brinton Averil Smith
Dan F. Smith
David C. Smith
Miss Ella Smith
Mrs. Eugene B. Smith
Dr. Kevin Smith
Frank C. Smith, Sr.
Frank C. Smith, Jr.
Mrs. Frank C. Smith
Mrs. Harry K. Smith
Jim R. Smith
Joseph Steven Smith
Mrs. Joseph S. Smith
Jule Smith
June D. Smith
Lester H. Smith
Lloyd H. Smith
Noyes D. Smith, Jr.
R. E. Smith
Mrs. R. E. Smith
Stewart P. Smith
Sue Smith
William A. Smith
Mrs. Sigmund Snelson
Mike Snow
Barry Snyder
Mrs. Edward H. Soderstrom
Kelly Somoza
Mrs. John Sorcic
Mary Nell Reck-Spaw
Leonard H. O. Spearman
Stacey Spears
Joseph F. Speelman
Ross H. Spicer
Roberta Sroka
Mrs. Frank St. Leger
Fred Staacke
Dunstan James Staas
Joel V. Staff
David Stanard
David Standridge
David G. Steakley
Jim Stein
Earle Steinberg
Michael Steinberg
David Steitz
Claude O. Stephens
Mrs. Robin Z. Stephenson
Miss Florence M. Sterling
William H. Stern
William P. Steven
Miss Lula M. Stevens
Karl Stewart
Mrs. Bess Stewart
Mrs. Esperson Stewart
Robert Stewart, Jr.
Wells Stewart
Sherman E. Stimley
Vernon M. Stockton, Sr.
Vernon M. Stockton, Jr.
E. E. Stokes
James E. Stone
Mrs. George M. Stone
George W. Strake
George W. Strake, Jr.
J. Terry Strange
Percy S. Straus, Jr.
Robert D. Straus
Neil Strauss
Robert Strauss
Hans F. Strohmer
Nancy Stopper Strohmer
W. Royce Stroud
Anita B. Stude
Henry Stude
Mike S. Stude*
Edward A. Stumpf III
Susan Pannill Campbell Stutts
John R. Suman
Ellen Susman
Karen H. Susman
W. D. Sutherland
Howard P. Swanson
R. Michael Swearingen
George B. Sweeney, Jr.
Jack Sweeney
Theodore E. Swigart
Mrs. Ira Sykes
H. Gardiner Symonds
Mrs. H. Gardiner Symonds

Antonio Szabo
David Tai
Mrs. C. M. Taliaferro
Leonard C. Tallerine, Jr.
C. Bradley Tashenberg
Henry J. N. Taub
Anne Taylor
Charles S. Taylor, Jr.
Walter J. Taylor
Latane Temple
John A. Tench
J. A. Tennant
Michael L. Tenzer
Arthur F. Thomas, Jr.
Dr. Fennoyee Thomas
Jay Thomas
L. Proctor "Terry" Thomas III
Mrs. Proctor Thomas
Mrs. Ernest L. Thompson
Mrs. J. L. Thompson
John Thorne
Mrs. Ron Tigner
Steven J. Tillinger
Glenn F. Tilton
Stephen G. Tipps
Kern Tips
Dr. David Tomatz
Mrs. Albert Michael Tomforde
Mrs. Allan J. Tomlinson
Alan K. Tomson
Glenda Toole
Mrs. Stanford O. Tostengard
Mrs. Charles Towery
Bart Townsend
P. Kevin Trautner
Darryl W. Traweek
Roger L. Tremblay
Ileana Treviño
Keith Trotman
Dr. R. A. Tsanoff
Mrs. Garrett R. Tucker, Jr.
Robert S. Tucker
Robert B. Tudor III*
Forrest W. Turner
Mrs. J. Harolde Turner
Michael Turner
Mrs. Percy Edwin Turner
Howard Turnley
Dr. Theo S. Tusa, Jr.
Betty Tutor*
Jesse B. Tutor*
Marshall C. Tyndall
A. Knox Tyson
Mrs. A. Knox Tyson
H. Michael Tyson
David M. Underwood
Milton R. Underwood
Mrs. Milton R. Underwood
Alice E. Valdez
Tony Vallone
Mrs. John Van de Mark
Steven T. Van Dorselaer
Astrid Van Dyke
Dr. Richard L. Van Horn
V. H. Van Horn
John Van Osdall
Matthew VanBesien
E. C. Vandagrift, Jr.
Mrs. E. C. Vandagrift, Jr.
Dr. Frank E. Vandiver
Nanik Vaswani
Roswell F. Vaughan III
Laurette Veres
William VerMeulen
C. Richard Vermillion, Jr.
Sid Victory
William Ashton Vinson
Art Vivar
Mrs. Richard W. Volk
Phillip Graf von Hardenberg
Mrs. Lewis C. Wade
Willard B. Wagner, Sr.
Dr. Richard E. Wainerdi
Dr. Margaret Waisman
K. M. Wald
Sidney J. Wald
Mrs. Gentry Waldo
M. C. "Bill" Walker III
Mimi Walker
Mrs. Robert B. Wall
Edward Gregg Wallace, Jr.
McClelland Wallace
Mrs. McClelland Wallace
Walter H. Walne

Mrs. Walter H. Walne
Mrs. James A. Walsh
M. E. Walter
Rabbi Roy A. Walter
Gary Wann
Danci Perugini Ware
Peter Wareing
Harry Warner
Phillip G. Warner
Howard C. Warren
Dr. William Charles Watters III
Frank A. Watts
Marcus A. Watts
Mrs. Larry Watts
Marsha Wayne
Mrs. William Wayne
Harry C. Webb
Frederic Alan Weber
Winston Webster
James D. Weeks
Mrs. Wharton E. Weems
Wharton Weems
Mrs. S. Conrad Weil, Jr.
Robert Weiner
Abe Weingarten
Bernard Weingarten
Joe Weingarten
R. W. Weir
Sid Weiss
The Honorable Louis Welch
Marshall F. Wells
Mrs. C. C. Wenzel
Mrs. Wesley West
Thomas L. West, Jr.
Vicki Creizis West
Wesley W. West
Shirley Wettling
Thomas H. Wharton
W. M. Wheless
George T. Whisman
Mr. Gail Whitcomb
Dr. David Ashley White
Mrs. Thomas C. White
Myra Bolen White
John E. Whitmore
Harmon Whittington
Mrs. Harmon Whittington
Fred Wichlep
A. Martin Wickliff, Jr.
Mrs. R. W. Wier
Harry C. Wiess
Miss Caroline Wiess
Mrs. Harry Carothers Wiess
Heywood Wilansky
Neil H. Wilcox
Mrs. Henry J. Wilkens, Jr.
G. T. Wilkinson
Dr. James T. Willerson
Nancy Willerson
Mrs. Bryan Williams
Margaret Alkek Williams*
Myron Williams
Stanley J. Williams
Steven Jay Williams
Mrs. Turner Williamson
Jan Wilson
Mrs. S. C. Wilson
Isabel Brown Wilson
Wallace S. Wilson
James O. Winston, Jr.
James P. Wise
Ms. Celia Lee Wittliff
Jennifer R. Wittman
Mrs. Erving Wolf
Cyvia Wolff
Mrs. Harris S. Wood
Mrs. James E. Wood, Jr.
Nancy Hollowell Wood
Bruce E. Woods
Mrs. Stanley C. Woods
Benjamin N. Woodson
Mrs. Benjamin N. Woodson
W. J. Wooten
Gus Sessions Wortham
Mrs. Gus S. Worthan
Mrs. Michael Wray
M. A. Wright
Mrs. Beth R. Wright
Mrs. M. A. Wright
R. Earle Wright
Thomas M. Wright
Ed Wulfe*
Scott Wulfe
David James Wuthrich

Lynn Wyatt
Oscar S. Wyatt, Jr.
Charity O'Connell Yarborough
Cary P. Yates
Judge Clarease Rankin Yates
Dr. Robert A. Yekovich
Glenn T. Young
Martha F. Zelsman
David Zerhusen
Judge Alvin Zimmerman
Janusz Zoltowski
Paul Zuest

HOUSTON SYMPHONY LEAGUE

PRESIDENTS

1937–39	Ima Hogg
1939–40	Homoiselle Grant
1940–42	Opal Parten
1942–44	Mary Rutter
1944–45	Marjorie Carter
1945–46	Katherine Sherar
1946–47	Vernon Burrows
1947–49	Hazel Ledbetter
1949–51	Nettie Jones
1951–53	Katherine Calhoun
1953–55	Virgie Lawhon
1955–57	Elizabeth Olsen
1957–59	Esme Gunn
1959–61	Jeannette Jaworski
1961–63	Phyllis Tucker
1963–65	Marion Launius
1965–67	Lucile McCleary
1967–69	George Cooper
1969–71	Ethel Carruth
1971–73	Catherine Hannah
1973–75	Mary Louis Murphy Kister
1975–78	Ellen Kelley
1978–80	Roblyn Herndon
1980–82	Rocky Franzen
1982–84	Judy DeMoss
1984–86	Frances Soderstrom
1986–88	Lilly Kucera Pryor Andress
1988–89	Marilou Bonner
1989–90	Betty Sellers
1990–91	Diane Gendel
1991–92	Gayle Eury
1992–93	Linda Vandagrift
1993–94	Mary Lynn Marks
1994–95	Terry Brown
1995–96	Nancy Stopper Strohmer
1996–97	Mary Ann McKeithan
1997–98	Ann Cavanaugh
1998–99	Helen Shaffer
1999–2000	Lucy Lewis
2000–01	Cathy McNamara
2001–02	Shirley MacGregor Pearson
2002–03	Paula Jarrett
2003–04	Cora Sue Mach
2004–05	Kathi Rovere
2005–06	Norma Jean Brown
2006–07	Barbara McCelvey
2007–08	Lori Sorcic Jansen
2008–09	Nancy Willerson
2009–10	Jane Clark
2010–11	Nancy Littlejohn
2011–12	Donna Shen
2012–13	Susan Osterberg
2013–14	Kelli Cohen Fein

HOUSTON SYMPHONY LEAGUE BAY AREA

PRESIDENTS

1976–77	Fran Strong
1977–79	Selma Neumann
1979–81	Julia Wells
1981–82	Dagmar Meeh
1982–84	Priscilla Heidbreder
1984–86	Harriett Small
1986–88	Nina Spencer
1988–90	Elizabeth Glenn
1990–91	Ebby Creden
1991–92	Charlotte Gaunt
1992–93	Norma Brady
1993–94	Cindy Kuenneke
1994–95	Helen Powell
1995–96	Sharon Dillard
1996–97	Diane McLaughlin
1997–98	Roberta Liston
1998–99	Suzanne Hicks
1999–2000	Sue Smith
2000–01	Shirley Wettling
2001–02	Jo Anne Mills
2002–03	Phyllis Molnar
2003–04	Pat Bertelli
2004–05	Emyre B. Robinson
2005–06	Dana Puddy
2006–07	Angela Buell
2007–08	Pat Brackett
2008–09	Joan Wade
2009–10	Yvonne Herring
2010–11	Deanna Lamoreux
2011–12	Glenda Toole
2012–13	Carole Murphy
2013–14	Patience Myers

HOUSTON SYMPHONY LEAGUE NORTH AREA

PRESIDENTS

1976–78	Carolyn Norris
1978–79	Jan Schurter
1979–81	Alice Flores
1981–82	Gloria Fawcett
1982–84	Andrea Garrity
1984–85	Andy Delery
1985–86	Joan Evans
1986–87	Sue Coffey
1987–88	Beverly Bland
1988–89	Debbie Harvill
1989–90	Rosalie Cross
1990–91	Nancy Stopper Strohmer
1991–93	Bonnie Lippincott
1993–94	Mary Lou Beauchamp
1994–95	Eileen Friesz
1995–96	Becky Blalock
1996–97	Susan Joerger
1997–98	Jeannette Loverdi
1998–99	Jan Glenz
1999–2000	Joan Cooley

WORLD PREMIERES AND COMMISSIONS

*Commissioned by or for the Houston Symphony

*November 1, 1948
Children's Suite from *The Red Pony*
Aaron Copland

*December 13, 1948
Elegy and Paean for Viola and Orchestra
Roy Harris

*February 28, 1949
Overture to *The Travelers*
Harold Shapero

*February 5, 1952
Texas – Symphonic Suite
David Guion

November 25, 1952
Offenbachiana
Offenbach-Rosenthal

January 5, 1953
Overture to *Androcles and the Lion*
William E. Rice

March 31, 1953
New Frontiers
Thomas Beversdorf

January 5, 1954
Symphony in One Movement
Merrills Lewis

January 25, 1954
Music in Memoriam – The Alamo
William E. Rice

October 31, 1955
Symphony No. 2, *Mysterious Mountain*
Alan Hovhaness

November 14, 1955
Symphony No. 6
Henry Cowell

November 28, 1955
Festive Poem
Aram Khachaturian

February 6, 1956
Concerto for Guitar and Orchestra
Heitor Villa-Lobos

April 10, 1956
Fable
Paul Holmes

October 30, 1956
Concerto for Wind and Percussion Instruments
William E. Rice

*March 12, 1957
Ad Lyram
Alan Hovhaness

March 18, 1957
Soliloquy for Oboe and Orchestra
Natasha Bender

November 4, 1957
Sinfonia No. 1
José Serebrier

November 11, 1957
Sinfonia Elegiaca
Andrzej Panufnik

October 20, 1958
Meditation on Orpheus
Alan Hovhaness

November 3, 1958
Atala
Serge de Gastyne

March 28, 1960
Symphony No. 12
Henry Cowell

November 4, 1963
Late Swallows
Delius-Fenby

December 6, 1965
Essay for Strings
John Williams

*October 3, 1966
Ode to the Temple of Sound
Alan Hovhaness

October 16, 1967
Concerto for Cello and Orchestra
André Previn

October 21, 1968
Symphony No. 1
John T. Williams

March 23, 1970
Clio, Symphonic Ode
Carlos Chávez

February 22, 1971
Black Requiem
Quincy Jones

March 13, 1972
Music for Orchestra
Ned Battista

April 23, 1973
Trumpet Concerto No. 1
Fisher Tull

*September 7, 1974
Rituals and Incantations
Hale Smith

October 28, 1974
Etudes for Piano and Orchestra
Benjamin Lees

July 10, 1975
Casey At The Bat
Robert Nelson

September 8, 1975
Symphony in Celebration (Ceremony V)
Paul Chihara

September 19, 1975
Symphony No. 4 – *Landscapes*
Paul Cooper

*July 1, 1977
The Gardens of Hieronymous B.
Michael Horvit

*July 5, 1977
Amenhotep III
Newton Strandberg

March 27, 1978
In Search of the Beyond
Joaquin Rodrigo

*April 12, 1980
Spectra for Small Orchestra
Stephen Paulus

*September 6, 1980
Fanfare and Celebration
Samuel Jones

September 21, 1980
Sondheim Melody
Stephen Sondheim

February 7, 1981
Paeans to Hyacinthus
Bruce Saylor

April 25, 1981
Overture For A Legacy
Fisher Tull

December 5, 1981
Star Captains
David Noon

May 22, 1982
A Yellow Rose Petal
Alvin Singleton

November 20, 1982
Flute Concerto
Paul Cooper

March 12, 1983
Amazon III
Joan Tower

September 10, 1983
Symphony in Two Movements
Paul Cooper

*October 8, 1983
Fantasy for Double Bass and
Orchestra
Frank Proto

September 14, 1984
Violin Concerto No. 2
Marc Neikrug

*November 21, 1984
Chiaroscuro
Ellsworth Milburn

*March 15, 1985
Concerto for Contrabassoon and
Orchestra
Donald Erb

September 28, 1985
Symphony No. 6 (first movement)
Ezra Laderman

*February 15, 1986
Jubilate
Paul Cooper

March 1, 1986
Jubileephony
Poul Ruders

*March 15, 1986
Fanfare
Charles Wuorinen

*April 5, 1986
Tromba Lontana
John Adams

April 12, 1986
2nd Concerto for Orchestra – *Icarus*
Henri Lazarof

*April 12, 1986
Frolic
Ned Rorem

May 3, 1986
Rosaceae
Marc Neikrug

*May 9, 1986
Old and Lost Rivers
Tobias Picker

*May 17, 1986
Fanfare, Opus 59
Aulis Sallinen

*July 4, 1986
Ringing
Victoria Bond

*September 4, 1986
Fanfare - In Celebration
John Williams

*September 13, 1986
Etude Fanfare
Christopher Rouse

*September 27, 1986
*Showcase: A Short Display for
Orchestra*
William Schuman

*October 11, 1986
Fanfare for Foley's
John Harbison

*October 25, 1986
Fanfare
Olly Wilson

*October 25, 1986
Symphony No. 2: *Aussöhnung* for
Soprano and Orchestra
Tobias Picker

*October 31, 1986
Symphonic Fanfare 1986
Josef Tal

*November 2, 1986
Fanfare: Salute
Steve Reich

*December 6, 1986
Continuoso
Carla Bley

*January 10, 1987
Fanfare for the Uncommon Woman
Joan Tower

*January 30, 1987
Texas Twilight
Marius Constant

*January 31, 1987
Paean
Jacob Druckman

*February 14, 1987
Flourishes
Carlisle Floyd

*April 10, 1987
*A Celebration of Some 100 X 150
Notes*
Elliott Carter

*May 16, 1987
Dance Overture
George Perle

*June 24, 1987
Interlude for Orchestra
George Burt

*September 18, 1987
Symphonic Transformations
Tristan Keuris

December 4, 1987
Favola for Cello and Orchestra
Oliver Knussen

*March 19, 1988
Symphony No. 6
Ezra Laderman

*June 28, 1988
Affinities
Richard Lavenda

*January 28, 1988
The Conch
Ann Witherspoon

*January 14, 1989
Symphony No. 3
Tobias Picker

*November 6, 1989
Old McDonald's Orchestra
Robert Nelson

December 15, 1989
The Little Match Girl
Robert Nelson

*January 6, 1990
Romances and Interludes for Oboe
Robert Schumann/
Tobias Picker

*February 24, 1990
Two Fantasies for Orchestra
Tobias Picker

September 9, 1990
Jagannath
Christopher Rouse

*March 14, 1992
Symphony No. 1
Marc Neikrug

June 2, 1993
The Lazy Lion
Kevin Scott

May 14, 1994
Nine Pieces for Orchestra
Aribert Reimann

July 2, 1994
The Rainmaker's Helper
Reynaldo Ochoa

*November 5, 1994
Prelude for Orchestra
Bright Sheng

*January 11, 1995
Future Tense
Paul Schleuse

*March 4, 1995
Symphony No. 2
Christopher Rouse

September 30, 1995
Blueskonzert for Piano and Orchestra
Alvin Singleton

*May 30, 1996
Alegría
Roberto Sierra

*June 3, 1997
Acrobatics
Michael Abels

*May 22, 1998
Variations for Orchestra
Hans-Jürgen von Bose

*January 19, 1999
Horntrio for Horn, Violin and Piano
Yehudi Wyner

*May 22, 1999
Flute Moon
Bright Sheng

*April 8, 2000
Rainbow Body 2000
Christopher Theofanidis

June 16, 2000
Another Time in America
Hannibal Lokumbe

November 11, 2000
Variations on the Tango
Stephen Margoshes

*January 18, 2002
Pierrot
Larry Lipkis

*February 8, 2003
Concerto for Horn
Samuel Adler

*December 11, 2003
Glad Tidings (The Story of Christmas)
Randol Alan Bass

*April 1, 2004
Concerto for Piccolo and
Contrabassoon
Damian Montano

*May 14, 2005
Concerto for Clarinet
Richard Lavenda

*January 13, 2006
big sky
Pierre Jalbert

*May 5, 2006
Concerto for Bass Viol
John Harbison

*February 23, 2007
La Llorona
Gabriela Lena Frank

*October 1, 2008
Solstice for Trombone and Orchestra
Cindy McTee

*January 22, 2009
*Absolute Ocean for Soprano, Harp
and Orchestra*
Augusta Read Thomas

*November 23, 2010
Kaddish: I Am Here (full-orchestra
version)
Lawrence Siegel

*September 16, 2011
Shades of Memory
Pierre Jalbert

*November 1, 2013
Symphony No. 3,
Ofrenda a los muertos
Juan Trigos

DISCOGRAPHY

Year of release	Title of album	Conductor	Guest artists	Record label
1950	South Pacific/Kiss Me Kate	Efrem Kurtz		Columbia Records
1957	Glière Symphony No. 3 in B minor	Leopold Stokowski		Capitol
1958	Shostakovich: Symphony No. 11, Opus 103 "The Year 1905"	Leopold Stokowski		Capitol
1959	Orff – Carmina Burana – Stokowski	Leopold Stokowski	Virginia Babikian, soprano; Clyde Hager, tenor; Guy Gardner, baritone; The Houston Chorale; Houston Youth Symphony Boy's Choir	Capitol
1959	Parsifal	Leopold Stokowski		Everest
1959	Brahms Symphony No. 3 in F major, Opus 90	Leopold Stokowski		Everest
1959	Scriabin : The poem of ecstasy, Opus 54 & Amirov: No. 2 : "Kyurdi ovshari" Azerbaijan Mugam	Leopold Stokowski		Everest
1960	Bartok Concerto for Orchestra/Stokowski	Leopold Stokowski		Everest
1960	Wagner, Chopin, Thomas Canning's Fantasy	Leopold Stokowski		Everest
1965	Painter of Orchestral Colors: Chopin, Strauss, Wagner	Leopold Stokowski		Everest
1966	Texas	Ezra Rachlin		Carsan Records
1975	Woody Herman and the Thundering Herd with the Houston Symphony Orchestra	Lawrence Foster		Fantasy Records
1976	American Contemporary	Samuel Jones		Composers Recordings, Inc.
1977	Paul Chihara: Symphony in Celebration, Missa Carminum	Lawrence Foster	Roger Wagner Chorale, Roger Wagner, conductor	Candide/Vox
1979	Woman: Burt Bacharach and the Houston Symphony	Burt Bacharach		A&M Records, Inc.
1982	Debussy – La Mer – Nocturnes	Sergiu Comissiona		Vanguard
1982	Cesar Franck: Symphony in D Minor	Sergiu Comissiona		Vanguard
1983	Ravel	Sergiu Comissiona		Vanguard
1983	Rimsky-Korsakov Scheherazade	Sergiu Comissiona	Ruben Gonzalez	Vanguard Audiophile
1983	Ravel	Sergiu Comissiona		Vanguard
1986	Tchaikovsky Waltzes	Sergiu Comissiona		Intersound
1987	America Swings	Newton Wayland		Intersound
1987	Symphonic Dreams	Erich Kunzel	Gerry Mulligan and His Quartet	Intersound
1990	Picker: Symphony No. 2 for Soprano & Orchestra; String Quartet; Fanfares	Mitchell - Comissiona		
1991	Tobias Picker: The Encantadas	Christoph Eschenbach	Sir John Gielgud, speaker; Robert Atherholt, oboe; Christoph Eschenbach, piano	Virgin Classics
1991	Dvorak Symphony No. 9 and Francesca da Rimini	Christoph Eschenbach		Virgin Classics
1992	Brahms: Symphony No. 1 in C minor, Opus 68; Academic Festival Overture, Opus 80	Christoph Eschenbach		Virgin Classics
1992	TV's Greatest Hits	Newton Wayland		Intersound

Year of release	Title of album	Conductor	Guest artists	Record label
1993	In the Mood: Big Band's Greatest Hits	Newton Wayland		Intersound
1993	Mozart Clarinet Concerto in A – Bassoon Concerto in B flat	Christoph Eschenbach	David Peck, clarinet; Benjamin Kamins, bassoon	IMP
1993	Mozart Wind Concertos	Christoph Eschenbach		I.M.P. Pickwick Group Ltd.
1994	Mozart Concerti for Horn & Orchestra	Christoph Eschenbach	William VerMeulen, horn	IMP
1995	Schoenberg: Pelleas und Melisande / Webern: Passacaglia	Christoph Eschenbach		Koch International
1996	Four Last Songs	Christoph Eschenbach	Renée Fleming	RCA Victor Red Seal
1996	Houston Symphony Chamber Players – Schoenberg, Webern, Berg	Christoph Eschenbach		Koch International
1996	Anton Bruckner: Symphony No. 2 in C minor	Christoph Eschenbach		Koch International Classics
1997	Schubert	Christoph Eschenbach		Koch International
1997	Christopher Rouse: Symphony No. 2, Flute Concerto, Phaethon	Christoph Eschenbach	Carol Wincenc, flute	Telarc
1997	Brahms: Symphonies Nos. 1–4	Christoph Eschenbach		Virgin Classics
1997	Bach Brahms Schoenberg Orchestrations	Christoph Eschenbach		RCA Victor Red Seal
1998	Mahler: Symphony No. 1	Christoph Eschenbach		Koch International Classics
1999	Messiaen Quartet for the End of Time	Christoph Eschenbach		Koch International Classics
1999	Violin Concertos of John Adams & Philip Glass	Christoph Eschenbach	Robert McDuffie, violin	
2000	Anton Bruckner – Symphony No. 6 in A	Christoph Eschenbach		Koch International Classics
2003	Houston Symphony Christmas Festival	Michael Krajewski	Charles Hausmann, chorus director, Houston Symphony Chorus	A Swineshead Production
2004	Houston Symphony Glad Tidings	Michael Krajewski	Houston Symphony Chorus; Houston Children's Chorus; Former President George H. W. Bush	Houston Symphony Media Productions
2005	Voices of the Symphony	Charles Hausmann		Houston Symphony Media Productions
2005	Bartók: The Wooden Prince/Stravinsky: La Baiser de la fée	Hans Graf		Koch International Classics
2006	The Gift	Randall Craig Fleisher		Houston Symphony Society
2009	Zemlinsky: Lyric Symphony / Berg: Three Pieces from the Lyric Suite	Hans Graf	Twyla Robinson, soprano; Roman Trekel, baritone	Naxos
2010	The Planets–An HD Odyssey	Hans Graf		Duncan Copp Ltd. and Houston Symphony
2011	Mahler: Das Lied von der Erde	Hans Graf	Jane Henschel, mezzo-soprano; Gregory Kunde, tenor	Naxos

ENDNOTES

Chapter 1 endnotes

1. Biographical information on Blitz was almost entirely obtained from his personal papers, located in the Dolph Briscoe Center for American History at the University of Texas, Austin.
2. The French term refers to the practice of solemnization, an ancient mnemonic practice of attaching syllables to musical pitches as an aid in singing a melody on the correct musical tones. The practice has existed in various forms among ancient musical cultures throughout the world. In Europe, its origin is attributed to the late 10th- and 11th-century Italian musical theorist Guido of Arezzo, though Blitz and his conservatory teachers may have traced their knowledge of it to the monumental seven-volume theoretical tract *Speculum musices* by the celebrated 13th- and 14th-century Franco-Flemish musical theorist Jacob of Liège.
3. This wealth may have been a factor in the sudden awareness of the need for major cultural and educational institutions at the time. The Museum of Fine Arts, Houston grew out of a Public Art League established by Houston's first professional artist, Emma Richardson Cherry, in 1900. The original wing of the building at Montrose Boulevard and Main Street opened in 1924. Rice University was founded in 1912, a year before the Houston Symphony. The land for the city's major park, Hermann Park, was not donated to the city until 1914. The Houston Junior College and the Houston Negro Junior College, predecessors of the publicly supported University of Houston and Texas Southern University, were established in 1927. Two Roman Catholic institutions, the former Sacred Heart Dominican College and the University of St. Thomas, were founded in 1945 and 1947, respectively. Houston Baptist College (now Houston Baptist University) was founded as recently as 1960.

Chapter 2 endnotes

1. Virginia Bernhard, *Ima Hogg: The Governor's Daughter* (Austin, Tex.: Texas Monthly Press, 1984), pp. 59–62.
2. *Who's Who in Music in California*, edited by W. Francis Gates (Los Angeles: Colby and Pryibil, 1920); William Reher brochure, Redpath Chautauqua Collection, University of Iowa; Sven Reher papers, Library Special Collections, Charles E. Young Research Library, University of California Los Angeles; William Reher to Josephine Boudreaux, Houston Symphony Archives.
3. Houston Symphony Archives.
4. Howard Shanet, *Philharmonic: A History of New York's Orchestra* (New York: Doubleday, 1975), pp. 222–223, 233.
5. Hubert Roussel, *The Houston Symphony Orchestra, 1913–1971* (Austin, Tex.: University of Texas Press, 1972), pp. 29–45, passim.
6. Ima Hogg to Alfredo Casella, and Alfredo Casella to Ima Hogg, telegrams, Ima Hogg Papers, Dolph Briscoe Center for American History, The University of Texas at Austin.
7. The number of concerts in a given season and the instruments a given performer played could vary widely. For instance, Willrich is listed as a second violinist in the December 19, 1913, program under Blitz, and a trombonist in the February 18, 1932, program under Nespoli. Patricio Gutierrez is best remembered as a pianist, but he is listed as a cellist in the 1913 program and as a horn player in the 1932 program. Multiple talents and multitasking were evidently quite common in the early days of the Houston Symphony.
8. Donald William Looser, "Music in Houston, 1930–1971" (Ph.D. diss., Florida State University, 1972), pp. 24–26; see also annotated index, p. 2, p. 93.

Chapter 3 endnotes

1. Much of the information in this chapter is owed to the comprehensive account in Hubert Roussel's earlier history *The Houston Symphony Orchestra, 1913–1971.*
2. Hoffmann family tree is courtesy of the conductor's grandson Andrew J. Hoffmann, Houston Symphony Archives.
3. George M. Logan, "The Bain Years," in *The Indiana University School of Music: A History* (Bloomington, Ind.: Indiana University Press, 2000), p. 149.

Chapter 4 endnotes

1. Roussel, Houston Symphony Orchestra, pp. 112–13, 118.
2. *The New Grove Dictionary of Music and Musicians*, edited by Stanley Sadie, vol. 14, 2nd ed. (New York: Oxford University Press, 2000), p. 50.
3. Rosters in Houston Symphony concert programs, 1947–48 and 1948–49.

Chapter 5 endnotes

1. Houston Symphony concert programs, 1913–18 and 1931–85. Other guest conductors that season included Maurice Abravanel, Ernest Ansermet, Erich Leinsdorf, Hugo Rignold and Andor Toth.
2. *Houston Post*, January 17, 1954; *Houston Chronicle*, January 17, 1954.
3. William Rice, "Houston Stirred by Fricsay Controversy," *Musical America*, January 15, 1955, p. 11. The press was divided over the nature of these proposals. The *Houston Post*'s Hubert Roussel referred to them as "conditions" for accepting a permanent position, while the *Houston Chronicle*'s Ann Holmes referred to them as "suggestions," to be spread over a five-year period.
4. Interview with Raphael Fliegel, *Houston Post* magazine, July 5, 1987.
5. Looser, "Music in Houston," p. 112.
6. David Waters, *A Labor History of the Houston Symphony* (pub. unknown), p. 3.
7. The matter is most fully covered in Chapter 69 of Oliver Daniel, *Stokowski: A Counterpoint of View* (New York: Dodd, Mead & Co., 1982).
8. There are varied estimates of City Auditorium's seating capacity. Early accounts and postcards dating from 1910, when the hall was built, indicate it held as many as 7,000 people, presumably to accommodate fans of the popular wrestling matches held there. However, a historical article in the *Houston Business Journal*, August 21–28, 1998, states that the seating capacity was ultimately reduced to 3,500 people, closer to the customary seating capacity associated with Houston Symphony performances.

Chapter 6 endnotes

1. David Llewellyn Jones, "Sir John Barbirolli and the Houston Symphony Orchestra," *The Barbirolli Society Journal*, no. 78 (Spring 2010), pp. 22–23.
2. Ibid., pp. 25–26.
3. *Houston Post*, February 14, 1967.
4. *Houston Chronicle*, July 2, 1967.
5. *Los Angeles Times*, April 18, 1966, and July 14, 1966.
6. Michael Kennedy, *Barbirolli* (New York: HarperCollins, 1971), pp. 292–295; interview with Lady Barbirolli, 1986, London.
7. Kennedy, *Barbirolli*, p. 292.
8. Crickmore had been Barbirolli's trusted manager since 1944, in addition to being manager of the Hallé Orchestra, which Barbirolli conducted from 1943 to 1968. In 1960, Crickmore left the Hallé, came to the United States and married Barbirolli's personal secretary, Rosalind Booth. At one point, Crickmore announced his intention to re-establish his musical management activities in Houston. However, the Crickmores moved on to the West Coast where a progressively worsening cancer cost him his leg and eventually his life in April 1965.

Chapter 7 endnotes

1. *Houston Post*, March 23, 1968.
2. Maurice Hirsch to Ronald Wilford, April 29, 1969, Hirsch papers, Houston Symphony Archives. Previn returned on May 24, 1986, as the conductor of the touring Los Angeles Philharmonic Orchestra, under Society for the Performing Arts auspices, and again in 2009 when the Houston Grand Opera gave the world premiere of his opera *Brief Encounter*. Hans Graf invited him to conduct a Houston Symphony subscription concert in connection with his second visit, and Previn accepted the invitation but later canceled, citing a need to devote all his energies to preparation for the opera.
3. Interview with Tom Johnson, August 18, 1987, Houston.
4. Interview with Antonio de Almeida, August 18, 1986, New York City.

Chapter 8 endnotes

1. *Houston Post*, December 19, 1972; *Houston Chronicle*, February 25, 1973. The list of some 200 candidates included Swiss conductor Niklaus Wyss, who became associate conductor more than a decade later (1987–1992). He held a dual professorship at the University of Houston. Endo returned to the American Ballet Theatre after less than a year.
2. Interview with Neil Martin, November 16, 1992, Houston. Many years later, Neil Martin, the attorney hired by the Houston Symphony Society, explained that it was a lockout, but that he understood it had been reviewed by the Houston office of the National Labor Relations Board, which found it to be a legally permissible action. For public relations purposes, the Symphony Society did not use the term "lockout" at the time, Martin said.
3. *Houston Post*, September 18, 1976; interview with Lawrence Foster, March 2, 1986, Houston. This was prompted not only by the fact that players were already leaving for better positions elsewhere, but also because he had heard rumors that the Symphony Society was considering a merger between its musicians and the Corpus Christi Symphony, a small regional orchestra several hundred miles away. The idea of an all-embracing Texas Symphony, playing in Houston, Dallas and San Antonio, had been floated among Houston Symphony board members during an earlier contract negotiation in the 1960s.
4. This request was made with special reference to Keith Robinson, assistant principal double bass player of the orchestra since 1948. He suffered a stroke during Foster's term and was left with limited benefits for himself, his wife and his five children.
5. With the Houston Grand Opera, the Houston Ballet and the Society for the Performing Arts competing for use of the stage, the Symphony was forced to rehearse in a basement rehearsal room, which failed to fulfill the acousticians' promise that it would duplicate the acoustics onstage. Thus, the orchestra had to spend three to four rehearsals in one acoustical environment, then change volume levels during the final onstage rehearsal for each concert.
6. *Houston Post*, November 9, 1976, and November 14, 1976. Previn had been scheduled for the revival, but was ill at the time.
7. Jones bristled when Foster was asked if the severance was initiated by him or by the Symphony Society, but the conductor merely answered, "It was mutual."
8. Bernhard, *Ima Hogg*, p. 1. Documents in the Houston Symphony Archives indicate Ima Hogg attended Symphony Society meetings as recently as a few months before her death. It was perhaps a blessing that the 93-year-old founder of the orchestra did not live through the terrible crisis of the following year. But she did foresee it. One afternoon (I don't remember the date), my telephone rang at the *Houston Post*, and it was a rare call from Miss Ima, who simply said, "I'm very worried about the Houston Symphony."
9. Houston Symphony concert program, May 14–16, 1978.

Chapter 9 endnotes

1. Traverse had originally come to Houston from the Royal Liverpool Orchestra as early as the fall of 1978, with the title of co-concertmaster. His appointment may have been connected to an effort to secure Walter Weller as conductor, but Weller went to the Royal Philharmonic Orchestra instead.
2. Johnson returned to Minneapolis following her Houston Symphony appointment, but she was hardly forgotten. Several years later, David Gockley, Houston Grand Opera (HGO) general director, appointed her as his managing director during the crucial time period spanning that company's move into the newly built Wortham Theater Center. Johnson spent an even more valuable 12 years keeping HGO's financial and operational affairs running smoothly.
3. Comissiona's appointment occurred during a time when there was a rash of dual appointments on the part of conductors—not only across America, but also internationally. Barbirolli's dual Hallé Orchestra and Houston Symphony appointment, and Previn's dual London Symphony and Houston Symphony appointment were two vivid local examples. The former brought cancellations and physical exhaustion to the end of Barbirolli's years here, and the latter resulted in schedule conflicts that led to the abrupt end of Previn's Houston Symphony career. Another prominent example involved Seiji Ozawa, who held simultaneous music directorships of the San Francisco and Boston Symphony Orchestras from 1973–1976.
4. Interview, *Houston Post* magazine, March 17, 1985.
5. At a western-themed concert in the summer of 1980, Harwood had the orchestra (including himself) dress in boots and jeans. At one Miller Outdoor Theatre concert of film music, an old English telephone booth from some antique store was placed at the edge of the stage during

intermission. When the concert resumed, out popped Harwood (who was hardly much more than five feet tall), attired in full Superman regalia, to conduct excerpts from John Williams' score to that movie.

6. The main reservation from Cunningham was his penchant for doubling all the woodwind parts in the symphonies, thus muddying Tchaikovsky's bright, clear orchestral textures.

7. The Mozart festivals continued under the early years of Eschenbach's tenure, until they were preempted by the orchestra's Japan tour in July 1991.

8. Legend has it that wealthy supporters of the early orchestra spent weekends in the surrounding countryside, where the men liked to go hunting.

9. The rehearsal room, constructed two levels below the stage, was roundly criticized for its failure to duplicate the acoustics of the stage. Thus, most of the orchestra's four to five weekly rehearsals had to be prepared in the rehearsal room, with only the dress rehearsal onstage the day of the concert. At that point, all of the orchestral balances between winds, brass, percussion and strings—and between the orchestra and the weekly soloist—had to be readjusted, causing great frustration and wasting valuable rehearsal time.

10. The historic Monday night series was not finally abandoned until 2006, when the Houston Symphony moved its subscribers to the present divided series of nine Thursday and nine Friday evenings.

11. Interview with Gideon Toeplitz, July 30, 1987, Houston.

12. Interview, *Houston Post* magazine, March 17, 1985. "We are finishing a performance we began in 1958," he said, referring to the night his dress rehearsal of the Tchaikovsky opera was interrupted and the Comissionas were dismissed from the Romanian State Opera.

13. The pan flute is akin to ancient panpipes, dating back to the fifth and sixth centuries BC, when they were popular in Anatolia. The instrument consists of a graduated row of tuned pipes placed on a rack. Air is blown over the holes at the ends of the pipes to produce a soft, flute-like tone.

14. Music directors rarely conducted Miller Outdoor Theatre performances, and those may have been the first performances of the Beethoven Ninth Symphony there. On June 21, 1983, Comissiona also shared the free outdoor concert podium with Leonard Bernstein, who happened to be in town on the orchestra's 70th anniversary, rehearsing the Houston Grand Opera for the world premiere of *A Quiet Place*. Notwithstanding a violent thunderstorm that soaked Houston the preceding afternoon, a huge mob of people sloshed through the flooded streets and trudged through the mud to reach the grassy hill fronting the theater.

15. Hans Graf revived eight of them during his tenure. Generous donors had paid to have the scores and parts recopied after the flooding from Tropical Storm Allison destroyed the Houston Symphony library in 2001.

16. It was later renamed the Williams Tower when the building changed hands. The series was called the Innova Concerts when it relocated to Houston's Innova Design Center during Christoph Eschenbach's early years as music director.

17. Interview with Tobias Picker, March 14, 2007, New York City. Picker also composed Two Fantasies for Orchestra, a Symphony for Strings and Romances and Interludes for Oboe and Orchestra, interwoven with Schumann's Three Romances for Oboe and Piano, Op. 94, during Christoph Eschenbach's tenure with the orchestra. However, a viola concerto commissioned for Pinchas Zukerman did not reach its premiere in Houston: Paul Neuberger, William McLaughlin and the Kansas City Symphony premiered the work in 1995.

Chapter 10 endnotes

1. *Houston Post*, March 4, 1988.

2. *Houston Post*, February 14, 1988. Comissiona had originally been scheduled as conductor for the Mahler Second Symphony when the 1988–89 75th anniversary season's programs were released. When Eschenbach was announced as the orchestra's new music director less than a month later, Comissiona had to cede the Mahler Second Symphony to him, in order to provide for Eschenbach's uninterrupted Mahler cycle. David Wax, the orchestra's new executive director, made several other program changes to redirect the focus of the 75th anniversary season toward Eschenbach. These included deleting several works the orchestra had originally commissioned, dating back at least as far as Stokowski's tenure.

3. *Houston Post*, February 20, 1990.

4. *New Grove Dictionary of Music*, p. 310.

5. Due to an injury he sustained, Lawrence Foster was unable to conduct the April 8–10 performances. Robert Page, assistant conductor of the Cleveland Orchestra and chorus director of the Cleveland Orchestra and the Pittsburgh Symphony, led the Symphony and Chorus in Lawrence Foster's place.

6. *Houston Post*, September 3, 1989.

7. A much more severe contraction was to come during the decade that followed.

8. She was on an extended leave during Barbirolli's directorship.

9. The pupils of Eschenbach's eyes took on a laser-like intensity during this conducting tactic when viewed head-on by the orchestra, as I learned while seated in the choral risers behind the stage in Hanover, Germany, during the 1992 tour. Eschenbach was not the only conductor to resort to such theatrics. As a graduate student hanging over the rail in the top balcony of the old Los Angeles Philharmonic Hall in the 1950s, I was fascinated to watch William Steinberg conduct the entire slow movement of Beethoven's *Eroica* Symphony with his left hand, while the right arm hung as though paralyzed at his side. And Fritz Reiner drew tiny pencil sketches in the air during a performance of the Divertimento from Stravinsky's ballet *The Fairy's Kiss*, suddenly causing a tonal explosion from the orchestra when he moved the baton barely 12 inches to the right or left.

10. Various conversations with Foster.

11. Interview with Wayne Crouse, 1989, Santa Fe, New Mexico. The string section was greatly heartened by Barbirolli's use of the word "we," since he had been a cellist in his youth, before taking up the baton.

12. It was a surprising disappointment to learn that the Virgin Classics recording company had chosen another American orchestra to record them, leaving the Houston Symphony with a Brahms cycle instead.

13. Undated notation, Ann Holmes Fine Arts Collection, Woodson Research Center, Rice University. A handwritten notation during an interview between *Houston Chronicle* critic-at-large Ann Holmes and Houston Symphony executive director David Wax indicated that Eschenbach's salary during that unspecified season was around $800,000 and that he was paid separate increments as conductor, piano soloist and music director. Wax told her that the following season he would only be paid around $500,000.

14. *Chicago Magazine* (July 1997), p. 16.

Chapter 11 endnotes

1. Thankfully, most of the orchestral instruments were safely stored in a van above ground, since they had been loaded for an outdoor concert that the Houston Symphony was scheduled to play. Please read the acknowledgments on p. XI for information concerning restoration of the Houston Symphony Archive.

2. Charles Ward, *Houston Chronicle*, September 17, 2001. Graf had been conducting the opening program of the Calgary Symphony's 2001–02 series during his final season with that orchestra. Fortunately, Houston-based Executive Air Charter had flown some passengers to Calgary and had empty seats available for the return flight. Graf and his wife arrived early Friday morning, September 14, and he had 36 hours to rehearse the orchestra and chorus for the sold-out opening concert on Saturday evening, September 15.

3. By happenstance, Enron had donated a fully equipped vacant floor of its office tower to the Houston Symphony for use by the orchestra's office staff after the flooding of their Jones Hall office space.

4. Before beginning the process, Wulfe consulted with Frank J. Macchiarola, president of St. Francis College in New York City, who had successfully mediated a strike by musicians of Local 802, American Federation of Musicians, against the League of American Theatres that had turned off the lights on Broadway. After settling the dispute between the Houston Symphony Society and its musicians, Wulfe jokingly compared the New York mediation process with the one in Houston: "The difference was, they didn't feed 'em until they finished, but we brought in more pizza."

5. Jennifer Mathieu, *Houston Press*, April 10, 2003.

6. The roster ranged from a high of 90 musicians when Kurtz arrived in 1948, down to 78 during his final season in 1953–54. Graf was not one to complain publicly, but at one annual meeting of the Houston Symphony Society during his years in Houston, he stood up and told board members, "We are just barely hanging on here."

7. Bartók's *The Wooden Prince* and the Divertimento from Stravinsky's *The Fairy's Kiss* were paired on a handsome CD by Graf and the Houston Symphony.

8. Interview with Hans Graf, September 19, 2012, Houston. Graf repeatedly felt he struggled to connect with his audience. He was particularly disappointed that the cultural/intellectual brain trust in Houston did not respond to his fairytale season with lectures by philosophers and literary experts, and with art exhibits in museums. He did not truly energize this segment of Houston's populace until the Houston Symphony's outreach staff organized a two-month citywide series of events preceding the orchestra's concert performances of Berg's *Wozzeck* at the beginning of March 2013, Graf's final season as music director. Also, he may not have realized that Americans fail to grasp the deep symbolism that Europeans naturally attach to fairytales.

9. Interview with Hans Graf, July 12, 2007, Houston.

Chapter 12 endnotes

1. Looser, "Music in Houston," p. 18.
2. Josephine Boudreaux Collection, Houston Symphony Archives.
3. Looser, "Music in Houston," p. 15.
4. Patricio Gutierrez Collection SC1310, Houston Metropolitan Research Center, Houston Public Library.
5. *Galveston Daily News*, November 15, 1942, p. 3.
6. Interview with George Illes, Houston Symphony Archives.
7. Sixteenth Census of the United States, 1940, T627, 4,643 rolls.
8. Estelle Hudson with Henry R. Maresh, *Czech Pioneers of the Southwest* (Dallas: Southwest Press, 1934), p. 333.
9. Houston Symphony concert program, November 4, 1946.
10. Materials from Washburn's daughter Melanie Richards, Houston Symphony Archives.
11. Houston Symphony concert program, February 10–11, 1975.
12. "Herman Randolph, 76, retired Houston Symphony Orchestra clarinetist," *Houston Chronicle*, August 10, 2007.
13. Houston Symphony concert program, May 2000.
14. "Bob Deutsch …Multifaceted Preservationist," *The Heights Pages*, November 5, 2000.

Chapter 15 endnotes

1. Correspondence 3B174, Ima Hogg Papers, Dolph Briscoe Center for American History, The University of Texas at Austin, Texas.
2. Ibid.

Chapter 16 endnotes

1. Minutes of the Auxiliary Committee of the Houston Symphony Orchestra Association, April 2, 1933, President's Records of the Houston Symphony League, Houston Symphony Archives.

Chapter 18 endnotes

1. *Houston Post*, October 26, 1941.
2. *Houston Chronicle*, November 26, 1960.
3. Houston Symphony concert program, February 13–14, 1961.

Chapter 19 endnotes

1. Interview with Red and Christine Pastorek, June 20, 2007, Houston Symphony Archives.
2. Interview with Don Jackson, February 6, 2006, Houston Symphony Archives.
3. Charles Ward, "The Symphony Goes to Mexico," *Houston Chronicle*, July 22, 1979.

CREDITS AND INDEX

LIST OF PHOTOGRAPHS AND ILLUSTRATIONS
(in the order of appearance)

Unless otherwise indicated, all photographs are courtesy Houston Symphony Archives.

p. 144, bottom, Photo by Jim Caldwell.
p. 146, top, left, Photo by Gittings.
p. 146, top, second from left, Photo by Eric Arbiter.
p. 146, top, second from right, Photo by Gittings.
p. 146, top, right, Photo by www.AlexandersPortraits.com.
p. 146, bottom, left, Photo by www.AlexandersPortraits.com.
p. 146, bottom, second from left, Photo by www.AlexandersPortraits.com.
p. 146, bottom, right, Photo by Gittings.
p. 147, top, left, Photo by Gittings.
p. 147, top, second from left, Photo by www.AlexandersPortraits.com.
p. 147, top, center, Photo by Anthony Rathbun.
p. 147, top, second from right, *Houston Press* Collection, RG D0005 F893,
Houston Metropolitan Research Center, Houston Public Library.
p. 147, top, right, Photo by Gittings.
p. 147, bottom, left, Photo by Gittings.
p. 147, bottom, center, Photo by Gittings.
p. 147, bottom, second from right, Photo by www.AlexandersPortraits.com.
p. 147, bottom, right, Photo by Gittings.

Chapter 16
p. 148, Photo by Jim Caldwell.
p. 149, Photo by Michelle Watson/Catchlight Group.
p. 150, center, Photo by Sheila Cunningham.
p. 150, bottom, Photo by E. Joseph Deering.
p. 152, bottom, Photo by Chinh Phan/CatchLight Group.

Chapter 17
p. 154, © *Houston Chronicle*. Used with permission.
p. 157, top, Photo by Bob Bailey Studios.
p. 157, bottom, Photo by Michelle Watson/Catchlight Group.
p. 159, top, Photo by John Brooks.
p. 159, bottom, Photo by Connie Juvan-Savoy.
p. 161, Photo by Jerry Click. © *Houston Chronicle*. Used with permission.
p. 162, Photo by Janice Rubin.
p. 163, top, Photo by Jamie Lupold.
p. 163, bottom, Photo by Jeff Fitlow.

Chapter 18
p. 164, Photo by Michael Tammaro.
p. 166, Leopold Meyer Papers, MSS 0067-272, Houston Metropolitan Research
Center, Houston Public Library.
p. 167, Photo by Anthony Rathbun.

Chapter 19
p. 169, Photo by Terry Brown.
p. 170, Photo by Herman Randolph.
p. 171, bottom left, Photo by Bruce Bennett.
p. 172, top, left, Photo by Eric Arbiter.
p. 172, top, center, Photo by Michelle Watson/CatchLight Group.
p. 172, center, Photo by Chinh Phan/CatchLight Group.
p. 172, bottom, left, Photo by Eric Arbiter.
p. 172, bottom, center, Photo by Jeff Fitlow.
p. 172, bottom, right, Photo by Eric Arbiter.

PUBLISHED MATERIALS:

Bernhard, Virginia. *Ima Hogg: The Governor's Daughter* (Third edition.) Denton: Texas State Historical Association, 2011.

Daniel, Oliver. *Stokowski: A Counterpoint of View*, New York: Dodd, Mead and Co., 1982.

Jones, David Llewellyn. "Sir John Barbirolli and the Houston Symphony Orchestra." The Barbirolli Society Journal (Issue Number 78, Spring 2010). Oxford: Design and Print, 2010.

Logan, George M. "The Bain Years." *The Indiana University School of Music: A History*. Bloomington: Indiana University Press, 2000.

Kennedy, Michael. *Barbirolli*. New York, London: Harper Collins, 1971.

Sadie, Stanley, ed. *New Grove Dictionary of Music and Musicians*. (Second Edition.) New York: Oxford University Press, 2000.

Maresh, Henry R. and Estelle Hudson. *The Czech Pioneers of the Southwest*. Houston: Western Lithograph, 1962.

Roussel, Hubert. *The Houston Symphony Orchestra, 1913–1971*. Austin and London: University of Texas Press, 1972.

Shanet, Howard. *Philharmonic: A History of New York's Orchestra*. Garden City, New York: Doubleday, 1975.

Welling, David, *Cinema Houston*. Austin: University of Texas Press, 2007.

UNPUBLISHED MATERIALS:

Blitz, Julien Paul: Papers. CAH—MS Blitz, Julien Paul. (1937, Dolph Briscoe Center for American History, University of Texas, Austin)

Hirsch, Maurice: Papers. (Houston Symphony Archives)

Looser, Donald William, PhD: *Music in Houston 1930-1971* (Florida State University, 1972)

Reher, Sven. Papers, 1918–1979. (Collection number: 1231, University of California at Los Angeles Library, Department of Special Collections, Manuscripts Division, Los Angeles)

Reher, William. Brochure. (MsC 150, Redpath Chautauqua Collection, University of Iowa)

Reher, William. Private letter to Josephine Boudreaux, October 14, 1921 (MS12 Josephine Boudreaux Collection, Houston Symphony Archives)

Waters, David: *A Labor History of the Houston Symphony*. (1997)

NEWSPAPERS AND PERIODICALS:

Chicago magazine, July 7, 1997

Houston Business Journal, August 21–28, 1998

Houston Chronicle, June 21, 1913–August 10, 2007

Houston Post, June 21, 1913–April 18, 1995

Houston Press, June 21, 1913–June 30, 1918

Los Angeles Times, April 18–July 14, 1966

Musical Courier, May 1916

Musical America, January 15, 1955

The Galveston Daily News, October 23, 1932–November 15, 1942

The Heights Pages, November 5, 2000

Uncredited. Houston Metropolitan Research Center, Houston Public Library, Patricio Gutierrez Collection SC1310.

AUDIOTAPE INTERVIEWS WITH CARL CUNNINGHAM:

Almeida, Antonio de: August 18, 1986, New York City

Crouse, Wayne: August, 1989, Santa Fe, New Mexico

Fliegel, Raphael: July 5, 1987

Foster, Lawrence: March 2, 1986

Graf, Hans: July 12, 2007; September 19, 2012, Houston, Texas

Johnson, Tom M.: August 18, 1987, Houston, Texas

Martin, Neil: November 12, 1992, Houston, Texas

Picker, Tobias: March 14, 2007